Contents

Tried & True Tutoring

SAT & ACT Experts

(747) 444-9907 | www.triedandtruetutoring.com | info@triedandtruetutoring.com

SAT Score Tracker

In-Home/Mock SAT Scores

Diagnostic Test Date: ___/___/___

R & W: _____ Math: _____
Total (Cumulative Score): _____
Essay R: ___ A: ___ W: ___

Practice Test 5 Date: ___/___/___

R & W: _____ Math: _____
Total (Cumulative Score): _____
Essay R: ___ A: ___ W: ___

Practice Test 6 Date: ___/___/___

R & W: _____ Math: _____
Total (Cumulative Score): _____
Essay R: ___ A: ___ W: ___

Practice Test 7 Date: ___/___/___

R & W: _____ Math: _____
Total (Cumulative Score): _____
Essay R: ___ A: ___ W: ___

Practice Test 8 Date: ___/___/___

R & W: _____ Math: _____
Total (Cumulative Score): _____
Essay R: ___ A: ___ W: ___

Official SAT Scores

First Test Date: ___/___/___

R & W: _____ Math: _____
Total (Cumulative Score): _____
Essay R: ___ A: ___ W: ___

Second Test Date: ___/___/___

R & W: _____ Math: _____
Total (Cumulative Score): _____
Essay R: ___ A: ___ W: ___

Third Test Date: ___/___/___

R & W: _____ Math: _____
Total (Cumulative Score): _____
Essay R: ___ A: ___ W: ___

Practice Test Login Information:
- Visit: triedandtruetutoring.com
- Select: "Online Score Tracker Login" at the bottom of the homepage.

Username:

_____

Password:

_____

College Board Login Information:
- Visit: collegereadiness.collegeboard.org

Username:

_____

Password:

_____

HOMEWORK

Session	Blue Book Practice	Timed Sections
1		
2		
3		
4		
5		
6		
7		
8		
9		
10		
11		
12		
13		
14		
15		

Tutor Information:

Name: _____ Phone: _____

E-Mail: _____

SAT Prep Checklist

9 months before the test:
- [ ] Take **diagnostic** test.
- [ ] Schedule **phone consultation**: www.triedandtruetutoring.com/why-tried-and-true-tutoring
- [ ] Decide your **test dates**. Pick two, but keep a third in mind, just in case!
- [ ] Choose your preferred form of **SAT prep**: Comprehensive class, boot camp, or 1-on-1.
- [ ] **Register** for your test ASAP so that you get your preferred location.

2 months before the test:
- [ ] Make sure test **registration** is complete.
- [ ] Make sure you have a valid **photo ID**. Don't leave this until the last minute! A student ID card, driver's license, or passport will work.
- [ ] Sign up for a **Boot Camp** if you think you'll need some last minute prep.

1 week before the test:
- [ ] Take a full-length **practice test** the weekend before your test, and simulate test conditions as much as possible to see what you need to do/change on test day.
- [ ] Do two timed practice sections each day
- [ ] Review your **#SAT_hacks**
- [ ] Practice **healthy sleep habits** – go to bed early and wake up at the same time you'll wake up on test day.
- [ ] Keep up with other classwork and chores to **prevent stress** or late nights.
- [ ] Eat healthy meals every day and get plenty of sleep. You need your brain and your body to be in tip-top shape. Don't get sick on test day because of bad habits!

The night before the test:
- [ ] Place your **testing supplies** in a bag:
  - [ ] PRINTED Admission Ticket
  - [ ] Photo ID
  - [ ] Sharpened #2 pencils (The College Board recommends 2, but we recommend bringing 6-10)
  - [ ] A big eraser
  - [ ] Calculator with fresh batteries – a list of College Board approved calculators can be found at **collegereadiness.collegeboard.org/sat/taking-the-test/calculator-policy**
  - [ ] Snacks (nuts or bars are good!)
  - [ ] A bottle of water
  - [ ] Tissues
- [ ] Do something relaxing.
- [ ] If you are testing at an unfamiliar location, make sure you know your route beforehand.
- [ ] Go to bed early, and turn off all electronics.

On Test Day:
- [ ] Get up as soon as your alarm goes off.
- [ ] Eat a healthy breakfast, avoiding too much sugar.
- [ ] Complete a few math problems to warm up your brain.
- [ ] Dress for success!
- [ ] Breathe deeply; you have prepped well!

SAT PREP CHECKLIST

College Admissions Exams Basics

- The SAT and ACT are the two most popular college entrance exams.
- High school students must take one of these two tests to be admitted to most 4-year, American colleges and universities.
- You must complete the SAT or ACT by _____ of your senior year.
- The SAT is offered 7 times each year.
- If you are applying to competitive colleges, you should plan to take the SAT two or three times.
- Dates can be found at collegereadiness.collegeboard.org.
- Use the chart below to plan your testing timeline.

Month	✓(Pick 2 + a backup)	Official Test Date	Sign up before...
December of junior year			
March of junior year			
May of junior year			
June of junior year			
August of senior year			
September of senior year			
October of senior year			
November of senior year			
December of senior year			

Registering for the SAT

- The deadline to register for the SAT is typically about _____ prior to the test date.
- Register early to lock in your preferred testing location.
- The registration process takes 30-minutes to an hour.
- To register visit www.sat.collegeboard.org.
- Click "Register" on the blue menu bar at the top of the page.
- Select the test date you wish to register for.
- You will be required to provide credit card information to reserve your spot.
- Some students are eligible to take the SAT for free. If you think you might qualify for a fee waiver, talk to your high school counselor.
- When registering, you will be asked where you want your scores reported. We recommend that you leave this section blank.

ACT: The Alternative to the SAT

- The ACT is the alternative to the SAT.
- The ACT is accepted at _____ college and university that accepts the SAT.
- Some students perform better on the SAT, while others perform better on the ACT.
- If you think the ACT might be a good fit for you, we recommend you take the **Free ACT Diagnostic Exam**.
- Once you have taken the SAT & ACT Diagnostics, we can help you determine which test is best for you.
- Directions to access the SAT & ACT Diagnostic Exams are on the next page.

Free Diagnostic Exams

- You can take a free, full-length SAT and/or ACT Diagnostic Exam through our website.
- Our experts will analyze your performance to determine what you should focus on to improve your score.
- If you take both the SAT and ACT, we will compare your scores and recommend which test is a better fit for you.

Taking Diagnostic Exams

1. Visit **www.triedandtruetutoring.com**.
2. Press the blue **Take a Free SAT or ACT Diagnostic** button on the right side of the home page.
3. Fill out the registration form.
4. Instructions and login credentials for our Online Score Tracker will be sent to you within 1 business day.
5. Each test takes approximately 4-hours.
6. You will be emailed a detailed score report the following business day.

Overview

- The SAT consists of 2-main sections: **Reading & Writing** and **Math**.
- Each section is scored from 200 to 800 points.
  - 200 is the lowest score.
  - _____ is approximately the average score.
  - 800 is the perfect score.
- Adding together the 2-main section scores creates the **Cumulative Score**.
  - 400 is the lowest cumulative score.
  - _____ is approximately the average cumulative score.
  - 1600 is the perfect cumulative score.

Reading & Writing

- This score is based on two timed sections: **Reading** and **Writing & Language**
  - The Reading Test is 65 minutes long and includes _____ passages and _____ multiple-choice questions. It tests your ability to read and understand passages.
  - The Writing & Language Test is 35 minutes long and includes _____ multiple-choice questions. It tests your grammar and writing structure skills.

Math

- This score is based on two timed sections: **Math without calculator** and **Math with calculator**
  - The Math Test – No Calculator is 25 minutes long and includes 15 multiple-choice questions and 5 student-produced response questions
  - The Math Test – Calculator is 55 minutes long and includes 30 multiple-choice questions and 8 student-produced response questions.

Optional Essay

- The Essay is optional.
- The essay lasts 50 minutes
- Some colleges and universities require the essay, some recommend it, and some do not look at it at all.
- If you are interested in applying to competitive schools, we recommend you take the essay.

#sat_hack
#what_is_a_sat_hack

Throughout this book, you will see SAT Hacks in bubbles like this. Pay close attention to these insider tips, tricks, and study strategies to boost your score quickly!

When To Guess

- The SAT scoring system works like this.

Correct Answer	
Incorrect Answer	
Blank Answer	

- You do not lose points for any incorrect answers, so you should _____ leave a question blank.

How To Guess

- If you don't know the answer to a question, what should you do?
  - **Elimination**: Cross out the answers that you know are wrong.
  - Make an **Educated Guess**: From the remaining choices, choose the one that seems "most correct."
  - Pick your **Favorite Letter:** If you have no idea or are running out of time or have to guess blindly, always choose the same letter to keep the odds on your side. Circle the letter below that you will use as your favorite letter.

A   B   C   D

Pacing

- Most students spend too much time on hard questions and not enough time on easy questions.
- Each of the questions is worth the same number of points.
- Do not rush on the easy questions just because they seem easy – making careless mistakes or reading the question wrong will cost you points.
- You do not have to answer the questions in order.
- If you are stumped, circle the question and move on.
- Come back to the questions you skipped after you have answered all the other questions.

Quiz

1. You get partial credit even if you make a careless mistake or bubble incorrectly. True/False
2. When should you leave an answer blank? _____

Reading Test

Tried & True Tutoring

Overview

- This test includes:
  - **5 passages** – it is hard to stay focused while reading these passages.
  - **52 multiple choice questions** – can be confusing and often more than one answer seems correct.
- You only get 65 minutes. This is not enough time to read the passages in detail and carefully answer each question.

- Take a look at the passage on page 15.
- If you are like most students, you probably do this:
  1. Try to read the passage from beginning to end.
  2. Go to the questions.
  3. Go back to the passage and reread while you answer the questions.

- We are going to learn a much better approach called **Score Zone Reading**.
- But first, let's break down the Reading Test.

Types of Passages

- There are _____ passages on this test:
  1. The **first** passage is always _____.
  2. The **second** and **fourth** passages are _____ passages:
     - One with a graphic
     - One that is a **pair of related passages** with different opinions about the same topic
  3. The **third** and **fifth** passages are _____ passages:
     - One with a graphic
     - One without a graphic

- Some students perform better on certain types of passages.
- You can always tell what genre you are reading by from the blurb at the beginning of the passage.
- As you practice for the SAT, pay attention to which types of passages you perform best on and which ones are your worst passages.

#sat_hack

#bubbling_for_reading

Bubble your answers in after completing each passage. This way, you are less likely to make bubbling errors if you complete the passages out-of-order.

Types of Questions

- There are two main categories of questions on this test:
  - **Whole passage** – these refer to the entire passage (#1 on page 15)
  - **Specific** – these refer to a specific part of the passage (#2 on page 16).

- There are also **two special types of Specific Questions** on this test:
  - **Words in Context** – these are vocabulary questions (#5 on page 16)
    - You do not need to memorize vocabulary words. The best way to prepare for these questions is to learn to use **context clues**.
  - **Command of Evidence** – these are pairs of questions (#7 and 8 on page 16)
    - The first question is a specific question
    - The second question asks you to support your answer with evidence from the text.

Reading for Points

- Reading on the SAT is different from reading in your high school classes.
- In school, you read to interpret and "find the deeper meaning"
- On the SAT…
  - You read to answer questions correctly and score points
  - You should not try to interpret or "find the deeper meaning"
  - You should only answer based on what is actually said in the passage – do not tie in outside or existing knowledge on these questions

- Score Zone Reading is a powerful technique that will boost your reading score by helping you…
  - Read the passages more quickly
  - Focus only on the parts of the passage that are needed to answer questions
  - Recognize and avoid trap answers
- Before you learn **Score Zone Reading**, there are three key terms you should be familiar with:
  1. **Deep Reading**
  2. **Answer Zone**
  3. **Your Own Answer**

Three Key Terms

- **Deep Reading** – reading slowly, carefully, and deliberately
  - Students often read too quickly on the SAT **Reading Test.**
  - Reading Quickly does not save time.
  - When you read too quickly, you end up having to read the same text more than once.
  - **Deep Reading** means reading carefully enough to "get the idea" the first time.
- **Answer Zone** – this is the small piece of the passage that you will read to find the answer to a Specific Question
  - It is usually about 12 lines long.
  - If a question gives you line number(s), the **Answer Zone** starts about 6 lines before and ends about 6 lines after the line number(s).
  - If a question doesn't give you line number(s), you will learn how to find it on the next page.
- **Your Own Answer** – this is the answer that you come up with before looking at the multiple-choice answers.
  - The SAT **Reading Test** tries to trap you with incorrect answers that "sound good."
  - If you figure out Your Own Answer before looking at theirs, you are less likely to be trapped by an answer that "sounds good."

Reading Overview Quiz

1. Question #1 on page 15 is a _____ question.

2. The three types of passages that appear on the Reading Test are _____,
   _____, and _____.

3. Questions 7 and 8 on page 16 are _____ questions.

4. How long is the Answer Zone? _____.

5. Where should you look for the answer zone if you are given line numbers?

   _____

   _____

6. _____ is the strategy you will be using to get through the passages more quickly and

   with more accuracy.

When you begin the SAT Reading Test...

1. Read the "blurbs" at the top of each passage, recognizing which type of passage each is: Prose, Social Studies, or Science?
2. Decide your test order.
3. Complete your strongest passages first, and end with your weakest.

Step One: Pre-Highlight the Passage

Follow the flow chart below to help you dissect the passage before you read.

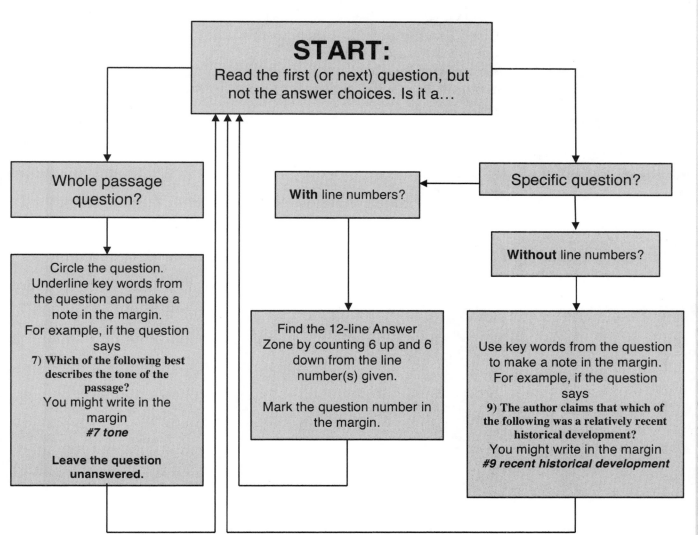

START:
Read the first (or next) question, but not the answer choices. Is it a...

Whole passage question?

Specific question?

With line numbers?

Without line numbers?

Circle the question. Underline key words from the question and make a note in the margin.
For example, if the question says
7) Which of the following best describes the tone of the passage?
You might write in the margin
#7 tone

Leave the question unanswered.

Find the 12-line Answer Zone by counting 6 up and 6 down from the line number(s) given.

Mark the question number in the margin.

Use key words from the question to make a note in the margin.
For example, if the question says
9) The author claims that which of the following was a relatively recent historical development?
You might write in the margin
#9 recent historical development

Step Two: Deep Read The Passage

1. **Deep Read** the passage as deliberately as possible.
2. As you read, keep in mind the notes that you wrote in the margins.
3. As you come across each **Answer Zone**, reread the question and think of **Your Own Answer** before you read the answer choices.
4. Read the answer choices. Select the one that best matches **Your Own Answer**.
   - Eliminate answers that "don't fit" with your answer.
   - If there are two answers that you are struggling to choose between, select the one that is most directly stated in the text.
   - Don't overthink your answers.
5. Circle your answers in your test booklet as you go.

Step Three: Clean Up

1. Go back and answer the Whole Passage questions.
2. Bubble in your answers once they are all circled.
3. Double check your bubbling-in. Does everything in your test booklet match your bubble sheet?
4. Go onto the next passage, starting with step one.

Questions 1-11 are based on the following passage.

This passage and the associated figure are adapted from Rachel Krantz-Kent, "Why Do You Ask." Originally published 2017 on the U.S. Department of Labor Blog.

On any given day, about 80 percent of the population age 15 and up watch television, and they watch for an average of 3 hours 29
Line minutes. That's an interesting piece of trivia, you
5 may be thinking, but why does the Bureau of Labor Statistics need to know that? Without context, TV watching may seem like an odd area of focus – but this is just one of many statistics the agency collects as part of the American Time
10 Use Survey. And Americans across the country use that information every day to get their jobs done.

The statistics above, for example, may be helpful to those promoting healthy behaviors
15 and products, such as those who work in the health and fitness industries. The data can also be useful to television producers in determining programming.

Unlike other BLS surveys that track
20 employment, wages and prices, the American Time Use Survey tracks a less conventional, but equally important, economic resource that we never have enough of: time. The survey compiles data on how much time Americans spend doing
25 paid work, unpaid household work (such as taking care of children or doing household chores) and all the other activities that compose a typical day.

Some of these measurements have
30 economic and policy-relevant significance. For example, the time people spend doing unpaid household work has implications for measures of national wealth. Information about eldercare providers and the time they spend providing this
35 care informs lawmakers. Measures of physical activity and social contact shed light on the health and wellbeing of the population. And information about leisure—how much people have and how they spend it—provides valuable insight into the
40 quality of life in the United States.

All of the data are publically available, and used by businesses, government agencies, employers, job seekers and private individuals to examine the different time choices and tradeoffs
45 that people make every day. Here are some other interesting facts the survey reveals about how Americans spend their time:

66 percent of women prepare food on a given day, compared with 40 percent of men.
50 These statistics measure one aspect of women's

and men's contributions to their families and households and help promote the value of all work people do, whether or not they are paid to perform it. Compared with men, women spend a
55 greater share of their time doing unpaid household work, such as food preparation, and statistics like these can shed light on barriers to equal opportunities for women. Parents whose youngest child is under age 6 spend 2 hours 8
60 minutes per day on average providing childcare as their main activity, compared to 1 hour for parents whose youngest child is between the ages of 6 and 12. (These estimates do not include the time parents spend supervising their children
65 while doing other activities.)

Parenting can be an intense experience for many reasons, including the time it demands of parents. These statistics provide average measures of the time involved in directly caring
70 for children, and they can be helpful to health and community workers whose work supports parents, as well as employers interested in developing ways to promote work-life balance and staff retention.
75 61 percent of unpaid eldercare providers are employed. Knowing the characteristics of those who provide unpaid care for aging family, friends and neighbors can help lawmakers create targeted policies and aid community workers in
80 developing supportive programs.

Employed people spend an average of 1 hour 6 minutes driving their vehicles, 7 minutes in the passenger seat, and 8 minutes traveling by another mode of transportation on days they
85 work.

Knowing how workers travel and the amount of time they spend using different modes of transportation can be useful to a variety of people, including city and transportation
90 planners, land and real estate developers, and designers in the automobile industry.

Figure 1

Minutes per day men spend more than women

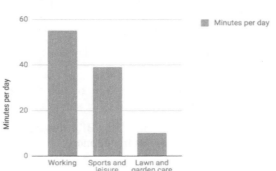

Figure 2

Minutes per day women spend more than men

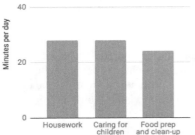

1

This passage primarily serves to

A) discuss the findings of recent surveys and advocate for wide-sweeping social changes based on these findings.

B) explain how seemingly trivial data is useful and to provide some interesting examples of that data.

C) provide vital data as part of a larger argument to lower the amount of time Americans spend in front of screens.

D) describe the drawbacks of traditional means of gathering data and make a push for more modern methods.

2

The primary purpose of the third paragraph is to

A) explain the importance of proper data collection when tracking employment and prices.

B) dispel a common misconception about BLS surveys.

C) describe a specific survey in part by pointing out a difference between it and other surveys.

D) give a detailed description of a BLS survey in order to demonstrate its importance.

3

Which of the following does the passage most clearly indicate?

A) Some methods of measuring economics have policy-relevant significance.

B) Unpaid household work is of great importance.

C) People who engage in more physical activity time tend to have less leisure time.

D) Activities that do not directly involve money can impact the measurement of national wealth.

4

Which choice provides the best evidence for the answer to the previous question?

A) Lines 30-33 ("For example… wealth")

B) Line 35-40 ("Measures of… United States")

C) Lines 50-54 ("These statistics… perform it")

D) Lines 86-91 ("Knowing how… automobile industry")

5

Based on the passage, the author most likely hopes the American Time Use Survey provides information that will

A) increase the number of eldercare providers in the US.

B) shed light on higher housing costs in some areas of the US.

C) lead to a reduction of impediments to equal job opportunities for women and men.

D) bring about a level playing field for people of all races to get into the colleges they want to get into.

6

Which choice provides the best evidence for the answer to the previous question?

A) Lines 33-35 ("Information about... informs lawmakers")

B) Lines 48-54 ("66 percent... perform it")

C) Lines 54-58 ("Compared with men... for women")

D) Lines 86-91 ("Knowing how workers... automobile industry")

7

As used in line 67, "demands" most nearly means

A) dictates.

B) requires.

C) requests.

D) beseeches.

8

As used in line 79, "targeted policies" most nearly means

A) laws put in place to hinder a specific person or group.

B) rules pushed quickly through the judicial system.

C) official courses of action specific to the situation.

D) legislation enacted for the good of all people.

9

Based on the graphs, which of the following is true of the demographic studied?

A) Dads spend more time working because moms spend more time with their children.

B) Moms spend less time on the computer than dads.

C) Dads spend more time working than moms spend on housework.

D) Moms spend more time on food prep and cleanup than dads do.

10

According to the graphs, within the demographic studied, the amount of time moms spend on housework

A) is, on average, the same amount of time they spend caring for children.

B) exceeds the amount of time dads spend on housework by the same amount of time as moms' time spent caring for children exceeds dads' time doing the same.

C) is roughly half the amount of time dads spend working.

D) increases, on average, by 28 minutes with each subsequent child.

11

Based on the passage and the graphs, to which of the following might the graph be most helpful?

A) "Eldercare providers" (lines 33-34)

B) "Job seekers and private individuals" (line 43)

C) "Health and community workers" (lines 70-71)

D) "Lawmakers" (line 78)

Blue Book Problem	My Answer	Correct Answer	Why did I miss?
P. 417 #1			
P. 417 #2			
P. 417 #3			
P. 417 #4			
P. 417 #5			
P. 417 #6			
P. 417 #7			
P. 418 #8			
P. 418 #9			
P. 418 #10			
P. 420 #11			
P. 420 #12			
P. 420 #13			
P. 420 #14			
P. 421 #15			
P. 421 #16			
P. 421 #17			
P. 421 #18			
P. 421 #19			
P. 421 #20			
P. 422 #21			
P. 426 #33			
P. 426 #34			
P. 426 #35			
P. 426 #36			
P. 426 #37			
P. 426 #38			
P. 426 #39			

Blue Book Problem	My Answer	Correct Answer	Why did I miss?
P. 426 #40			
P. 427 #41			
P. 427 #42			
P. 429 #43			
P. 429 #44			
P. 429 #45			
P. 429 #46			
P. 430 #47			
P. 430 #48			
P. 430 #49			
P. 430 #50			
P. 430 #51			
P. 430 #52			

CORRECT OUT OF TOTAL: _____/41

NOTES:

It's A Trap!

- The hardest part of the SAT Reading Test is avoiding the **Trap Answers.**
- On the Reading Test, the questions are fairly straightforward, but the answers will try to throw you off.
- Now that you have learned Score Zone Reading, you are going to learn some strategies to avoid the SAT's seven types of Trap Answers:
  - **Word-For-Word Hook**
  - **Extreme Statements**
  - **Opposite**
  - **Bogus Comparisons**
  - **True, But So What?**
  - **Half-Right, Half-Wrong**
  - **Implied, Literally?**

#sat_hack

#three_wrongs_make_a_right

If you are stumped on a question, or none of the choices match your answer, eliminate the ones you know are wrong.

Sometimes it's easier to spot a wrong answer than a right answer, and you improve your odds with each answer you eliminate. You might be able to eliminate three choices to determine the correct answer!

Word-For-Word Hook

- These answer choices use the exact same wording as the passage, but do not answer the question correctly.
- Always double check that your answer choice is really answering the question.
- Can you tell which choice below contains the **Word-For-Word Hook**?

Last night, thousands of eager Beliebers lined up outside of the Staples Center to get tickets for Justin Bieber's annual tour. This year has been the first instance that the Biebs and his management have not allowed any online sales of tickets, to many fans' dismay. Despite the three-day wait and the near-freezing temperature – last night set a record low for Los Angeles – fans are camping out in the hopes that they will be one of the lucky many who get their hands on a ticket at the Sunday morning release.

1

Why are fans upset?

A) There is a three-day wait for the tickets to be released.

B) The near-freezing temperature is a record low.

C) The artist's management team did not offer ticket sales online.

D) There is a limited number of tickets for the concert.

Extreme Statements

- These are answer choices that take a statement in the passage and generalize or overstate it.
- Always double check that the answer choice is stating ONLY what is said in the passage, and beware of answer choices that jump to conclusions.
- Can you tell which choice below is correct by eliminating all of the **Extreme Statements**?

A recent survey conducted by the RIAA (Recording Industry Association of America) found that eighty-four percent of Justin Bieber fans were also fans of Taylor Swift. A mere 4% of Taylor Swift fans also admitted to listening to Kanye West – this comes as no surprise due to the messy history between the Pop Queen and the King of Hip Hop which dates all the way back nearly a decade to the 2009 VMAs. Some may be too young to remember when Kanye stole the microphone during T-Swizzle's acceptance speech. Kanye gave no comment on these survey results, but later Tweeted that "Haters gonna hate."

2

According to the passage, what is true of Taylor Swift fans?

A) There is a large overlap between Taylor Swift and Justin Bieber fans.

B) They are probably too young to remember why they dislike Kanye West.

C) None of them like Kanye West.

D) They hope that Taylor Swift and Kanye West mend their relationship soon.

Total Reversal

- Some answer choices use similar words or phrases from the passage, but actually state the opposite.
- Can you tell which of the choices below is a **Total Reversal**?

Kanye West is facing a serious financial crisis. In recent years, he has lost billions of his hard-earned dollars investing in a new fashion line and other extravagant business ideas. While his platinum records continue to earn him plenty of income to support a more-than-lavish lifestyle, if he continues to make poor financial decisions, he will likely be flat broke by the year 2020. His accountant made no comment, but an inside source states that "for richer or poorer" was left out of the vows in his wedding to Kim Kardashian, so stay tuned on the future of the Kardashian-West Empire.

3

What current issue is Kanye West currently facing?

A) His records sales are not earning enough revenue to support his more-than-lavish lifestyle.

B) He has made poor investment decisions.

C) He is sad that nobody likes his records.

D) Kim Kardashian might divorce him.

#sat_hack

#lesser_of_two_evils

During the SAT, there may be questions where you find yourself choosing between two answers.

In this situation, see if you can spot a **Trap** in either of these choices. While they might both "sound" right, one is probably a **Trap**!

Bogus Comparisons

- You will see these when you are asked to identify a comparison between two things in the passage.
- These answer choices might include two things mentioned in the passage, but not actually compared.
- Always double check that the answer choice presents a comparison that was actually made in the passage.
- Can you tell which of the choices below is a **Bogus Comparison**? There might be more than one.

What exactly is the Boy Band Phenomenon? Sociologists have been studying this pattern for years – what qualities make teenage girls go crazy for singing and dancing groups of young guys? Sociologist Michael Mallaley recently commented in a PBS documentary that the One-Direction hysteria that gripped the world earlier this decade was similar to that which we saw in the 1960s when the Beatles were at the height of their popularity. Experts are after an answer as to why solo artists from the group Harry Styles, Zayn Malik, and Liam Payne have seen such greater success than other members of the group since the beginning of their "hiatus" in 2016.

4

What comparison does the author make in this paragraph?

A) One Direction was not quite as popular as the Beatles were in the 1960s.

B) Some members of One Direction are having better solo careers than others.

C) Harry Styles and Zayn Malik have been more successful than Liam Payne.

D) Teenaged girls like boy bands more than teenaged boys.

True, But So What?

- These are answer choices that might be a true statement, but have nothing to do with the questions being asked.
- Always double check that an answer choice is answering the question with direct evidence, rather than just being a true statement.
- Can you tell which of the choices below is a **True, But So What** Trap?

In 2013, Kanye West released his famous album *Yeezus*, which has earned him both critical acclaim and adoration from his fans. Some West fans have said that Kanye can do more with his words two and a half minutes than Abraham Lincoln did in his three-minute *Gettysburg Address*, which was given a century and a half before the release of *Yeezus*. Historians do agree that Yeezus has earned more immediate attention than did the Gettysburg address, which was largely forgotten for nearly ten years after it was given.

5

According to the passage, what statement would historians agree with?

A) Abraham Lincoln was an incredible orator.

B) Kanye West is a better wordsmith than Abraham Lincoln was.

C) Yeezus was more popular after its release than the Gettysburg address was.

D) Abraham Lincoln received widespread acclaim for his *Gettysburg Address*.

Half-Right, Half-Wrong

- The answer choices for these questions usually have multiple elements, one of which is wrong.
- Remember that even if an answer is "mostly" correct, if any part is wrong, the whole answer is wrong.
- Can you tell which of the choices below is **Half-Right, Half Wrong**?

Since the beginning of the 21ˢᵗ century, our society has seen a huge shift in musical technology. Between early 2000s hip hop artists' fascination with autotune and the recent craze in electro-pop music, the days of organic music production are far behind us. This makes for an interesting concert experience for younger generations. Unlike the simple, pure musical experiences that previous generations experienced, concerts now are often more about the visual spectacle rather than the quality of the music itself. Voices like Justin Bieber's and Taylor Swift's sound much different live than on a recording. This doesn't seem to deter fans, however; both artists continue to sell out arenas and grow their fan bases.

6

Which of the following best identifies the author's attitude towards the subject of the passage?

A) admiring but condescending

B) appreciative but discouraging

C) fascinated but fearful

D) straightforward but nostalgic

Implied, Literally?

- These answer choices usually follow a question that asks what can be "implied". When you see this word, it is the only time you should look for something that was **not directly stated in the passage**.
- Remember that "imply" means to suggest something without saying it directly.
- Can you tell which of the choices below is an **Implied, Literally** Trap?

On the morning of her 16ᵗʰ birthday, Natalie was certain that it wouldn't be anything special. She hadn't had a birthday party since she was in elementary school, and usually her mom just gave Natalie and her siblings some money on their birthday. She was certain it would be like any other birthday, but when she came to the table for breakfast, there was a big banner and her mom and brothers stood up and shouted "Surprise!" When she sat down at her place at the table, she noticed a thick envelope on her plate, and when she opened it, the usual birthday check fell out… Along with two tickets to the Justin Bieber concert at the Staples Center! She was so blown away – she had waited all night with her sister but the tickets sold out before they made it to the front of the line.

7

Which of the following can be implied about Natalie?

A) She has more than one sister.

B) Birthdays are usually nothing special in her family.

C) She is a huge Justin Bieber fan.

D) Her favorite meal is breakfast.

Questions 1-10 are based on the following passage.

This passage is adapted from Saki, "The Disappearance of Crispina Umberleigh." Originally published in 1919.

In a first-class carriage of a train speeding Balkanward across the flat, green Hungarian plain two Britons sat in friendly, fitful

Line converse. Neither man was talkative and each
5 was grateful to the other for not being talkative. That is why from time to time they talked.

One topic of conversation naturally thrust itself forward in front of all others. In Vienna the previous day they had learned of the
10 mysterious vanishing of a world-famous picture from the walls of the Louvre.

"A dramatic disappearance of that sort is sure to produce a crop of imitations," said the Journalist.
15 "I was thinking," replied the Wine Merchant, "of the spiriting away of human beings rather than pictures. In particular I was thinking of the case of my aunt, Crispina Umberleigh."

"I remember hearing something of the
20 affair," said the Journalist, "but I was away from England at the time. I never quite knew what was supposed to have happened."

"You may hear what really happened if you will respect it as a confidence," said the Wine
25 Merchant. "In the first place I may say that the disappearance of Mrs. Umberleigh was not regarded by the family entirely as a bereavement. My uncle, Edward Umberleigh, was not by any means a weak-kneed individual, in fact in the
30 world of politics he had to be reckoned with more or less as a strong man, but he was unmistakably dominated by Crispina; indeed I never met any human being who was not frozen into subjection when brought into prolonged contact with her.
35 From the kitchen regions upwards every one in the household came under her despotic sway and stayed there with the submissiveness of molluscs involved in a glacial epoch. As a nephew on a footing of only occasional visits she affected me
40 merely as an epidemic, disagreeable while it lasted, but without any permanent effect; but her own sons and daughters stood in mortal awe of her; their studies, friendships, diet, amusements, religious observances, and way of doing their hair
45 were all regulated and ordained according to the august lady's will and pleasure. This will help you to understand the sensation of stupefaction which was caused in the family when she unobtrusively and inexplicably vanished.

50 "Of course the matter was put in the hands of the police, but as far as possible it was kept out of the papers, and the generally accepted explanation of her withdrawal from her social circle was that she had gone into a nursing
55 home."

"And what was the immediate effect on the home circle?" asked the Journalist.

"All the girls bought themselves bicycles; the feminine cycling craze was still in
60 existence, and Crispina had rigidly vetoed any participation in it among the members of her household. The youngest boy let himself go to such an extent during his next term that it had to be his last as far as that particular establishment
65 was concerned. The elder boys propounded a theory that their mother might be wandering somewhere abroad, and searched for her assiduously, chiefly, it must be admitted, in a class of Montmartre resort where it was
70 extremely improbable that she would be found."

"And all this while couldn't your uncle get hold of the least clue?"

"As a matter of fact he had received some information, though of course I did not
75 know of it at the time. He got a message one day telling him that his wife had been kidnapped, and with the information came a demand for money; a lump sum of 2000 pounds was to be paid yearly. Failing this she would be immediately
80 restored to her family."

The Journalist was silent for a moment. "It was certainly an inverted form of holding to ransom," he said.

"If you had known my aunt," said the
85 Wine Merchant, "you would have wondered that they didn't put the figure higher."

1

Which choice best summarizes the passage?

A) Passengers on a train describe relatives they dislike.

B) A journalist interviews a man on a train about the strange disappearance of his aunt for a story he is writing.

C) One man describes the details of a case to another man who hopes to solve it.

D) Men discuss what seems to be a very strange kidnapping.

2

As used in line 24, "confidence" most nearly means

A) assurance.

B) insurance.

C) secret.

D) poise.

3

The passage indicates that Edward Umberleigh

A) was weak-kneed and dominated.

B) showed strength in some areas but not others.

C) had a career in politics that was overshadowed by his wife's.

D) would have divorced his wife if he wasn't afraid of her.

4

Which of the following does the wine merchant indicate about his aunt?

A) She had a stronger effect on those who spent more time with her.

B) she charmed everyone in the household, from the kitchen regions upward.

C) She showed true concern for each and every one of her children.

D) She controlled everyone in the house with a loud voice and harsh words.

5

Which choice provides the best evidence for the answer to the previous question?

A) Lines 28-34 ("My uncle... contact with her")

B) Lines 35-38 ("From the kitchen...glacial epoch")

C) Lines 38-43 ("As a nephew... awe of her")

D) Lines 58-62 ("All the girls... her household")

6

As used in line 46, "august" most nearly means

A) loud.

B) imposing.

C) angry.

D) celebrated.

7

The main purpose of the ninth paragraph (lines 58-70) is to

A) advance the theme of people doing what they want.

B) demonstrate the importance of strong female figures to children, especially girls.

C) show some people's unusual reactions to what would usually be a sad event.

D) portray the power of peer pressure and fads.

Which of the following does the wine merchant most strongly imply about the disappearance of Crispina Umberleigh?

A) It remained a complete and utter mystery at the time of the telling of this story.

B) She had merely gone to a nursing home.

C) The police didn't really like Crispina Umberleigh so didn't work as hard as they could have to solve the case.

D) Some people lied about trying to find her.

Which choice provides the best evidence for the answer to the previous question?

A) Lines 43-49 ("their studies… vanished")

B) Lines 50-55 ("Of course…nursing home")

C) Lines 65-70 ("The elder boys… found")

D) Lines 75-79 ("He got… paid yearly")

It can be most reasonably inferred from the passage that the kidnappers

A) needed a lot of money.

B) knew something about the dynamics of the Umberleigh family.

C) were unaware of how a ransom typically works, so were probably kidnapping for the first time.

D) had a personal vendetta against Edward Umberleigh and his children.

Blue Book Problem	My Answer	Correct Answer	Why did I miss?
P. 529 #1			
P. 529 #2			
P. 529 #3			
P. 529 #4			
P. 530 #5			
P. 530 #6			
P. 530 #7			
P. 530 #8			
P. 530 #9			
P. 530 #10			
P. 532 #11			
P. 532 #12			
P. 533 #13			
P. 533 #14			
P. 533 #15			
P. 533 #16			
P. 533 #17			
P. 533 #18			
P. 533 #19			
P. 533 #20			
P. 535 #21			
P. 535 #22			
P. 535 #23			
P. 535 #24			
P. 535 #25			
P. 535 #26			
P. 535 #27			
P. 536 #28			
P. 536 #29			
P. 536 #30			

Blue Book Problem	My Answer	Correct Answer	Why did I miss?
P. 540 #42			
P. 540 #43			
P. 540 #44			
P. 540 #45			
P. 540 #46			
P. 540 #47			
P. 540 #48			
P. 541 #59			
P. 541 #50			
P. 541 #51			
P. 430 #52			

CORRECT OUT OF TOTAL: _____/41

NOTES:

Paired Passages

- The second or fourth passage will be a set of Paired Passages on the same social studies topic, but with different points of view.
- Score Zone Reading is still very effective on Paired Passages, with a few modifications to the approach.
- Follow the same steps as before, paying attention to the modifications:
  - You will complete all the questions for **Passage 1** before you look at **Passage 2**.
  - Once you have answered all the single-passage questions, answer the ones that relate to both passages.

Step One: Pre-Highlight Passage 1

Follow the flow chart below to help you dissect the passage before you read.

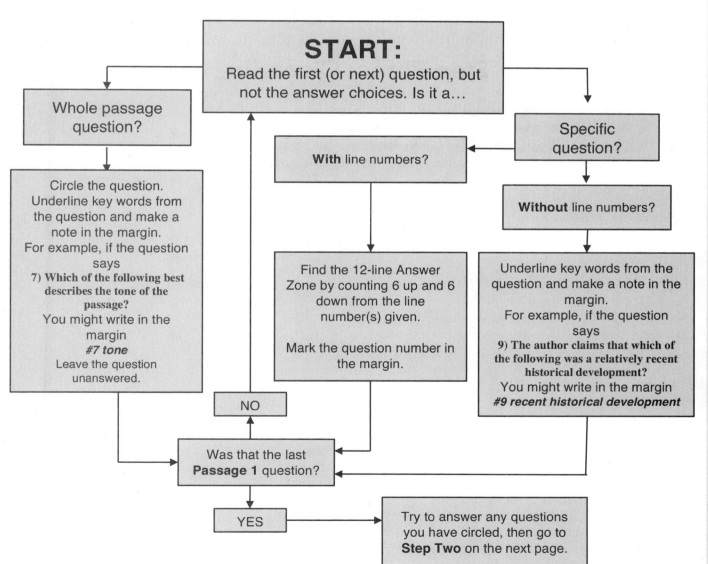

START:
Read the first (or next) question, but not the answer choices. Is it a…

Whole passage question?

Specific question?

With line numbers?

Without line numbers?

Circle the question. Underline key words from the question and make a note in the margin.
For example, if the question says
7) Which of the following best describes the tone of the passage?
You might write in the margin
#7 tone
Leave the question unanswered.

Find the 12-line Answer Zone by counting 6 up and 6 down from the line number(s) given.

Mark the question number in the margin.

Underline key words from the question and make a note in the margin.
For example, if the question says
9) The author claims that which of the following was a relatively recent historical development?
You might write in the margin
#9 recent historical development

NO

Was that the last **Passage 1** question?

YES

Try to answer any questions you have circled, then go to **Step Two** on the next page.

Step Two: Deep Read Passage 1

1. Read the passage as deliberately as possible.
2. As you read, keep in mind the notes that you wrote in the margins.
3. As you come across each **Answer Zone**, reread the question and come up with Your Own Answer before you look at the answer choices. This will keep you from falling into any of the **Traps**.
4. Read the answer choices. Select the one that best matches **Your Own Answer**.
   - Eliminate answers that "don't fit" with your answer.
   - If there are two answers that you are struggling to choose between, select the one that is most directly stated in the text.
   - Don't overthink your answers.
5. Circle your answers in your test booklet as you go. You will bubble in your answers after you have completed the questions for both passages.
6. Once you have answered all of the questions for Passage 1, continue to Passage 2, starting at the beginning of the flow chart.

Step Three: Clean Up

1. Answer any of the questions that relate to both passages.
2. Bubble in your answers once they are all circled.
3. Double check your bubbling-in. Does everything in your test booklet match your bubble sheet?
4. Go onto the next passage, starting at the beginning of Step One.

Questions 1-10 are based on the following passages.

Passage 1 is adapted from a speech entitled "Declaration of Sentiments" delivered by Elizabeth Cady Stanton to the Seneca Falls Convention, a historic assembly of women, in 1848. Passage 2 is adapted from Louis Godey, "How to be a Perfect Housewife" from *Godey's Lady's Book*. Originally published in 1859.

Passage 1

The history of mankind is a history of repeated injuries and usurpations on the part of man toward woman, having in direct object the establishment of an absolute tyranny over her. To prove this, let facts be submitted to a candid world.

He has never permitted her to exercise her inalienable right to the elective franchise.

He has compelled her to submit to laws, in the formation of which she had no voice.

He has withheld from her rights which are given to the most ignorant and degraded men—both natives and foreigners.

He has so framed the laws of divorce, as to what shall be the proper causes of divorce, in case of separation, to whom the guardianship of the children shall be given; as to be wholly regardless of the happiness of the women - the law, in all cases, going upon a false supposition of the supremacy of man, and giving all power into his hands.

He has monopolized nearly all the profitable employments, and from those she is permitted to follow, she receives but a scanty remuneration.

He closes against her all the avenues to wealth and distinction, which he considers most honorable to himself. As a teacher of theology, medicine, or law, she is not known.

He has denied her the facilities for obtaining a thorough education—all colleges being closed against her.

He has endeavored, in every way that he could to destroy her confidence in her own powers, to lessen her self-respect, and to make her willing to lead a dependent and abject life.

Now, in view of this entire disfranchisement of one-half the people of this country, their social and religious degradation, in view of the unjust laws above mentioned, and because women do feel themselves aggrieved, oppressed, and fraudulently deprived of their most sacred rights, we insist that they have immediate admission to all the rights and privileges which belong to them as citizens of these United States.

In entering upon the great work before us, we anticipate no small amount of misconception, misrepresentation, and ridicule; but we shall use every instrumentality within our power to effect our object. We shall employ agents, circulate tracts, petition the State and national Legislatures, and endeavor to enlist the pulpit and the press in our behalf. We hope this Convention will be followed by a series of Conventions, embracing every part of the country.

Firmly relying upon the final triumph of the Right and the True, we do this day affix our signatures to this declaration.

Passage 2

Having before suggested what is or should be the position of a wife, let us next consider her province as a housewife. What is her first duty?

To ascertain her husband's income, its resources, its limits, the amount beyond which she cannot pass without entailing ruin upon him and misery on herself.

But, alas! She has had no direction--no counsel--no lessons in household economy; she is at a loss what to do, save that she has a cook and a housemaid.

It is a certain fact that servants are like soldiers in a field of battle: upon them depend the success of well-ordered arrangements. It is useless to expect regularity or good management if the orders are not properly executed, and, therefore, it becomes important to exercise the utmost care in taking any person into the family as a domestic.

The servants having been chosen, and well chosen, rather for their knowledge in the strict and economical performance of their duties--it will be understood that these remarks apply to one servant as to five, or ten, or more-- the next thing will be to see that the kitchen is properly provided.

You will know how you can afford to live by the amount of your income; you will know your husband cannot expect to live beyond the amount which he has allowed you to keep his house with; but it must be your ambition to know how to make the best appearance; with small means to appear--without improper assumption-- richer than you are, or at least quite as rich as you are. Even at a tete-a-tete dinner with your husband, there is an air of clean comfort about it, while your own kinds words and tender smiles make him feel that he cannot by friendship or purchase obtain the felicity elsewhere he meets with at home.

105   The direction of the table is especially the province of the lady, for it involves not only her judgement in expenditure, a respectability of appearance, but the comfort of her husband and those who may have a seat at her table.

1

The examples given in paragraphs 6 and 7 of Passage 1 (lines 22-29) primarily serve to

A) explain her reasons for mistrusting men.

B) demonstrate how men have worked to make women unable to live without men.

C) describe how women can begin to take back power from men.

D) indicate her disdain for profitable employment (paragraph 6) and certain occupations (paragraph 7).

2

Which choice provides the best evidence for the answer to the previous question?

A) Lines 1-4 ("The history… over her")

B) Lines 14-21 ("He has so… his hands")

C) Lines 33-37 ("He has endeavored… abject life")

D) Lines 46-50 ("In entering… our object")

3

As used in line 36, "abject" most nearly means

A) extreme.

B) humble.

C) objectified.

D) prideless.

4

The author of Passage 1 anticipates

A) resistance in fighting for women's rights.

B) a small amount of misconception in her efforts to achieve her goal.

C) firm reliance from the Right and True.

D) immediate admission to the rights and privileges afforded to all citizens of the United States.

5

As used in line 66, "province" most nearly means

A) town.

B) region.

C) privilege.

D) responsibility.

6

According to the author of Passage 2, one of the duties of a housewife is to

A) increase her husband's wealth as much as possible.

B) look wealthy while spending very little money.

C) set the table.

D) give orders directly to all servants.

7

Which choice best states the relationship between the two passages?

A) Passage 2 directly refutes claims made in Passage 1.

B) Passage 2 explains the difficulties of demands made in Passage 1.

C) Passage 1 explains a problem that Passage 2 does not seem to see as a problem.

D) Passage 1 hints at some issues that Passage 2 states more openly.

8

Based on the passages, both authors would likely agree with which of the following claims?

A) Women should have the opportunity to be better educated.

B) Women should have the opportunity to make more money.

C) Men are tyrants.

D) It is important for women to tell the truth.

9

The author of Passage 2 would mostly likely respond to the first sentence of Passage 1 by stating that

A) men are usually gentle rulers over women.

B) women should stand up and fight against tyranny.

C) women have willingly and knowingly given power to men as a result of their humble natures.

D) men and women are merely in charge in different areas of life, men outside the house and women inside the house.

10

Which choice provides the best evidence for the answer to the previous question?

A) Lines 72-75 ("But alas… a housemaid")

B) Lines 76-83 ("It is a certain… as a domestic")

C) Lines 87-88 ("it will be understood… ten, or more")

D) Lines 91-95 ("You will know… his house with")

Blue Book Problem	My Answer	Correct Answer	Why did I miss?
P. 423 #22			
P. 423 #23			
P. 423 #24			
P. 423 #25			
P. 424 #26			
P. 424 #27			
P. 424 #28			
P. 424 #29			
P. 424 #30			
P. 424 #31			
P. 424 #32			
P. 537 #31			
P. 537 #32			
P. 537 #33			
P. 537 #34			
P. 538 #35			
P. 538 #36			
P. 538 #37			
P. 538 #38			
P. 538 #39			
P. 538 #40			
P. 538 #41			

CORRECT OUT OF TOTAL: _____/21

NOTES:

Questions 1-10 are based on the following passage.

This passage is adapted from H. G. Wells, *The War of the Worlds*. Originally published in 1898.

No one would have believed in the last years of the nineteenth century that this world was being watched keenly and closely by
Line intelligences greater than man's and yet as mortal
5 as his own; that as men busied themselves about their various concerns they were scrutinised and studied, perhaps almost as narrowly as a man with a microscope might scrutinise the transient creatures that swarm and multiply in a drop of
10 water. With infinite complacency men went to and fro over this globe about their little affairs, serene in their assurance of their empire over matter. It is possible that the infusoria under the microscope do the same. No one gave a thought
15 to the older worlds of space as sources of human danger, or thought of them only to dismiss the idea of life upon them as impossible or improbable. It is curious to recall some of the mental habits of those departed days. At most
20 terrestrial men fancied there might be other men upon Mars, perhaps inferior to themselves and ready to welcome a missionary enterprise. Yet across the gulf of space, minds that are to our minds as ours are to those of the beasts that
25 perish, intellects vast and cool and unsympathetic, regarded this earth with envious eyes, and slowly and surely drew their plans against us. And early in the twentieth century came the great disillusionment.
30 The planet Mars, I scarcely need remind the reader, revolves about the sun at a mean distance of 140,000,000 miles, and the light and heat it receives from the sun is barely half of that received by this world. It must be, if the nebular
35 hypothesis has any truth, older than our world; and long before this earth ceased to be molten, life upon its surface must have begun its course. The fact that it is scarcely one seventh of the volume of the earth must have accelerated its
40 cooling to the temperature at which life could begin. It has air and water and all that is necessary for the support of animated existence.

Yet so vain is man, and so blinded by his vanity, that no writer, up to the very end of the
45 nineteenth century, expressed any idea that intelligent life might have developed there far, or indeed at all, beyond its earthly level.

And we men, the creatures who inhabit this earth, must be to those on Mars at least as
50 alien and lowly as are the monkeys and lemurs to us. The intellectual side of man already admits that life is an incessant struggle for existence, and it would seem that this too is the belief of the minds upon Mars. Their world is far gone in its
55 cooling and this world is still crowded with life, but crowded only with what they regard as inferior animals. To carry warfare sunward is, indeed, their only escape from the destruction that, generation after generation, creeps upon
60 them.

And before we judge of them too harshly we must remember what ruthless and utter destruction our own species has wrought, not only upon animals, such as the vanished
65 bison and the dodo, but upon other races. The Tasmanians, in spite of their human likeness, were entirely swept out of existence in a war of extermination waged by European immigrants, in the space of fifty years. Are we such apostles of
70 mercy as to complain if the Martians warred in the same spirit?

The Martians seem to have calculated their descent with amazing subtlety—their mathematical learning is evidently far in excess
75 of ours—and to have carried out their preparations with a well-nigh perfect unanimity. Had our instruments permitted it, we might have seen the gathering trouble far back in the nineteenth century. Men like Schiaparelli
80 watched the red planet—it is odd, by-the-bye, that for countless centuries Mars has been the star of war—but failed to interpret the fluctuating appearances of the markings they mapped so well. All that time the Martians must have been
85 getting ready.

1

Which choice best describes a motif of the passage?

A) The extinction of species

B) The relative closeness of planets

C) Human beings as animals compared to the Martians

D) Human beings scrutinizing transient creatures

2

The narrator most likely uses the phrase "serene in their assurance of their empire" in line 12 to portray human beings as

A) complacent and arrogant.

B) malevolent and tyrannical.

C) peaceful rulers.

D) tranquil after a recent conquest.

3

When is this passage supposed to have been written?

A) in the last years of the nineteenth century

B) right around the time human beings realized there was life on other planets

C) early in the twentieth century

D) after mankind was given a reason to think of other worlds as threatening

4

Which choice provides the best evidence for the answer to the previous question?

A) Lines 1-10 ("No one… drop of water")

B) Lines 14-19 ("No one… departed days")

C) Lines 28-29 ("And early… disillusionment")

D) Lines 61-65 ("And before… other races")

5

As used in line 20, "terrestial" most nearly means

A) prognosticating.

B) Earth-dwelling.

C) terrified.

D) alien.

6

The main purpose of the second paragraph (lines 30-42) is to

A) indicate that life on Mars has had longer to evolve than life on Earth.

B) remind the reader of Mars's distance from the sun and subsequent temperature.

C) give more information on the setting of the passage.

D) demonstrate that, although suitable for life, Mars is unsuitable for human life.

7

Based on the passage, which choice gives the most likely reason for Mars attacking Earth?

A) Mars's harsh climate has produced particularly aggressive beings.

B) Mars is very slowly becoming uninhabitable.

C) The Martians must escape an immediate threat to their planet.

D) Earth has precious metals and other resources the Martians need to advance.

8

Which choice provides the best evidence for the answer to the previous question?

A) Lines 34-41 ("It must be… could begin")

B) Lines 48-54 ("And we men… upon Mars")

C) Lines 57-60 ("To carry… creeps upon them")

D) Lines 72-76 ("The Martians… perfect unanimity")

9

The narrator portrays the invaders as

A) ruthless beyond comparison.

B) having instruments that can see dangers to their world.

C) no more merciless than Earth dwellers.

D) apostles of mercy.

10

The first sentence of the last paragraph (lines 72-76) serves mainly to

A) give more detail about an event that has been hinted at throughout the passage.

B) emphasize the significance of an invasion from another planet.

C) convince the reader of the importance of planning.

D) add an element of danger and surprise to the passage.

Questions 1-11 are based on the following passage.

This passage is adapted from "Metallic Glass Gears Make for Graceful Robots." Originally published 2016 on NASA's website.

Throw a baseball, and you might say it's all in the wrist.

For robots, it's all in the gears.

Line 5 Gears are essential for precision robotics. They allow limbs to turn smoothly and stop on command; low-quality gears cause limbs to jerk or shake. If you're designing a robot to scoop samples or grip a ledge, the kind of gears you'll need won't come from a hardware store.

10 At NASA's Jet Propulsion Laboratory in Pasadena, California, technologist Douglas Hofmann and his collaborators are building a better gear. Hofmann is the lead author of two recent papers on gears made from bulk metallic 15 glass (BMG), a specially crafted alloy with properties that make it ideal for robotics.

"Although BMGs have been explored for a long time, understanding how to design and implement them into structural hardware has 20 proven elusive," said Hofmann. "Our team of researchers and engineers at JPL, in collaboration with groups at Caltech and UC San Diego, have finally put BMGs through the necessary testing to demonstrate their potential benefits for NASA 25 spacecraft. These materials may be able to offer us solutions for mobility in harsh environments, like on Jupiter's moon Europa."

How can this mystery material be both a metal and a glass? The secret is in its atomic 30 structure. Metals have an organized, crystalline arrangement. But if you heat them up into a liquid, they melt and the atoms become randomized. Cool them rapidly enough --about 1,832 degrees Fahrenheit (1,000 degrees Celsius) 35 per second -- and you can trap their non-crystalline, "liquid" form in place.

By virtue of being cooled so rapidly, the material is technically a glass. It can flow easily and be blow-molded when heated, just like 40 windowpane glass. When this glassy material is produced in parts greater than about .04 inches (1 millimeter), it's called "bulk" metallic glass, or BMG.

Metallic glasses were originally 45 developed at Caltech in Pasadena, California, in 1960. Since then, they've been used to manufacture everything from cellphones to golf clubs.

Among their attractive qualities, BMGs 50 have low melting temperatures. That allows parts to be cast using injection-molding technology, similar to what's used in the plastics industry, but with much higher strength and wear-resistance. BMGs also don't get brittle in extreme cold, a 55 factor which can lead to a gear's teeth fracturing. This last quality makes the material particularly useful for the kinds of robotics done at JPL.

Hofmann said that gears made from BMGs can "run cold and dry": initial testing has 60 demonstrated strong torque and smooth turning without lubricant, even at -328 degrees Fahrenheit (-200 degrees Celsius). For robots sent to frozen landscapes, that can be a power-saving advantage. NASA's Mars Curiosity rover, 65 for example, expends energy heating up grease lubricant every time it needs to move.

"Being able to operate gears at the low temperature of icy moons, like Europa, is a potential game changer for scientists," said R. 70 Peter Dillon, a technologist and program manager in JPL's Materials Development and Manufacturing Technology Group. "Power no longer needs to be siphoned away from the science instruments for heating gearbox 75 lubricant, which preserves precious battery power."

Not only can BMGs allow these gears to perform at low temperatures, but they can also be manufactured at a fraction of the cost of their 80 steel versions without sacrificing performance. This is potentially game changing for reducing the cost of robots that use strain wave gears, since they are often their most expensive part.

85 "Mass producing strain wave gears using BMGs may have a major impact on the consumer robotics market," Hofmann said. "This is especially true for humanoid robots, where gears in the joints can be very expensive but are 90 required to prevent shaking arms. The performance at low temperatures for JPL spacecraft and rovers seems to be a happy added benefit."

1

The main purpose of the passage is to

A) highlight similarities and differences between people and robots.

B) argue the importance of new innovations in robotic science.

C) explain how an important part of robots works.

D) describe a material that is or will be used in robots.

2

According to the passage, the process of proving bulk metallic glass's value for NASA has involved

A) experimentation and a high level of funding.

B) cooperation and trials to check quality and/or performance.

C) exploring and solving anticipated gravitational problems associated with robotics in space.

D) teamwork and seemingly unrelated innovations.

3

Which choice provides the best evidence for the answer to the previous question?

A) Lines 17-20 ("Although BMGs... said Hoffmann")

B) Lines 20-25 ("Our team... NASA spacecraft")

C) Lines 28-36 ("How can this... in place")

D) Lines 44-48 ("Metallic glasses... golf clubs")

4

The author most likely includes specific temperatures in lines 33-35 ("about 1,832... per second") to

A) demonstrate how much heat is necessary to create bulk metal glass.

B) point out how rapid current technology can cool materials.

C) emphasize how extremely resilient bulk metal glass is to temperature change.

D) specify how fast metal must change temperature to become bulk metal glass.

5

The main purpose of lines 28 to 48 ("How can... golf clubs") is to

A) support a claim with facts.

B) demonstrate the value of a material.

C) clarify something that might be confusing.

D) answer a question that previously puzzled scientists.

6

Based on information in the passage, which of the following might pose a problem for bulk metal glass?

A) extremely high temperatures

B) exceptionally high gravity

C) severely unstable terrain

D) wet environments

7

Which choice provides the best evidence for the answer to the previous question?

A) Lines 49-53 ("Among their attractive... and wear-resistance")

B) Lines 58-62 ("Hoffmann said... degrees Celsius")

C) Lines 67-72 ("Being able to... Technology Group")

D) Lines 76-84 ("Not only can... expensive part")

8

As used in line 51, "cast" most nearly means

A) thrown.

B) formed.

C) heated.

D) changed.

The passage implies that NASA's Mars Curiosity rover

A) would add torque by incorporating bulk metal glass gears.

B) in its present state requires a restrictive amount of lubricant in extremely low temperatures.

C) could run in cold environments for a longer period of time by using different materials.

D) needs the capacity to cool its parts to -328 degrees Fahrenheit.

According to the passage, in what area do bulk metal glass gears have a significant advantage over steel gears?

A) efficiency

B) performance

C) price

D) malleability

Hoffmann uses the phrase "happy added benefit" (lines 92-93) most likely to

A) clarify how NASA and JPL personnel feel about an aspect of bulk metal glass gears.

B) convince consumer robotics manufacturers of a benefit of bulk metal glass they might not have considered.

C) emphasize that there are many reasons to use bulk metal glass gears in robots.

D) indicate that performance at low temperatures was not NASA's primary objective in working with bulk metal glass.

Questions 1-10 are based on the following passage.

This passage is adapted from Robert Stawell Ball, *Great Astronomers: Isaac Newton.* Originally published in 1907.

The earliest of Newton's great achievements in natural philosophy was his detection of the composite character of light. That
Line a beam of ordinary sunlight is, in fact, a mixture
5 of a very great number of different-colored lights, is a doctrine now familiar to everyone who has theslightest education in physical science. We must, however, remember that this discovery was really a tremendous advance in knowledge at the
10 time when Newton announced it.

We here explain the experiment by which he first learned the composition of light. A sunbeam is admitted into a darkened room through an opening in a shutter. This beam, when
15 not interfered with, will travel in a straight line to the screen, and there reproduce a bright spot of the same shape as the hole in the shutter. If, however, a prism of glass be introduced so that the beam traverse it, then it will be seen at once
20 that the light is deflected from its original track. There is, however, a further and most important change which takes place. The spot of light is not alone removed to another part of the screen, but it becomes spread out into a long band, beautifully
25 colored and exhibiting the hues of the rainbow. At the top are the violet rays, and then in descending order we have the indigo, blue, green, yellow, orange, and red.

The circumstance in this phenomenon
30 which appears to have particularly arrested Newton's attention was the elongation which the luminous spot underwent in consequence of its passage through the prism. When the prism was absent the spot was nearly circular, but when the
35 prism was introduced the spot was about five times as long as it was broad. To ascertain the explanation of this was the first problem to be solved. He discovered that though the beam of white light looks so pure and so simple, yet in
40 reality it is composed of differently colored lights blended together. These are, of course, indistinguishable in the compound beam, but they are separated or disentangled, so to speak, by the action of the prism. The rays at the blue end of
45 the spectrum are more powerfully deflected by the action of the glass than are the rays at the red end. Thus, the rays variously colored red, orange, yellow, green, blue, indigo, violet, are each conducted to a different part of the screen. In this
50 way the prism has the effect of exhibiting the constitution of the composite beam of light.

To us this now seems quite obvious, but Newton did not adopt it hastily. With
55 characteristic caution he verified the explanation by many different experiments, all of which confirmed his discovery. One of these may be mentioned. He made a hole in the screen at that part on which the violet rays fell. Thus a violet
60 ray was allowed to pass through, all the rest of the light being intercepted, and on this beam so isolated he was able to try further experiments. For instance, when he interposed another prism in its path, he found, as he expected, that it was
65 again deflected, and he measured the amount of the deflection. Again he tried the same experiment with one of the red rays from the opposite end of the colored band. He allowed it to pass through the same aperture in the screen,
70 and he tested the amount by which the second prism was capable of producing deflection. He thus found, as he had expected to find, that the second prism was more efficacious in bending the violet rays than in bending the red rays. Thus
75 he confirmed the fact that the various hues of the rainbow were each bent by a prism to a different extent, violet being acted upon the most, and red the least.

Not only did Newton decompose a
80 white beam into its constituent colors, but conversely by interposing a second prism with its angle turned upwards, he reunited the different colors, and thus reproduced the original beam of white light.

Figure 1 shows the spectrum of visible and invisible light rays along with their wavelength.

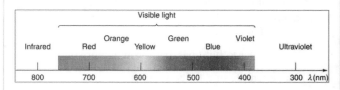

1

Which choice best describes the overall structure of the passage?

A) an introduction to a surprising property of light, the experiment that determined this strange property, and resistance to this experiment at the time it was conducted

B) a detailed account of Newton's achievements and a list of his most famous experiments

C) a conclusion about light, a description of a series of experiment that led to that conclusion, and a brief account of some follow-up experiments

D) an announcement of a famous achievement, the reaction to that achievement, and the effects of

2

The use of the words "great," "doctrine," and "tremendous" in the first paragraph establish a tone that is

A) informal.

B) respectful.

C) sensationalized.

D) scornful.

3

The author describes a sunbeam that has not been interfered with in lines 12-17 ("A sunbeam... hole in the shutter)" most likely as

A) a contrast to light passing through a prism.

B) an example of a failed version of the prism experiment.

C) context for the prism experiment.

D) a reason to doubt the results of the prism experiment.

4

As used in line 30, "arrested" most nearly means

A) stopped.

B) imprisoned.

C) distracted.

D) caught.

5

Which of the following does the passage indicate about Newton's discovery?

A) Newton succeeded in designing and executing an experiment to determine why a sunbeam going through a prism yields so many colors.

B) Newton discovered why a beam of light going through a prism yields so many colors while attempting to solve a different but related mystery about light.

C) Newton's discovery about the nature of light was only possible because of the many scientists who came before him.

D) Newton's discovery led to many important inventions.

6

Which choice provides the best evidence for the answer to the previous question?

A) Lines 17-25 ("If, however... of the rainbow")

B) Lines 34-41 ("When the prism... blended together")

C) Lines 42-47 ("These are... the the red end")

D) Lines 63-67 ("For instance... red rays")

Which of the following is NOT true according to the passage?

A) Beams of different colored light passing through a prism always spread further apart.

B) A blue ray of light bends more going through a prism than an orange ray of light.

C) Yellow light passing through a prism can come out red and green on the other side.

D) Newton took a long time to accept what he had discovered about light.

Which choice provides the best evidence for the answer to the previous question?

A) Lines 38-47 ("He discovered... the red end")

B) Lines 47-57 ("Thus, the rays... his discovery")

C) Lines 71-78 ("He thus found... red the least")

D) Lines 79-83 ("Not only... white light")

Based on the figure and the passage, one can most reasonably infer that

A) green light passing through a prism would deflect less than ultraviolet light passing through a prism.

B) visible light is the only light that deflects when passing through a prism.

C) doubling the wavelength of a beam of light will cause it to deflect half as much on passing through a prism.

D) if infrared light were visible, it would deflect less than yellow light on passing through a prism.

Which of the following is true according to the figure?

A) Light with a wavelength of 650 nanometers is yellow.

B) Light with a wavelength of 720 nanometers is not visible.

C) Infrared light waves are approximately twice as long as violet light waves.

D) Yellow light waves are approximately half as long as infrared light waves.

Questions 1-11 are based on the following passage.

This passage is adapted from "NASA Tests Robotic Ice Tools." Originally published 2017 on NASA's website.

Want to go ice fishing on Jupiter's moon Europa? There's no promising you'll catch anything, but a new set of robotic prototypes could help.

Line 5   Since 2015, NASA's Jet Propulsion Laboratory in Pasadena, California, has been developing new technologies for use on future missions to ocean worlds. That includes a subsurface probe that could burrow through
10   miles of ice, taking samples along the way, robotic arms that unfold to reach faraway objects, and a projectile launcher for even more distant samples.

"In the future, we want to answer the
15   question of whether there's life on the moons of the outer planets—on Europa, Enceladus and Titan," said Tom Cwik, who leads JPL's Space Technology Program. "We're working with NASA Headquarters to identify the specific
20   systems we need to build now, so that in 10 or 15 years, they could be ready for a spacecraft."

Those systems would face a variety of challenging environments. Temperatures can reach hundreds of degrees below freezing.
25   Rover wheels might cross ice that behaves like sand. On Europa, surfaces are bathed in radiation.

"Robotic systems would face cryogenic temperatures and rugged terrain and
30   have to meet strict planetary protection requirements," said Hari Nayar, who leads the robotics group that oversaw the research. "One of the most exciting places we can go is deep into subsurface oceans—but doing so requires
35   new technologies that don't exist yet."

Brian Wilcox, an engineering fellow at JPL, designed a prototype inspired by so-called "melt probes" used here on Earth. Since the late 1960s, these probes have been used to melt
40   through snow and ice to explore subsurface regions.

The problem is that they use heat inefficiently. Europa's crust could be 6.2 miles deep or it could be 12.4 miles deep (10 to 20
45   kilometers); a probe that doesn't manage its energy would cool down until it stopped frozen in the ice.

Wilcox innovated a different idea: a capsule insulated by a vacuum, the same way a
50   thermos bottle is insulated. Instead of radiating heat outwards, it would retain energy from a chunk of heat-source plutonium as the probe sinks into the ice.

A rotating sawblade on the bottom of
55   the probe would slowly turn and cut through the ice. As it does so, it would throw ice chips back into the probe's body, where they would be melted by the plutonium and pumped out behind it.
60   Removing the ice chips would ensure the probe drills steadily through the ice without blockages. The ice water could also be sampled and sent through a spool of aluminum tubing to a lander on the surface. Once there,
65   the water samples could be checked for biosignatures.

"We think there are glacier-like ice flows deep within Europa's frozen crust," Wilcox said. "Those flows churn up material
70   from the ocean down below. As this probe tunnels into the crust, it could be sampling waters that may contain biosignatures, if any exist."

To ensure no Earth microbes hitched a
75   ride, the probe would heat itself to over 900 degrees Fahrenheit (482 degrees Celsius) during its cruise on a spacecraft. That would kill any residual organisms and decompose complex organic molecules that could affect
80   science results.

These and concurrent innovations and experiments are just starting points. With the ocean worlds study complete, researchers will now consider whether these inventions can be
85   further refined. A second phase of development is being considered by NASA. Those efforts could eventually produce the technologies that might fly on future missions to the outer solar system.
90   This research was funded by NASA's Space Technology Mission Directorate's Game Changing Development Program, which investigates ideas and approaches that could solve significant technological problems and
95   revolutionize future space endeavors.

1

The main purpose of the passage is to

A) explain technology that private citizens will be using on planets and moons in our solar system soon.

B) introduce innovations that will hopefully allow NASA to perform new missions in difficult environments.

C) explain surprising methods of collecting data from around our solar system.

D) put forth a hypothesis about life on other planets and moons.

2

The first sentence of the passage establishes a tone that is

A) churlish.

B) scholarly.

C) inviting.

D) earnest.

3

As used in line 29, "cryogenic" most nearly means

A) life-preserving.

B) quickly changing.

C) extreme.

D) very cold.

4

Which of the following can be most reasonably inferred from information in the passage?

A) Some members of NASA think evidence of life on other planets' moons might be found deep in their subsurface oceans.

B) NASA is preparing to found human colonies on other planets and moons.

C) NASA expects to find life on the moons of other planets within 15 years.

D) A team at NASA is developing systems that, in 10 to 15 years, will hopefully allow an astronaut to dive deep into the subsurface oceans existing on some planets' moons.

5

Which choice provides the best evidence for the answer to the previous question?

A) Lines 5-13 ("Since 2015... distant samples")

B) Lines 22-27 ("Those systems... bathed in radiation")

C) Lines 32-35 ("One of the... don't exist yet")

D) Lines 82-89 ("With the ocean... solar system")

6

The passage indicates that new technologies developed by NASA

A) can inspire innovations used on Earth.

B) tend to elements that are kept secret.

C) sometimes utilize technology used on Earth.

D) are tested many times to ensure NASA's high standard.

7

Which choice provides the best evidence for the answer to the previous question?

A) Lines 32-35 ("One of the most... don't exist yet")

B) Lines 36-41 ("Brian Wilcox... subsurface regions")

C) Lines 48-53 ("Wilcox innovated... sinks into the ice")

D) Lines 74-80 ("To ensure no... science results")

8

The eighth and ninth paragraphs (lines 48-59) serve primarily to

A) explain clever developments to an existing technology that will prepare it for a broad range of environments and uses.

B) enumerate the possible issues a heat probe might encounter on Europa.

C) give context that will help the reader understand the importance of probing deep into Europa's ice.

D) describe changes to a machine that will hopefully mitigate or solve a potential problem.

9

Which choice best describes a possible method of collecting water samples explained in the passage?

A) Water samples could be sucked from a subsurface ocean through tubing into the lander.

B) Ice thrown by a sawblade, once melted, could be sampled.

C) Once back on the spacecraft, the probe could heat itself to over 900 degrees Fahrenheit to melt the ice it had captured for sampling.

D) Robotic arms could collect scoops of ice and water for sampling.

10

The primary purpose of the eleventh paragraph (lines 67-73) is to

A) give a reason for the process described in the previous paragraph.

B) illuminate a potential drawback to the process described in the previous paragraph.

C) assure the reader that contingencies to plan described earlier in the passage have been considered.

D) explain why further developments to the heat probe than those described in the preceding paragraphs must be made.

11

From the final two paragraphs of the passage (lines 81-95), it can most reasonably be inferred that

A) NASA will further refine the innovations discussed in this passage to send to space on future missions.

B) NASA will plan future missions mostly based on the success or failure of the missions discussed in this passage.

C) funding for NASA's Space Technology Mission Directorate's Game Changing Development Program depends partly upon the successful use of the innovations discussed in this passage.

D) NASA believes the innovations described in this passage might revolutionize future missions.

Questions 1-10 are based on the following passages.

Passage 1 is adapted from H. Clay Trumbull, *A Lie Never Justifiable: A Study in Ethics.* Originally published in 1856. Passage 2 is adapted from Mark Twain, "On the Decay of the Art of Lying." Originally delivered as a speech in 1880 and published in 1882.

Passage 1

Whether a lie is ever justifiable is a question that has been in discussion, not only in all the Christian centuries, but ever since
Line questions concerning human conduct were first a
5 possibility.

In the summer of 1863 I was a prisoner of war in Columbia, South Carolina. An escape plan proposed to me by a fellow-officer seemed to offer peculiar chances of success, and I gladly
10 joined in it. But as its fuller details were considered, I found that a probable contingency would involve the telling of a lie to an enemy, or a failure of the whole plan. At this my moral sense recoiled, and I expressed my unwillingness
15 to tell a lie, even to regain my personal liberty or to advantage my government by a return to its army.

My friend asked me whether I would hesitate to kill an enemy who was on guard over
20 me, or whom I met outside, if it were essential to our escape. I replied that I would not hesitate to do so, any more than I would hesitate at it if we were over against each other in battle. My friend then asked me on what principle I
25 could justify the taking of a man's life as an enemy, and yet not feel justified in telling him a lie in order to save his life and secure our liberty.

In my careful study of the principles involved in this question, I came upon what
30 seemed to me the conclusion of the whole matter. God is the author of life. He who gives life has the right to take it again. What God can do by himself, God can authorize another to do. Human governments derive their just powers from God.
35 If a war waged by a human government be righteous, the officers of that government take life, in the prosecution of the war, as God's agents.

On the other hand, God, who can justly
40 take life, cannot lie. A lie is contrary to the very nature of God. And if God cannot lie, God cannot authorize another to lie. What is unjustifiable in God's sight, is without a possibility of justification in the universe. No personal or social
45 emergency can justify a lie, whatever may be its apparent gain, or whatever harm may seem to be involved in a refusal to speak it.

Passage 2

No fact is more firmly established than that lying is a necessity of our circumstances—
50 the deduction that it is then a Virtue goes without saying. No virtue can reach its highest usefulness without careful and diligent cultivation— therefore, it goes without saying that this one ought to be taught in the public schools—even in
55 the newspapers.

In a far country where I once lived the ladies used to go around paying calls, under the humane and kindly pretence of wanting to see each other; and when they returned home, they
60 would cry out with a glad voice, saying, "We made sixteen calls and found fourteen of them out"—not meaning that they found out anything important against the fourteen—no, that was only a colloquial phrase to signify that they were not
65 at home—and their manner of saying it expressed their lively satisfaction in that fact. Now their pretence of wanting to see the fourteen—and the other two whom they had been less lucky with— was that commonest and mildest form of lying
70 which is sufficiently described as a deflection from the truth.

I think that all this courteous lying is a sweet and loving art, and should be cultivated.
75 What I bemoan is the growing prevalence of the brutal truth. An injurious truth has no merit over an injurious lie. Neither should ever be uttered. The man who speaks an injurious truth lest his soul be not saved if he do otherwise,
80 should reflect that that sort of a soul is not strictly worth saving. The man who tells a lie to help a poor devil out of trouble, is one of whom the angels doubtless say, "Lo, here is an heroic soul who casts his own welfare in jeopardy to succor
85 his neighbor's; let us exalt this magnanimous liar."

An injurious lie is an uncommendable thing; and so, also, and in the same degree, is an injurious truth—a fact that is recognized by the
90 law of libel.

Lying is universal—we <u>all</u> do it. Therefore, the wise thing is for us diligently to train ourselves to lie thoughtfully, judiciously; to lie with a good object, and not an evil one; to lie
95 for others' advantage, and not our own; to lie healingly, charitably, humanely, not cruelly, hurtfully, maliciously; to lie gracefully and graciously, not awkwardly and clumsily; to lie firmly, frankly, squarely, with head erect, not
100 haltingly, tortuously, with pusillanimous mien, as being ashamed of our high calling.

1

As used in line 37, "prosecution" most nearly means

A) arresting.

B) legal action against.

C) torturing.

D) carrying out.

2

Which of the following provides the most direct evidence in support of Trumbull's stance on lying?

A) "Whether a lie... first a possibility" (lines 1-5)

B) "But as its fuller... return to its army" (lines 10-17)

C) "God is the author of life... as God's agents" (lines 31-38)

D) "On the other hand... in the universe" (lines 39-44)

3

The second paragraph of Passage 2 (lines 56-71) primarily serves to

A) introduce the author's opinion on the ethical nature of lying.

B) describe a routine that the author considers to be a positive form of lying.

C) tell a story involving lies that seem harmless but are not.

D) relate a custom that caused the author to begin deliberating the ethical nature of lying.

4

It can be inferred from Passage 2 that Twain believes most strongly that, before speaking, a person should consider

A) the wellbeing of others.

B) the facts in question.

C) how he/she (the speaker) will be affected.

D) how to tell the truth without being injurious.

5

Which choice provides the best evidence for the answer to the previous question?

A) Lines 48-55 ("No fact... in the newspapers")

B) Lines 72-76 ("I think that all... brutal truth")

C) Lines 78-86 ("The man who... magnanimous liar")

D) Lines 91-93 ("Lying is universal... ourselves to lie")

6

As used in line 100, "pusillanimous" most nearly means

A) overt.

B) timid.

C) courageous.

D) angry.

Which choice best states the relationship between the two passages?

A) Passage 2 gives important context to Passage 1 but ultimately disagrees with it.

B) Passage 2 offers a logical continuation of the argument started in Passage 1.

C) The passages give nearly opposite opinions on the same issue, each for moral reasons.

D) Both passages discuss the ethics of lying, but Passage 2 takes a much more self-centered stance.

8

Based on Passage 1, Trumbull would most likely respond to the third paragraph of Passage 2 (lines 72-74) by saying that

A) no one should ever lie no matter how much good the lie might do or how much harm it might stop.

B) lying can never be loving or courteous.

C) if one must tell a lie, the more courteous lie one can tell, the better.

D) God gives those who tell the truth authority to take the lives of those who lie.

The second paragraph of each passage serves primarily to

A) tell a story from the author's life to help the audience relate to the author.

B) relate part or all of an incident that prompted the author to think about lies.

C) establish the importance of the author's argument by relating it to a pivotal moment in the author's life.

D) refute a likely counterargument to the author's main claim.

10

Based on these two passages, which seems the most likely way each author decides what is ethical?

A) Both authors try to determine what would be best for the largest number of people.

B) Trumbull follows God's example, and Twain aims to keep others from getting mad at him.

C) Twain aspires to do what will make him look the best; Trumbull strives to make others as comfortable as possible.

D) Trumbull tries to interpret God's will while Twain considers what would bring about the most good for others.

Questions 1-11 are based on the following passage and the corresponding graphic.

This passage and the associated figure are adapted from Steve Henderson, "Ice Cream v. Bacon." Originally published 2017 on the U.S. Department of Labor Blog.

How much did you spend on ice cream last year? According to the Bureau of Labor Statistics, the average U.S. household spent
Line
5 around $54. But why does BLS need to know that?

Let's take a deep dive into that ice cream. That's just one of thousands of data we collect to calculate the Consumer Price Index, a monthly assessment of price changes for goods
10 and services in the United States. The CPI has separate inflation indexes for just about everything people purchase. For example, the CPI has an index for "Bacon and related products," and lots of other itemized food
15 categories, including "Ice cream and related products."

Why so many indexes? The CPI needs to carefully track how the prices of food, and just about everything else, change because not every
20 item's price goes up or down at the same rate. For example, bacon has increased in price almost 32 percent over the past 10 years while ice cream went up 21 percent over the same time period.

Looking at how prices have moved over
25 the last year, bacon is slightly less expensive than it was in January 2016, while the price of ice cream has gone up slightly. This information is helpful for families looking to see where their food budget money went, as well as researchers
30 investigating changing food prices and other indicators of inflation.

Most importantly, the CPI needs to know how much the average U.S. household spends on both of those two food items in order to measure
35 the impact different inflation rates have on *total* inflation. If everybody spent the same number of dollars on ice cream as they do on bacon, then you could just use a simple average of the two inflation rates to get a total. Here is where BLS's
40 Consumer Expenditure Survey comes in. It measures, in great detail, all the different goods and services consumers purchase in a year, and passes these numbers to the CPI to form a "market basket" – that is, a list of everything
45 people buy and what percentage of their total spending goes to each item.

The latest spending numbers showed that the average dollar amount per year that all U.S. households spent on ice cream was $54.04,
50 while the average amount on bacon was $39.07. That means that ice cream has a greater importance than bacon when tracking inflation, not only in the Henderson household, but in the CPI. In other words, the more people spend on an
55 item, the more inflationary changes to its cost will affect the total inflation rate.

Policymakers, researchers, journalists, government bodies and others use the CPI to make important decisions that directly affect
60 American citizens. Census Bureau analysts use CPI data to adjust the official poverty thresholds for inflation, and it's one of several factors the Federal Reserve Board considers when deciding whether to raise or lower interest rates.
65 Employers may use it to determine whether to give cost-of-living increases, and policymakers use the CPI when considering changes to allotments for things like Social Security, military benefits or school lunch programs.
70 I hope this deep dive into ice cream spending helps you understand why the Consumer Expenditure Survey is so detailed.

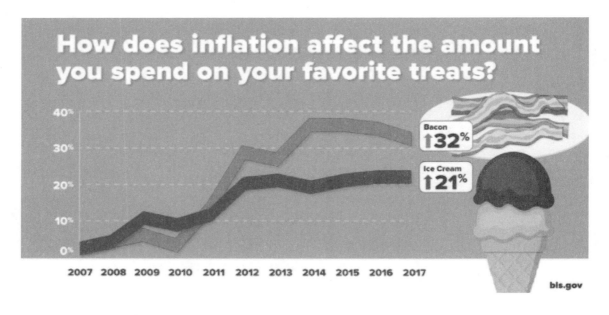

1

The main purpose of this passage is to

A) show the calculation of total inflation in the US for the years 2007 to 2017.

B) compare the relative effect of ice cream and bacon on total inflation in the U.S.

C) convince the reader of the importance of a government agency.

D) explain how a complicated calculation is made using two example products.

The third paragraph serves primarily to

A) introduce a reason for such detailed data collection.

B) indicate an alarming trend.

C) shift focus from a problem to a solution.

D) pose a question about the relative inflation of ice cream and bacon.

The passage indicates that it is important to find out how much people are spending on bacon mostly to

A) calculate the Consumer Price Index (CPI).

B) determine how much influence the change in price of bacon will have on total inflation.

C) help them decide what role, if any, bacon will play in the "market basket."

D) estimate income in different areas.

Which choice provides the best evidence for the answer to the previous question?

A) Lines 10-16 ("The CPI... related products")

B) Lines 17-23 ("The CPI... time period")

C) Lines 32-36 ("Most importantly... total inflation")

D) Lines 39-46 ("Here is where... each item")

As used in line 52, "tracking" most nearly means

A) searching for.

B) separating into categories.

C) seeking.

D) monitoring.

Which statement is most likely given information in the passage?

A) A change in the price of toilet paper will affect the total inflation rate more than a similar change in price of steel hammers.

B) If 51% of the items in the "market basket" experience an increase in price, total inflation will rise.

C) A change in the price of a $60 item will have a greater impact on total inflation than a change in the price of a $50 item.

D) Bacon had a greater impact on total inflation than ice cream in 2009 and 2010.

Which choice provides the best evidence for the answer to the previous question?

A) Lines 40-46 ("It measures... each item")

B) Lines 51-56 ("That means... inflation rate")

C) Lines 57-64 ("Policymakers... interest rates")

D) Lines 65-69 ("Employers may... lunch programs")

As used in line 68, "allotments for" most nearly means

A) expected income from.

B) allocation of funds for.

C) distribution of.

D) policies to benefit.

According to the graph, which of the following occurred between 2012 and 2013?

A) Bacon had a greater effect on inflation than ice cream did.

B) Bacon's effect on the market basket increased.

C) The cost of bacon fell.

D) Bacon lost some of its influence on total inflation.

The intersection on the graph between 2010 and 2011 represents

A) a point in time when bacon and ice cream had equal impacts on total inflation.

B) a point in time when bacon and ice cream cost the same amount.

C) a point in time when the average consumer began to spend more money on bacon than on ice cream in a year.

D) a point in time when bacon and ice cream had both increased the same percentage from their 2007 prices.

11

Based on the passage, which of the following information would be necessary in addition to the graph to calculate the total inflation for a bacon and ice cream "market basket" from 2007 to 2017?

A) The amount per pound the average consumer spent on ice cream and bacon every year between 2007 and 2017

B) The percentage of his/her income each consumer spent on ice cream and bacon every year between 2007 and 2017

C) The amount of money the average consumer spent on ice cream and bacon every year between 2007 and 2017

D) The change in spending on bacon and ice cream from 2007 to 2017

Questions 1-10 are based on the following passage and corresponding graphics.

This passage is adapted from "Worth the Weight: New Table Aims to Clarify Variable Atomic Weight Values" from the U.S. Geological Survey (USGS) website. The USGS is a branch of the Department of the Interior. Originally published 2017.

Those left confused by recent updates to the table of standard atomic weights, whose values appear on the periodic table of elements, have reason to celebrate.

Three scientists from the U.S. Geological Survey, the International Union of Pure and Applied Chemistry (IUPAC), and the Brookhaven National Laboratory have prepared a new table meant to clarify atomic weights.

For the first time, a single table containing both four-digit standard atomic weight values and conventional atomic weight values, for those elements with standard atomic weights given as intervals, is available, making it easier for teachers to demonstrate that the atomic weights of many elements have natural variation and are not constants of nature. Additionally, students and others can select a single value for molecular calculations.

The atomic weights of more than half of the elements have some variability. To indicate this, in 2009 and 2011 the Commission on Isotopic Abundances and Atomic Weights, of the IUPAC, replaced single-value standard atomic weight values with atomic weight intervals for 12 elements, whose variations are well known: hydrogen, lithium, boron, carbon, nitrogen, oxygen, magnesium, silicon, sulfur, chlorine, bromine, and thallium. For example, the four-digit standard atomic weight of sulfur became the interval [32.06, 32.08].

"This new table presents the best of both worlds—single values for use in calculations and the more complex intervals for stable isotope applications," said Coplen. For example, interval values can be used to highlight the variability of atomic weights arising from variations in abundances of stable isotopes in different sources of elements, such as variations in atomic weights of hydrogen and oxygen in precipitation, rivers, and groundwater.

This change, while representative of the true atomic weights of elements, presented its own problem: teachers and students did not know what value to use in classroom problems, like molecular calculations. With the new table, teachers can easily demonstrate to students that several chemical elements have variable atomic weight values depending upon their source, and when a single value is needed, such as for molecular calculations, the same row in the table indicates that the single-value conventional atomic weight can be used.

"As a young student of chemistry, I was taught that the atomic weights of the elements on the periodic table were constants of nature," said Tyler Coplen, director of the Reston Stable Isotope Laboratory. "It took me decades to discover that standard atomic weights of a dozen elements are variable and should be displayed as intervals to highlight these natural variations."

Figure 1.

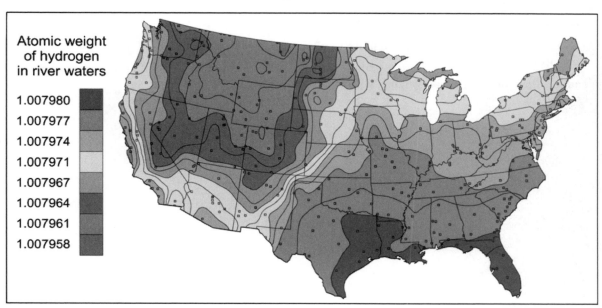

Figure 2.

1

The primary purpose of the passage is to

A) announce a new scientific discovery.

B) correct a long-standing error in the way chemistry has been taught.

C) garner support for a change in teaching proposed by the author.

D) introduce a new way of presenting information.

2

Which benefit of the new table does the author indicate?

A) a greater level of precision

B) ease in education

C) a new organization that allows users to find elements much faster

D) intuitive flow for greater understanding without explanation

3

Which choice provides the best evidence for the answer to the previous question?

A) Lines 10-14 ("For the first... is available")

B) Lines 14-19 ("making it... molecular calculations")

C) Lines 21-31 ("To indicate... 32.06, 32.08]")

D) Lines 42-46 ("This change... molecular calculations")

4

Based on information in the passage, in which situation would the periodic table from before 2009 be more useful than the table with changes made "in 2009 and 2011 [by] the Commission on Isotopic Abundances and Atomic Weights" (line 22-23)?

A) illustrating that atomic weights are not constants of nature

B) making quick decisions in the field

C) solving problems in class

D) tying chemistry to real-world experiences

5

Which choice provides the best evidence for the answer to the previous question?

A) Lines 10-17 ("For the first... constants of nature")

B) Lines 32-35 ("This new table... said Coplen")

C) Lines 42-52 ("This change... can be used")

D) Lines 53-60 ("As a young... natural variations")

6

Which statement best describes a technique the author uses in the sixth and seventh paragraphs (lines 32-52) to support to main purpose of the passage?

A) The author relates a scientist's personal experience to indicate the importance of the new table.

B) The author recounts a story from his own education to demonstrate the value of the updated table.

C) The author gives specific examples of ways the new table has been used as a way of demonstrating its usefulness.

D) The author quotes a relatable person to make the reader feel that this information is relevant to him/her.

7

In the quotation in the first sentence of the last paragraph (lines 53-60), the author gives the information after the dash ("single values… isotope applications") to

A) give additional examples like the one before the dash.

B) clarify the definition of a term that came before the dash.

C) explain information that came before the dash.

D) add interesting but unrelated information.

As used in line 37, "arising from" most nearly means

A) caused by.

B) growing out of.

C) originating in.

D) resulting in.

Given information in the figures and passage and assuming that the hydrogen in the river waters of the United States is representative of the hydrogen in the rest of the world, which of the following will most likely be true of hydrogen on the new periodic table?

A) The new entry will list 8 possible atomic weights for hydrogen.

B) The new entry means that students in Florida will use a higher atomic weight for hydrogen in their classroom calculations than students in the middle of the US.

C) The atomic weight will be listed differently depending on where the table is made.

D) The atomic weight will be written as a single number since the four-digit weight will always be rounded to the same number.

10

The author most likely included Figure 2 in order to

A) show why water is different in different parts of the US.

B) give a picture that shows the importance of a single, settled value for atomic weight.

C) emphasize the range in values of atomic weight across the elements.

D) provide an illustration of variation in the atomic weight of individual elements.

Timed Assignments

Reading Summary

1. **Overview**
   - 5 Passages & 52 Questions
   - Types of Passages
   - Types of Questions
   - Reading for Points
   - Three Key Terms: Deep Reading, Answer Zone, & Your Own Answer
2. **Score Zone Reading**
   - Step One: Pre-Highlight The Passage
   - Step Two: Deep Read the Passage
   - Step Three: Clean Up
3. **Paired Passages**
   - Step One: Pre-Highlight The Passage
   - Step Two: Deep Read the Passage
   - Step Three: Clean Up
4. **It's A Trap!**
   - Word-For-Word Hook
   - Extreme Statements
   - Opposite
   - Bogus Comparison
   - True, But So What?
   - Half-Right, Half-Wrong
   - Implied, Literally?

Writing & Language Test

Tried & True Tutoring

What is the Writing & Language Test?

- The Writing and Language test measures your writing ability by testing your changes to another writer's work.
- This test includes:
  - 4 passages – these passages contain grammar and structural errors
  - 44 questions – these will refer to the grammar and structural errors and may not include an actual "question"
- You will have 35 minutes to complete this test.

Types of Questions

- There are 2 general types of questions on this test:
  - **Grammar questions** – these test you on a specific rule
    - These are the "questions" that don't seem to include an actual question – just answer choices
    - Example: Page 64 #1
  - **Question questions** – these include actual questions on a range of concepts concerning the structure of the passage
- There are many categories of **Grammar** and **Question Questions** that you will learn to recognize.
- The ability to recognize types of questions quickly is one of the most important skills on the **Writing and Language Test.**

#sat_hack

#pacing

On the Writing and Language test, you have less than a minute per question.

Try to spend around 30 seconds on each **Grammar Question**, and save time for the longer **Question Questions**.

Review

Fill in the blank.

1. How can you quickly determine whether a question is a **Grammar Question** or a **Question Question**?

_____

2. Question #1 on page 64 is an example of a _____ Question.

3. What is one of the most important skills on the **Writing and Language Test**?

_____

Grammar Guessing Strategy

- Even though Grammar Questions don't include a "question," you can easily figure out which error is being tested.
- Look at the answer choices and notice what differs from one choice to the next.
- The element that is changing in the answer choices indicates which grammar error is being tested.
- Take a look at these Grammar Questions and see if you can figure out what is being tested.

1

A) NO CHANGE

B) dentists: and

C) dentists, and

D) dentists, and,

What do you think is being tested?

_____

2

A) NO CHANGE

B) sleeps

C) will sleep

D) slept

What do you think is being tested?

_____

When you encounter a Grammar Question, first look at the choices and decide what is being tested. This will make it easier to recall specific rules and choose an answer.

#sat_hack
#step_number_one

More Than One Error

- Some Grammar Questions will test more than one error at a time.
- See if you can find more than one error being tested in the questions below.

3

A) NO CHANGE

B) can pollute the sea's

C) could have polluted the seas

D) has polluted sea's

What do you think is being tested?

_____

3

A) NO CHANGE

B) whom wants

C) who wanted

D) she wanted

What do you think is being tested?

_____

Punctuation

- There are three main types of Punctuation errors that appear in the Grammar Questions:
  1. **Sentence Punctuation**
  2. **Commas**
  3. **Apostrophes**

Complete Sentences

- Before we can talk about proper Sentence Punctuation, recall what a Complete Sentence is.
- For a sentence to be complete, it must:
  - Be a complete thought
  - Have a subject and a verb
- Take a look at the sentences below. Are these complete sentences or are they fragments (independent or dependent clauses)?

1

On Saturday morning, on his way to take the SAT, Jonathan stopped to get coffee.

Circle one: **complete / fragment**

2

When he arrived at the café and ordered his coffee in a hurry.

Circle one: **complete / fragment**

3

Because he was in a hurry, and he spilled his coffee.

Circle one: **complete / fragment**

4

Even though Jonathan spilled his coffee, he managed to not only make it to the SAT on time but to also score a 1600.

Circle one: **complete / fragment**

#sat_hack

#strong_independent_clause

To be complete, a sentence must contain at least one independent clause – a clause that is a complete sentence on its own.

For example, "**When I needed groceries, so I went to the store,**" is not a complete sentence because neither "**When I needed groceries**" nor "**so I went to the store**" is a complete sentence on its own.

You need to know conjunctions before learning Sentence Punctuation. There are 7 conjunctions you need to know:

For, **A**nd, **N**or, **B**ut, **O**r, **Y**et, **S**o

Remember these by using **FANBOYS.**

Sentence Punctuation

- When determining punctuation, first identify the different parts of the sentence.
  - **Two complete sentences**? You can use:
    - A period, exclamation mark, or question mark (. ! ?) to split them into two separate sentences.
    - A semicolon
    - A comma with a conjunction (, FANBOYS)
  - One **complete sentence** followed by **either a fragment or another complete sentence**? You can use:
    - A colon (:)
    - A dash (–)
  - Only **one complete sentence**? You can use:
    - A comma alone (,)
- Here's a chart to break down all of this information:

Both Complete	First Complete (Second either Complete or Incomplete)	Only One Complete
. ! ?	:	,
;	–	
,FANBOYS		

- Test your understanding. In the problems below, list all the types of punctuations that could go in the ▨

1

Some students prefer listening to Beyoncé's music ▨ [o]thers prefer Adele's.

Possible Punctuation:

_____

2

You might be a fan of Justin Bieber, Kendrick Lamar, or even Adele ▨ all inspiring artists.

Possible Punctuation:

_____

3

Even though some people don't consider rap to be "real music" ▨ most experts agree that artists like Jay-Z have changed pop culture.

Possible Punctuation:

_____

4

However, lesser known artists also help shape popular culture but receive less attention ▨ we have to give them credit, too.

Possible Punctuation:

_____

61

Commas

- In general, **commas** are overused on the SAT. There are only four reasons to use a comma:
  1. To join a fragment and a complete thought
  2. With a conjunction (FANBOYS) to join two complete thoughts
  3. In a list
  4. To surround "unnecessary" information
- We already discussed the first two back in **Sentence Punctuation**, so let's review the others.

Commas in a List

- Use **commas** if there are 3 or more items in the list
  Example: "At the top of my shopping list were milk, bread, and eggs."
- Use a comma after **every item in a list** (the Oxford comma that comes before "and")

#sat_hack

#commas_with_adjectives

There is only one circumstance where you should use a comma in a list of two items: between two adjectives whose order can be changed.

Commas To "Surround" Unnecessary Information

- You can also position commas around extra information.
- You can **only** do this if you can remove the phrase and still have a complete sentence.
  - Example: "Avocados, **loaded with beneficial nutrients**, are a great addition to any dish."
- This "unnecessary information" is called a modifier, and usually describes what follows.
- Practice these comma rules in the sentences below.

1

Some days when it is very sunny my mom brother and I like to go to the small private beach near our house and collect shells but we stay home if it's raining.

2

Neil DeGrasse Tyson an author astrophysicist and researcher is a very interesting funny man.

Apostrophes

- Apostrophes are used for **contractions** and to show **possession**.
- Contractions are words that are combined together (**can not → can't**)
- Possession means ownership (a **hat** that belongs to **Steven → Steven's hat**)
- Do <u>NOT</u> use an apostrophe for plural nouns ("I have two **puppies**." <u>NOT</u> "I have two **puppy's**.")

1

Its Kanye Wests first platinum record.

2

Throughout our nations history, our Presidents actions havent had as much of an impact as our Congresses actions.

3

Within the next decade, we will be celebrating our countries two-hundred-and-fiftieth anniversary.

4

Congresses actions have had even more of an impact than Kanye Wests Platinum Records.

Some students often confuse "**its**" and "**it's**"...

Its = possessive (does not **possess** an apostrophe)
It's = contraction of "it is" (imagine the apostrophe is a miniature of the i it is replacing)

Its' is not a word because there is no plural form of "it".

#sat_hack
#which_its_is_it

Punctuation Practice 1

Select from the following error types:
1. Incomplete Sentences
2. Sentence Punctuation
3. Commas
4. Apostrophes

On a 1 <u>cold dark day</u> in the winter of many adoring 2 <u>fans' existence,</u> One Direction 3 <u>announced that their</u> temporary hiatus would become a permanent split. 4 <u>When asked, what dragged them down and ultimately made them all ready to run their separate ways,</u> a source close to the manboys commented, "It was a lot of 5 <u>things; little things."</u> Already 6 <u>rumors—which</u> the UK

1

A) NO CHANGE

B) cold, dark day

C) cold dark day,

D) cold, and dark, day

Error Type: _____

2

A) NO CHANGE

B) fan's existence,

C) fans' existence;

D) fans' existence

Error Type: _____

3

A) NO CHANGE

B) announced, that their

C) announced: their

D) announced; that their

Error Type: _____

4

A) NO CHANGE

B) When asked what dragged them down and ultimately made them all ready to run their separate ways,

C) When asked what dragged them down and ultimately made them all ready to run their separate ways

D) When asked, what dragged them down and ultimately made them all ready to run their separate ways—

Error Type: _____

5

A) NO CHANGE

B) things little things."

C) things, they were all little things."

D) things—little things."

Error Type: _____

singers refer to as *rumours*, have surfaced about a reunion tour that would even include 7 <u>Zayn who</u> fans often describe as "irresistible," or even "perfect." In response to these allegations, one 1D member insisted, "Na na na. They don't know about 8 <u>us. Its</u> time for me to act my age. If 9 <u>that's is</u> true, where do broken hearts go to find solace? While some fans have turned to alternatives 10 <u>such as Forever in Your Mind, The</u>

A) NO CHANGE

B) rumors; which

C) rumors, which

D) rumors;

Error Type: _____

A) NO CHANGE

B) Zayn whom

C) Zayn: who

D) Zayn, whom

Error Type: _____

A) NO CHANGE

B) us, it's

C) us. It's

D) us, its

Error Type: _____

A) NO CHANGE

B) thats is

C) thats

D) that's

Error Type: _____

A) NO CHANGE

B) such as: Forever in Your Mind, The Vamps, or

C) such as, Forever in Your Mind, The Vamps, or

D) such as Forever in Your Mind, The Vamps, or,

Error Type: _____

Vamps, or 11 <u>Waterparks but</u> most recognize these others are a long way down from 12 <u>1D and they</u> just have to move on and live while they're young. 13 <u>Many on the other hand</u> have returned to the origin of the 14 <u>heartthrobs. *The X-Factor*.</u> Asked what he thought fans of 1D should 15 <u>do, Justin Bieber, Canadian pop legend and tattoo enthusiast</u> said, "What do you mean? Love

12

A) NO CHANGE

B) 1D, and they

C) 1D, they

D) 1D so they

Error Type: _____

13

A) NO CHANGE

B) Many, on the other hand,

C) Many on the other hand,

D) (Many on the other hand)

Error Type: _____

14

A) NO CHANGE

B) heartthrobs':

C) heartthrobs;

D) heartthrobs:

Error Type: _____

11

A) NO CHANGE

B) Waterparks, but

C) Waterparks, although

D) Waterparks,

Error Type: _____

15

A) NO CHANGE

B) do, Justin Bieber: Canadian pop legend and tattoo enthusiast

C) do; Justin Bieber, Canadian pop legend and tattoo enthusiast

D) do, Justin Bieber, Canadian pop legend and tattoo enthusiast,

Error Type: _____

me." Taylor Swift offered harsher advice on how to fill the blank space left by 16 <u>1D;</u> "Shake it off. They are never getting back together." Tay Tay added that she would welcome 17 <u>fans' of One Directions'</u> allegiance, telling them, "You belong with me." When asked if he had anything to say to his billions of 18 <u>fans, then</u> One Direction's Liam Payne said, "I want to write you a song." Even though this and other similar statements are likely little white 19 <u>lies: your</u> fans would like to say this back to 20 <u>you Liam. That's</u> what makes you beautiful.

16

A) NO CHANGE

B) 1D, she said,

C) 1D:

D) 1D(;

Error Type: _____

17

A) NO CHANGE

B) One Direction's fans'

C) fans of One Direction's

D) One Directions' fans'

Error Type: _____

18

A) NO CHANGE

B) fans.

C) fans,

D) fans:

Error Type: _____

19

A) NO CHANGE

B) lies. Your

C) lies, your

D) lies; your

Error Type: _____

20

A) NO CHANGE

B) you Liam: that's

C) you, Liam, that's

D) you, Liam: that's

Error Type: _____

PUNCTUATION PRACTICE 1

Punctuation Practice 2

Select from the following error types:
1. Incopmplete Sentences
2. Sentence Punctuation
3. Commas
4, Apostrophes.

1 When Hollywood announced an eighth movie in the _Fast and Furious_ franchise the news met with mixed reactions. One Tried & True 2 student on being asked about her level of excitement over the sequel, commented, "I know the first one is a 3 classic. I like stuff thats not super old better." Another student had this to say about the 4 franchises' star; "Isn't Vin Diesel like a hundred?"

1

A) NO CHANGE

B) When Hollywood announced an eighth movie in the _Fast and Furious_ franchise, the news meeting

C) Hollywood announced an eighth movie in the _Fast and Furious_ franchise, the news met

D) When Hollywood announced an eighth movie in the _Fast and Furious_ franchise, the news met

Error Type: _____

2

A) NO CHANGE

B) student; on

C) student, on

D) student—on

Error Type: _____

3

A) NO CHANGE

B) classic, but I like stuff that's

C) classic; but I like stuff that's

D) classic; I like stuff thats

Error Type: _____

4

A) NO CHANGE

B) franchise's star;

C) franchises' star:

D) franchise's star:

Error Type: _____

While 5 its true, his head has grown less 6 shiny, but Vin Diesel is still just as furious as ever. Whereas before in his movies the action 7 megastar's character's anger was generally directed at those bent on his 8 destruction, such as: aliens, hijackers, or the FBI, now he's garnering roles with more age-appropriate gripes. "I just didn't really buy that he was still mad at those guys for something that happened a million years ago," confided a Hollywood source.

5

A) NO CHANGE
B) it's true that
C) its true that
D) it's true—

Error Type: _____

6

A) NO CHANGE
B) shiny, nonetheless
C) shiny;
D) shiny,

Error Type: _____

7

A) NO CHANGE
B) megastar's characters'
C) megastars' character's
D) megastars' characters'

Error Type: _____

8

A) NO CHANGE
B) destruction, such as aliens, hijackers, or the FBI, now
C) destruction, such as aliens, hijackers, or the FBI. Now
D) destruction (such as, aliens, hijackers, or the FBI) now

Error Type: _____

9 "He started complaining about his 10 neighbors music after 9 PM, he reached new levels of fury and 11 believability. Hes' really come into his own as an actor." Experts 12 speculate that: Vin Diesel's upcoming roles will feature anger at topics ranging from his aching

9

A) NO CHANGE
B) When he
C) Then he
D) Eventually, he

Error Type: _____

10

A) NO CHANGE
B) neighbors—they play music
C) neighbors playing music
D) neighbors' music:

Error Type: _____

11

A) NO CHANGE
B) believability, he's
C) believability; hes'
D) believability—he's

Error Type: _____

12

A) NO CHANGE
B) agree:
C) agree that,
D) agree: that

Error Type: _____

back to why the kids haven't 13 <u>called, this is one</u> of the actor's current favorite topics of conversation. The buzz around Hollywood says that Vin Diesel can only grow as a star as he becomes more angry about more things. A movie bigshot told Tried & True that she's excited for Vin's family, saying, 14 <u>"The Diesel's ship has come in."</u> She went on to say that she couldn't wait for Vin to tackle his greatest 15 <u>frustration, milk, he's</u> been lactose intolerant for most of his life. Though this time when he meets his old 16 <u>rival he won't just be intolerant, he'll be furious.</u>

A) NO CHANGE

B) called; because this is one

C) called; one

D) called, one

Error Type: _____

A) NO CHANGE

B) the Diesel's ship has come in.

C) The Diesels' ship has come in.

D) the Diesels' ship has come in.

Error Type: _____

A) NO CHANGE

B) frustration: milk, he's

C) frustration; milk—he's

D) frustration: milk—he's

Error Type: _____

A) NO CHANGE

B) rival; he won't just be intolerant: he'll be furious.

C) rival, he won't just be intolerant—he'll be furious.

D) rival—he won't just be intolerant, he'll be furious.

Error Type: _____

PUNCTUATION PRACTICE 2

71

Punctuation Practice 3

Select from the following error types:
1. Incomplete Sentences
2. Sentence Punctuation
3. Commas
4. Apostrophes

Elementary school students 1 <u>arriving cheering with excitement but</u> ended up 2 <u>sighing, some even cried,</u> through 3 <u>yesterday's assembly on piracy</u>. Many students entered the auditorium 4 <u>wearing homemade eyepatches, wooden legs, or</u> hooks

1

A) NO CHANGE

B) arrived cheering with excitement; but

C) arrived cheering with excitement but

D) arriving cheering with excitement. They

Error Type: _____

2

A) NO CHANGE

B) sighing (some even cried)

C) sighing; some even cried,

D) sighing. Some crying

Error Type: _____

3

A) NO CHANGE

B) yesterday's assembly: on piracy.

C) yesterdays assembly on piracy.

D) the principal called an assembly on piracy.

Error Type: _____

4

A) NO CHANGE

B) wearing, homemade eyepatches, wooden legs, or

C) wearing: homemade eyepatches, wooden legs, or

D) wearing, homemade eyepatches, wooden legs,

Error Type: _____

for 5 <u>hands; others</u> brought crackers to attract the 6

<u>pirates' parrot's</u> attention. When Principal 7 <u>Jeffries;</u>

<u>who was briefly enjoying the highest level of popularity</u>

<u>he'd ever experienced</u> asked, "Who's ready for

pirates?!" the 8 <u>crowd—prepared for the greatest</u>

<u>moment of it's collective life,</u> shouted an affirmative

5

A) NO CHANGE

B) hands. Other's

C) hands, others

D) hands; while others

Error Type: _____

6

A) NO CHANGE

B) pirate's parrots'

C) ALL OF THE ABOVE

D) NONE OF THE ABOVE

Error Type: _____

7

A) NO CHANGE

B) Jeffries: who was briefly enjoying the highest level of popularity he'd ever experienced;

C) Jeffries—who was briefly enjoying the highest level of popularity he'd ever experienced,

D) Jeffries, who was briefly enjoying the highest level of popularity he'd ever experienced,

Error Type: _____

8

A) NO CHANGE

B) crowd prepared for the greatest moment of its collective life

C) crowd, prepared for the greatest moment of it's collective life,

D) crowd—prepared for the greatest moment of its collective life—

Error Type: _____

"Rrrrrr!" The students quickly belayed their response when 9 <u>three pale wrinkled</u> men in polo 10 <u>shirts:</u> six eyes, legs, and hands between 11 <u>them, although one did have an earring</u>—took the stage. They'd been hornswoggled. The three landlubbers droned about the detriments of illegally downloading 12 <u>content for example, music, videos, and games,</u>

9

A) NO CHANGE

B) three, pale, wrinkled

C) three pale, wrinkled,

D) three pale, wrinkled

Error Type: _____

10

A) NO CHANGE

B) shirts with

C) shirts;

D) shirts. They had

Error Type: _____

11

A) NO CHANGE

B) them, one did have an earring,

C) them (although one did have an earring)

D) them. One did have an earring

Error Type: _____

12

A) NO CHANGE

B) content, such as music, videos, and games,

C) content, music, videos, and games

D) content, such as: music, videos and games

Error Type: _____

13 for, in one of Miss Smiths' third-graders' estimations "like a hundred years." One of the **14** pirates, earlier he'd made a terrible pirate joke about getting seasick, ended the assembly with a rare moment of **15** clarity; saying "I used to think being a pirate was cool. I quickly realized that it's super lame." **16** That's an opinion the

A) NO CHANGE

B) for—in one of Miss Smith's third-graders' estimations—

C) for (in one of Miss Smiths' third-graders' estimations)

D) for—in one of Miss Smith's third-grader's estimations—

Error Type: _____

A) NO CHANGE

B) pirates, who earlier had made a terrible pirate joke about getting seasick

C) pirates (whod already made a terrible pirate joke about getting seasick)

D) pirates, who'd earlier made a terrible pirate joke about getting seasick,

Error Type: _____

A) NO CHANGE

B) clarity,

C) clarity:

D) clarity, he said,

Error Type: _____

A) NO CHANGE

B) Thats an

C) An

D) That's is an

Error Type: _____

PUNCTUATION PRACTICE 3

former pirate now shares with 17 300 extremely disappointed children. Lets hope they temper their expectations about 18 next weeks assembly—Red Dwarfs: The Tiny Masters of Outer Space.

17

A) NO CHANGE

B) 300 extremely disappointed children, I

C) 300, extremely disappointed, children. Let's

D) 300 extremely disappointed children. Let's

Error Type: _____

18

A) NO CHANGE

B) next week's assembly—

C) next week's assembly;

D) next weeks assembly entitled

Error Type: _____

Blue Book Problem	My answer	Correct answer	Why did I miss?
P. 434 #8			
P. 436 #13			
P. 436 #14			
P. 440 #23			
P. 441 #29			
P. 442 #33			
P. 443 #35			
P. 543 #4			
P. 545 #10			
P. 546 #14			
P. 548 #21			
P. 550 #24			
P. 551 #29			
P. 554 #34			
P. 554 #35			
P. 556 #41			
P. 654 #1			
P. 655 #3			
P. 661 #22			
P. 662 #24			
P. 663 #26			
P. 663 #29			
P. 665 #35			
P. 665 #36			

CORRECT OUT OF TOTAL: _____/24

NOTES:

Pronouns & Verbs

- The SAT tests you on verb and pronoun usage.
- You need to know the following **Pronoun** and **Verb Errors**:
  1. **Pronoun Number**
  2. **Pronoun Clarity**
  3. **Subject Pronouns vs Object Pronouns**
  4. **Subject-Verb Agreement**
  5. **Verb tense**

Pronoun Number

- A pronoun is a word that _____ a noun.
- Be careful when deciding between singular and plural pronouns.

  • Some examples of singular pronouns are _____

  • Some examples of plural pronouns are _____

#sat_hack

#pronoun_numbers

Sometimes the SAT will use complex phrases to try to confuse you. When choosing a pronoun, first identify the word it is replacing.

Words such as **everyone**, **each**, and **every** are <u>singular</u>
Words such as **all**, **any**, and **most**, are <u>plural</u>

1

None of brothers could fit into his soccer gear from last year.

2

The ASB celebrated when they met the year's fundraising goal.

3

Each of the Lakers complained about their injuries.

4

In addition to keeping you healthy, high-cardio activities – like running and swimming – may also boost emotional health, since it produces endorphins.

Clear Pronouns

- It must be clear which noun the pronoun is replacing.

1

When Tom, Maria, and Jackson returned from Egypt, he put a new poster of the Great Pyramids up on his wall.

2

Both Olivia and her mother were surprised by just how lucky she had been.

Subject Pronouns vs. Object Pronouns

- In a sentence, the noun "doing" the action is called the _____.

- The noun that is being acted upon is called the _____.

  - Example: In the sentence "David went to the store," _____ is the subject and _____ is the object.

- We use different pronouns to replace subjects and objects.

  - Some examples of subject pronouns are _____

  - Some examples of object pronouns are _____

#sat_hack
#hit_the_ball

If a pronoun fits into the sentence "_____ **hit the ball**," then it is a subject pronoun.

If it fits into "**The ball hit** _____," then it is an object pronoun.

Try it this trick with the tricky pronouns **who** and **whom**. Which is a subject and which is an object?

3

My parents allowed my brother and I to borrow the car to run errands.

4

Between you and I, Justin Bieber is my favorite celebrity.

Subject-Verb Agreement

- A verb is an action word. Some examples of verbs include: _____
- Verbs must agree with the nouns that are "doing" them.
- Correct the sentences below.

1

The three of us is running the Boston Marathon next year.

2

In the election yesterday, the number of voters were at an all-time high.

Verb Tense

- The tense of a verb indicates _____.
- In addition to the past, present, and future tenses, there are many other tenses in the English language.
- The two others you need to know for the SAT are:
  - Present Perfect: Indicates something has been going on and is still currently going on.
    Example: "I have been studying for the SAT for several months now."
  - Past Perfect: Indicates something happened for a length of time in the past and stopped happening.
    Example: I had been studying for the SAT for several months when I decided to switch and try the ACT."
- Correct the sentences below.

#sat_hack

#verb_tense_hints   If you come across a verb tense question, try looking at the other verbs in the passage. Is there a hint as to what tense the verb should be?

3

Although she graduated with a degree in biology, she has started college as a journalism major.

4

Over the past several months, the relationship between the coworkers was improving greatly.

Pronouns & Verbs Practice 1

Select from the following error types:
1. Pronoun Number
2. Clear Pronouns
3. Subject vs. Object Pronouns
4. Subject-Verb Agreement
5. Verb Tense

1 Us humans stand on the precipice of an important decision. If we 2 had chosen to be making incredibly smart robots, 3 we risks these robots 4 looking down on us.

1

A) NO CHANGE

B) We humans will of stood

C) Us humans will have stood

D) We humans stand

Error Type: _____

2

A) NO CHANGE

B) choose to be making

C) will have chosen to make

D) choose to make

Error Type: _____

3

A) NO CHANGE

B) we'll take a risk

C) we risk

D) we were risking

Error Type: _____

4

A) NO CHANGE

B) look down on us

C) looking down on him/her

D) looking down on ourselves

Error Type: _____

5 <u>Whom can stand</u> a robot's biting sarcasm and snarky, condescending tone? Worse than that, what if 6 <u>robots will have pitied</u> us for our feeble human minds? 7 <u>Those are</u> what I fear most. If, in the future, robots openly mock my relative lack of intelligence, 8 <u>it's just a jerk,</u> 9 <u>that</u> I can accept. If, on the other hand, a well-

5

A) NO CHANGE

B) Who stands

C) Who could stand

D) Whom could stand

Error Type: _____

6

A) NO CHANGE

B) robots pitying

C) robot pities

D) robots pity

Error Type: _____

7

A) NO CHANGE

B) These are

C) Which is

D) That is

Error Type: _____

8

A) NO CHANGE

B) their just jerks

C) they're just jerks

D) there just jerks

Error Type: _____

9

A) NO CHANGE

B) this

C) who

D) which

Error Type: _____

intentioned robot 10 <u>were to struggle for finding</u> the simplest words to describe something which I don't understand but is elementary to it, 11 <u>which</u> would feel terrible. 12 <u>It seemed</u> most likely, though, that robots 13 <u>will just be</u> obnoxiously patronizing most of the time.

　　　　You may be thinking that the number of super intelligent robots 14 <u>are</u> zero, and realistically speaking

A) NO CHANGE

B) were struggling at finding

C) were to struggle to find

D) struggled

Error Type: _____

A) NO CHANGE

B) I

C) he or she

D) they

Error Type: _____

A) NO CHANGE

B) It will seem

C) It seems

D) Robots seem

Error Type: _____

A) NO CHANGE

B) are just

C) were just

D) act in way that will feel

Error Type: _____

A) NO CHANGE

B) is

C) were

D) should

Error Type: _____

15 one will have kept it this way. Consider this: if aliens find us, they probably will be way smarter than **16** us, it would be bad enough if we do have awesome robots, but bad and also extremely embarrassing if we don't. I **17** will assume that, if a contingent of aliens **18** do arrive, they either will want to obliterate all of humanity as we know it, in **19** that case a robot may or may not be

15

A) NO CHANGE

B) we kept

C) we should keep

D) he or she should keep

Error Type: _____

16

A) NO CHANGE

B) us, which

C) we, that

D) we, which

Error Type: _____

17

A) NO CHANGE

B) will make the assumption

C) am to assume

D) assume

Error Type: _____

18

A) NO CHANGE

B) are arriving, they

C) will arrive, the aliens

D) does arrive, the aliens

Error Type: _____

19

A) NO CHANGE

B) which

C) what

D) DELETE THE UNDERLINED SECTION

Error Type: _____

helpful, or they 20 are enlightened enough to not speak

condescendingly or patronizingly like 21 these jerk

robots. Of course, the aliens would still be thinking, 22

"Which poor, robotless fools."

The future 23 will then have been upon us.

Everyone must ask 24 ourselves: would we prefer

animatronic arrogance or extraterrestrial

embarrassment?

A) NO CHANGE

B) is

C) will be

D) should

Error Type: _____

A) NO CHANGE

B) that

C) those

D) them

Error Type: _____

A) NO CHANGE

B) was then

C) were

D) will then be

Error Type: _____

A) NO CHANGE

B) will make the assumption

C) am to assume

D) assume

Error Type: _____

A) NO CHANGE

B) themselves: would I

C) oneself: would I

D) himself or herself: would I

Error Type: _____

Pronouns & Verbs Practice 2

Select from the following error types:
1. Pronoun Number
2. Clear Pronouns
3. Subject vs. Object Pronouns
4. Subject-Verb Agreement
5. Verb Tense

The fat, ugly ashtray 1 <u>squats</u> in the middle of the table. It is a porcelain monstrosity, the insides of 2 <u>it</u> <u>have blackened</u> with ashes and time. Into it 3 <u>have</u> <u>heaped</u> cigarettes, crusts of bread, and poems 4 <u>wrote</u> on

1

A) NO CHANGE

B) squatting

C) squat

D) have been squatting

Error Type: _____

2

A) NO CHANGE

B) the ashtray have been blackened

C) which have been blackened

D) that have blackened

Error Type: _____

3

A) NO CHANGE

B) have been heaped

C) will heap

D) has been heaped

Error Type: _____

4

A) NO CHANGE

B) write

C) to write

D) written

Error Type: _____

paper napkins. 5 It accepts all offerings with indifference. The author of the poems, covered with tattoos, even now 6 crumples a napkin, adds his tears to 7 it. All around the author of these poems 8 lay mementos from his admirers: letters, chocolate hearts, and locks of hair, some of 9 them were sent by a

5

A) NO CHANGE
B) They accept
C) Accepting
D) Now accepting

Error Type: _____

6

A) NO CHANGE
B) crumpling
C) will crumple
D) crumpled

Error Type: _____

7

A) NO CHANGE
B) this.
C) which.
D) the ashtray.

Error Type: _____

8

A) NO CHANGE
B) lies
C) laid
D) lie

Error Type: _____

9

A) NO CHANGE
B) them have been sent
C) which were
D) which are

Error Type: _____

nameless fan 10 <u>which</u> hoped to put some part of 11 <u>them</u> close to 12 <u>their</u> idol. Seven billion people 13 <u>populating</u> this lonely globe—seven billion Beliebers. The artist sits atop the charts and in front of an ashtray, an ugly monstrosity of porcelain, 14 <u>he contemplates</u> the

10

A) NO CHANGE

B) that

C) who

D) whom

Error Type: _____

11

A) NO CHANGE

B) it

C) him or her

D) himself or herself

Error Type: _____

12

A) NO CHANGE

B) him or her

C) his or her

D) they're

Error Type: _____

13

A) NO CHANGE

B) populate

C) population

D) to populate

Error Type: _____

14

A) NO CHANGE

B) he contemplated

C) to contemplate

D) contemplating

Error Type: _____

words of Hans Gruber: "And 15 <u>when Alexander seeing</u> the breadth of his domain, he wept...for 16 <u>there were</u> no more worlds 17 <u>conquering.</u>"

A) NO CHANGE

B) Alexander saw

C) when Alexander saw

D) Alexander, in seeing

Error Type: _____

A) NO CHANGE

B) they're

C) their were

D) there are

Error Type: _____

A) NO CHANGE

B) to conquer.

C) needed conquering.

D) of conquer.

Error Type: _____

Pronouns and Verbs Practice 3

Select from the following error types:
1. Pronoun Number
2. Clear Pronouns
3. Subject vs. Object Pronouns
4. Subject-Verb Agreement
5. Verb Tense

Amid loud cheers from fans and onlookers, the bigwigs of Tried and True Tutoring unveiled **1** it's first mascot. Marc Meinhardt, CEO and founder of the Calabasas-based company, **2** warmed the crowd up **3** by when he dropped an ill math rap. Meinhardt **4** going on to give a

1

A) NO CHANGE

B) its

C) their

D) they're

Error Type: _____

2

A) NO CHANGE

B) warms

C) is warming

D) warm

Error Type: _____

3

A) NO CHANGE

B) when dropping

C) by dropping

D) he dropped

Error Type: _____

4

A) NO CHANGE

B) went on to give

C) went on giving

D) goes on, giving

Error Type: _____

brief history of the company, 5 <u>that</u> really fired up the crowd. Then, rather than dropping 6 <u>them</u>, he handed the mic over to Jonathan Mallaley, COO and other founder. Mallaley 7 <u>keeps</u> the crowd going with some quick SAT, ACT, and Taylor Swift stats, then rolled straight into the story of the mascot search: "We 8 <u>are tinkering</u> with the idea of completely making something up like Virginia Tech and Penn State 9 <u>done</u> with

5

A) NO CHANGE

B) what

C) who

D) which

Error Type: _____

6

A) NO CHANGE

B) him or her

C) himself

D) it

Error Type: _____

7

A) NO CHANGE

B) kept

C) had kept

D) will keep

Error Type: _____

8

A) NO CHANGE

B) tinker

C) were tinkering

D) will tinker

Error Type: _____

9

A) NO CHANGE

B) do

C) did

D) is doing

Error Type: _____

10 they're Hokies and Nittany Lions, but then we

decided 11 on making the pick of a mascot from the

company's base, Calabasas. "Mallaley went on to

explain that many believe *Calabasas* 12 come from the

Spanish *calabaza* for "pumpkin," "squash," or "gourd,"

so 13 him and Meinhardt considered but 14 rejecting

10

A) NO CHANGE

B) there

C) their

D) its

Error Type: _____

11

A) NO CHANGE

B) picking

C) to pick

D) that picking

Error Type: _____

12

A) NO CHANGE

B) has come

C) comes

D) were

Error Type: _____

13

A) NO CHANGE

B) he and Meinhardt

C) they

D) those two

Error Type: _____

14

A) NO CHANGE

B) reject

C) had rejected

D) rejected

Error Type: _____

Jack O. Lantern, Simon Squash, and Lord Gourd. None 15 of those seeming quite right. The founders 16 explain which name, Calabasas, 17 believed by some to come from a Chumash word 18 designed to mean "the wild geese on the gentle breeze 19 flies."

15

A) NO CHANGE
B) of these seem
C) o' those worked
D) of these seemed

Error Type: _____

16

A) NO CHANGE
B) explained which
C) explained that that
D) explain that that

Error Type: _____

17

A) NO CHANGE
B) believes
C) is believed
D) are believed

Error Type: _____

18

A) NO CHANGE
B) that means
C) that has a meaning of
D) which is meaning

Error Type: _____

19

A) NO CHANGE
B) fly
C) is flying
D) flown

Error Type: _____

Nearly 20 <u>not being able to</u> contain 21 <u>himself or</u>

<u>herself,</u> Mallaley and Meinhardt broke into an

impassioned speech about the beauty of the way geese

fly together, conforming. "What," 22 <u>finishing</u>

<u>Meinhardt, "has been</u> more thematically appropriate for

a standardized testing company? Tried and True

Tutoring is proud to present: Gary the Scholastic

Goose!" Mallaley added that, after months 23 <u>of</u>

<u>searching,</u> neither 24 <u>him nor Meinhardt have</u> any

20

A) NO CHANGE

B) they couldn't

C) unable to

D) bursting with glee and without

Error Type: _____

21

A) NO CHANGE

B) theirselves,

C) themselves,

D) Mallaley and Meinhardt

Error Type: _____

22

A) NO CHANGE

B) finished Meinhardt, "has been

C) finising Meinhardt, "could be

D) finished Meinhardt, "could be

Error Type: _____

23

A) NO CHANGE

B) when we searched,

C) we searched,

D) to search,

Error Type: _____

24

A) NO CHANGE

B) of them will have

C) he nor Meinhardt has

D) he nor Meinhardt have

Error Type: _____

doubts that they made the right choice. "Nothing in Calabasas," declared the founders in melodic unison, 25 "was a better representative for our fine company!" The excitement of the crowd 26 could reach a fever pitch. The noise 27 was deafened. Then a sobering truth, hurled like Polyphemus' boulder from somewhere near the back of the crowd, soared above the din, reached 28 it's pinnacle, then slammed the ground, coming to rest in the center of the mass, 29 hushed the twilight frenzy: "Justin Bieber lives in Calabasas!"

25

A) NO CHANGE
B) "is being
C) "could be
D) "are judged to be

Error Type: _____

26

A) NO CHANGE
B) reaches
C) reaching
D) reached

Error Type: _____

27

A) NO CHANGE
B) was deaf
C) was deafening
D) mos def

Error Type: _____

28

A) NO CHANGE
B) its
C) which
D) their

Error Type: _____

29

A) NO CHANGE
B) it hushed
C) that hushed
D) hushing

Error Type: _____

Blue Book Problem	My Answer	Correct Answer	Why did I miss?
P. 439 #20			
P. 441 #29			
P. 442 #30			
P. 444 #39			
P. 444 #41			
P. 543 #5			
P. 546 #12			
P. 546 #15			
P. 547 #19			
P. 550 #26			
P. 550 #27			
P. 550 #28			
P. 554 #36			
P. 555 #38			

CORRECT OUT OF TOTAL: _____/14

NOTES:

VERBS AND PRONOUNS: BLUE BOOK PRACTICE

Writing Logically

- Often, the words we write don't express what we are "really trying to say."
- **Logic Issues** occur when sentences don't. . .
  - mean what they are "supposed to mean."
  - make sense.
- There are four types of **Logic Issues** that appear in the **Grammar Questions**:
  1. **Redundancy**
  2. **Parallelism**
  3. **Faulty Comparisons**
  4. **Misplaced Modifiers**

Redundancy

- **Redundancy** means saying the same thing more than once.
  - Example: In the sentence "He is fast and quick," "fast" and "quick" mean the same thing, so this sentence is repeating itself.
- The SAT wants us to make sure ideas are not **Redundant**.

1

Each year, Kanye West has an annual world tour.

2

The biggest problem I have with public speaking is that I am too self-aware of myself.

#sat_hack
#pronoun_numbers

On the SAT, you may be asked to choose between two seemingly-correct choices; with redundancy errors, the shortest choice is usually the correct one.

Parallelism

- Every item in a list or comparison must have the same structure.

3

The DJ played Kanye West, Kendrick Lamar, and even the music of Justin Bieber.

4

Beyoncé is just as good a rapper as she is at singing.

Faulty Comparisons

- On the SAT, make sure that comparisons only compare things that are of the "same kind.
  - For example: You can make a comparison between Coke and Pepsi because they are both colas.
- The SAT wants you to avoid making Faulty Comparisons, or comparing things that are not the "same kind"
  - For example: You cannot make a comparison between Coke and "loyalty" because Coke is a cola and "loyalty" is a character trait.

1

Like Justin Bieber, Miley Cyrus's music also makes me happy to be alive.

2

The popularity of *Avatar* in 2010 was similar to *Star Wars* in 1977.

3

Marc hoped his SAT score would be better than his sister.

4

Young readers prefer the novels of J. K Rowling to Jane Austen.

Misplaced Modifiers

- Remember when we learned about the "unnecessary information" that you must surround with commas? These are called modifiers.
- A modifier is usually a phrase that clarifies the word or words that it follows.
- "David, **usually a fast runner**, ran slowly today." ➔ "**usually a fast runner**" is modifying "**David**"
- Modifiers must be correctly placed within a sentence, so that it is obvious what they are describing.

5

Despite having finished his homework, Skylar's dad would not allow him to attend the concert.

6

This morning I saw a dog riding my bike.

7

After camping for the weekend, Jonathan's clothes and hair smelled like a campfire.

8

Hiking towards the summit, blisters started to form from my boots.

Writing Logically Practice 1

Select from the following error types:
1. Redundancy
2. Parallelism
3. Faulty Comparisons
4. Misplaced Modifiers

Snubbed four classes in a row, **1** the honor of receiving even a single $5 gift card was slipping away from Wanda Ramirez. "Sure," said the Los Angeles junior in an interview, "I'm pleased to have learned **2** Score Zone Reading, some dominant general guessing techniques, several ways to tackle tough math questions, and a powerful method for dealing with the reading section, but I haven't yet achieved my **3** ultimate goal that I really want: caffeine." **4** Determined to keep hope alive, a strict training regimen was the answer for the Los Angeles junior.

1

A) NO CHANGE

B) that $5 gift card was slipping away from Wanda Ramirez.

C) Wanda Ramirez felt the honor of receiving even a single $5 gift card slipping away after she didn't get it at first.

D) Wanda Ramirez felt the honor of receiving even a single $5 gift card slipping away.

Error Type: _____

2

A) NO CHANGE

B) the Plug and Chug method,

C) a way to increase my odds by elimination,

D) DELETE THE UNDERLINED SECTION

Error Type: _____

3

A) NO CHANGE

B) much-coveted ultimate goal:

C) most important ultimate goal:

D) ultimate goal:

Error Type: _____

4

A) NO CHANGE

B) The Los Angeles junior, determined to keep hope alive, instituted a strict training regimen.

C) A strict training regimen, determined to keep hope alive, was instituted by the Los Angeles junior.

D) Determined, through training, to keep hope alive, the Los Angeles junior instituted a regimen.

Error Type: _____

Having lost the most recent raffle, 5 <u>a picture of a venti, soy, six-pump orange mocha Frappuccino with whipped cream and a chocolate drizzle was taped to Wanda's mirror,</u> which Wanda looks at 6 <u>every morning</u> daily. She's made a simulated classroom at home where she practices the skills necessary to earn tickets, 7 <u>skills she desperately needs to achieve her goal.</u> Her most frequent drills focus on the vital skill of hand raising. 8 <u>She does them often</u>—some for speed, some for height,

---

A) NO CHANGE

B) Wanda's mirror had taped to it a picture of a trenta, iced, sugar-free, five-shot Madagascar vanilla latte with foam and a light raspberry fudge drizzle,

C) Wanda taped a picture of a grande, extra hot, coconut-milk, half-caff, 8-pump hazelnut macchiato with a caramel-salted rim to her mirror,

D) DELETE THE UNDERLINED SECTION

Error Type: _____

A) NO CHANGE

B) frequently and

C) often

D) DELETE THE UNDERLINED SECTION

Error Type: _____

A) NO CHANGE

B) such as the ability to answer questions and the art of flattery

C) such as the ability to answer questions and flattering the teacher

D) the ability to answer questions, and the art of flattery.

Error Type: _____

A) NO CHANGE

B) Hand raising is very important, so she does some exercises

C) She takes a deep breath and performs these exercises, doing some

D) She does some exercises to help with hand-raising, some

Error Type: _____

and 9 <u>some to see how long she can hold her hand in the air.</u> Because Wanda is faster at raising her right hand than 10 <u>she is a left-hand raiser</u> but better at holding the left for 11 <u>longer, so</u> she will use different hands for different situations. 12 <u>Wanda has performed thousands of reps of hand switching,</u> a technique she will only employ if the teacher

A) NO CHANGE

B) for seeing how long she can keep her and in the air.

C) some for length of time she can hold her hand in the air.

D) for length of time she can hold her hand in the air.

Error Type: _____

A) NO CHANGE

B) her left

C) at raising her left hand

D) B OR C

Error Type: _____

A) NO CHANGE

B) longer, therefore

C) longer:

D) longer,

Error Type: _____

A) NO CHANGE

B) Wanda has performed thousands of hand-switching reps,

C) Thousands of reps of hand switching have been performed by Wanda,

D) Wanda has switched hands for thousands of repetitions,

Error Type: _____

says, "Let's see some new hands." 13 <u>A remarkable and insightful competitor, hand raising is only half of the gift-card game, Wanda realizes.</u> "Half of winning that raffle is mental. You gotta stay hungry, y'know? That's why I've been starving myself for caffeine by cutting down on sleep and 14 <u>I don't drink coffee.</u> I'm hungry, baby. I'm straight up *ravenous!* "Wanda went on to say that psyching herself up 15 <u>is really important to fire herself up every morning,</u> but declined to comment on the specifics of this ritual. Not being a real reporter, 16 <u>speculation is fine.</u> I like to imagine Wanda looking in the mirror and saying things like, "You're good enough, you're smart enough, and, darn it, Wanda Ramirez, you're a winner," "And the winner of the most important gift-card raffle in Tried & True Tutoring history… Wanda Ramirez!" or

13

A) NO CHANGE

B) Hand raising is only half of the gift-card game Wanda realizes, a remarkable and insightful competitor.

C) Wanda realizes that hand raising is only half of the gift-card game, a remarkable and insightful competitor.

D) A remarkable and insightful competitor, Wanda realizes that hand raising is only half of the gift-card game.

Error Type: _____

14

A) NO CHANGE

B) avoiding coffee.

C) staying awake more.

D) not napping.

Error Type: _____

15

A) NO CHANGE

B) is essential and really important,

C) in the morning is a vital part of her day,

D) in the morning is something she does before noon,

Error Type: _____

16

A) NO CHANGE

B) let the speculation fly!

C) allow me to speculate.

D) I am free to speculate.

Error Type: _____

17 like "Wanda Ramirez, you are one baaaaad standardized-test-taker!" I further imagine that she stares herself down in the mirror, going through pump-up techniques, such as 18 psyching herself up in various ways, lightly bouncing back and forth, cracking her neck, and 19 she pictures the moment when her teacher lifts Wanda's hand in the air and declares her the winner. On the morning of the big raffle, she will crumple the Frappuccino picture in her hand to demonstrate her dominance over the whole Starbucks corporation, 20 she'll look into the mirror, and see only one thing: the cold, steel eyes of a winner.

17

A) NO CHANGE
B) such as
C) including but not limited to
D) DELETE THE UNDERLINED SECTION

Error Type: _____

18

A) NO CHANGE
B) imagining herself winning,
C) listening to intense Bieber remixes,
D) getting fired up,

Error Type: _____

19

A) NO CHANGE
B) imagines
C) picturing
D) DELETE THE UNDERLINED SECTION

Error Type: _____

20

A) NO CHANGE
B) taking a look
C) looking
D) look

Error Type: _____

Writing Logically Practice 2

Select from the following error types:
1. Redundancy
2. Parallelism
3. Faulty Comparisons
4. Misplaced Modifiers

SAT Teacher Makes Outdated Reference

1 In a startling, strange, and surprising turn of events, Tried & True Tutoring founder, COO, and **2** also a teacher for it, Jonathan Mallaley, **3** referenced a bit of popular culture that none of his students understood, usually on top of the current scene. Since Mallaley frequently mentions currently relevant artists **4** all the time

---

1

A) NO CHANGE

B) In a startling turn of events that was also surprising,

C) In a startling, surprising turn of events,

D) In a startling and strange turn of events,

Error Type: _____

2

A) NO CHANGE

B) a teacher,

C) also a teacher,

D) teacher,

Error Type: _____

3

A) NO CHANGE

B) referenced a bit of popular culture, usually on top of the current scene, that none of his students understood.

C) usually on top of the current scene, referenced a bit of popular culture that none of his students understood.

D) DELETE THE UNDERLINED SECTION

Error Type: _____

4

A) NO CHANGE

B) who still matter

C) and singers

D) DELETE THE UNDERLINED SECTION

Error Type: _____

such as Taylor Swift, 5 the music of MC Hammer, and Justin 6 Bieber, so the students were taken aback when he compared one student's work to 7 the Black Eyed Peas. When the students became confused and 8 had absolutely no idea what he was talking about, Mallaley explained, "They're like the Digital Underground of the two thousands." The situation didn't improve when he described Digital Underground as "The Sugarhill Gang of the 9 nineties," which just made things worse.

5

A) NO CHANGE
B) Kanye West's children,
C) MC Hammer's children,
D) Kanye West,

Error Type: _____

6

A) NO CHANGE
B) Bieber, therefore
C) Bieber:
D) Bieber,

Error Type: _____

7

A) NO CHANGE
B) the Spice Girls.
C) that of the Black Eyed Peas.
D) himself.

Error Type: _____

8

A) NO CHANGE
B) stared blankly,
C) did not understand,
D) Mallaley decided to say something,

Error Type: _____

9

A) NO CHANGE
B) nineties," which was not helpful.
C) nineties," who sang "Rapper's Delight."
D) nineties."

Error Type: _____

The situation, which Mallaley would later describe to several SAT and ACT teachers as "a Lawnmower Man-like descent into darkness—the 1992 film, not the short story or the '87 film"—an unnecessary distinction as none of the teachers had heard of any of these—and a student 10 labeled "#outofcontrol," went downhill from there. Mallaley searched in movies, 11 in music, and TV shows for some sort of cultural connection with students. He recited lines, Rain Man style, from sources like *Seinfeld*, *Braveheart*, and 12 pop culture, eventually finding some common ground 13 in the end by shouting, "Hey you guuuuys!" Noting recognition on their faces, 14 the students heard Mallaley say, "Oh good, at least you've seen *Goonies*."

10

A) NO CHANGE
B) also described as
C) would label
D) tweeted

Error Type: _____

11

A) NO CHANGE
B) also in music,
C) music,
D) Kanye West,

Error Type: _____

12

A) NO CHANGE
B) movies,
C) Netflix,
D) "U Can't Touch This,"

Error Type: _____

13

A) NO CHANGE
B) finally
C) that everyone recognized
D) they could all stand on

Error Type: _____

14

A) NO CHANGE
B) the smiles gave it away. Mallaley said,
C) Mallaley said,
D) Kanye West said,

Error Type: _____

A student promptly 15 responded right away, "No, Mr. Mallaley—it's a meme." Mallaley indicated that he was "going to ask [the students] a bunch of questions [and that he wanted] to have them answered immediately: what is a meme, and what does it do?" Over the course of the next hour, the following 16 then became perfectly clear: Mallaley would never understand memes, 17 that he may possibly never, in fact, understand any part of popular culture past 2010, and he could love Justin Bieber and Taylor Swift, even so. Mallaley ended the class oldly by breathing heavily, 18 he made some weird space noises, too, and saying, "The circle is now complete. When I left you, you were but learners. Now you are the masters."

15

A) NO CHANGE

B) replied back,

C) responded back,

D) corrected him, saying,

Error Type: _____

16

A) NO CHANGE

B) three things subsequently became clear:

C) became clear, clear as a clear crystal in a fountain of pure, clean clear spring water:

D) became perfectly clear:

Error Type: _____

17

A) NO CHANGE

B) might never,

C) that he might never,

D) he might never,

Error Type: _____

18

A) NO CHANGE

B) making some weird space noises, and saying,

C) making some weird space noises, and said,

D) and saying,

Error Type: _____

Blue Book Problem	My answer	Correct Answer	Why did I miss?
P. 433 #6			
P. 437 #16			
P. 439 #21			
P. 445 #44			
P. 542 #1			
P. 544 #8			
P. 547 #18			

CORRECT OUT OF TOTAL: _____/7

NOTES:

Word Choice

- The SAT will ask questions about wording errors. These can be tricky, because there aren't always specific rules we can apply.
- There are a few specific concepts may help you with SAT wording questions:
  1. **Concise wording**
  2. **Idiomatic Phrases** & their prepositions
  3. **Commonly Confused Words**
  4. **Transition Words**

Concise Wording

- Both the Writing & Language Test and Essay require concise writing.
- When writing concisely, the shortest choice is **often** (but not always) the correct answer.
- It's important, however, to still think critically and make sure that the answer makes sense in the sentence and the paragraph.
- Practice with the sentences below – can you reword these sentences to be more "tight"?

1

Being that she wanted to score a 1550 on the SAT, Jackie studied for one hour every day in the several days that were leading up to the test.

2

In spite of the fact that she was so nervous that she couldn't sleep the night before the test, Jackie was still able to score well on her test.

Idiomatic Phrases & Their Prepositions

- Many Idiomatic phrases that we use in English require specific prepositions.
- On the next page, there is a list of commonly misused phrases. You don't have to memorize them, but you may want to read through them and take note of which ones on which you tend to make errors.
- Use the list to correct the sentences below.

1

Even though Michael had fantastic test scores and an outstanding GPA, his parents insisted at him applying to several safety schools, as a means to make sure he was accepted to at least one school.

2

In order that Jesse would not miss the bus, he arrived at the station an extra half-hour ahead for time, because last time he missed the bus on accident.

Idioms

- at least
- at length
- at play
- at the beginning
- at times
- at work
- by accident
- by all means
- by chance
- by definition
- by force
- by hand
- by mistake
- by no means
- by request
- by surprise
- by way of
- for certain
- for granted
- for hire
- for lack of
- for the good of
- for the sake of
- from experience
- from memory
- in a hurry
- in addition to
- in advance
- in agony
- in bulk
- in character
- in charge of
- in code
- in collaboration with
- in command of
- in common
- in conclusion
- in confusion
- in conjunction with
- in contact with
- in contrast with
- in control of
- in danger
- in demand
- in detail
- in doubt
- in effect
- in error
- in essence
- in exchange for
- in fact
- in fairness
- in fear of
- in general
- in good faith
- in memory of
- in mind
- in moderation
- in opposition to
- in other words
- in particular
- in practice
- in preparation for
- in principle
- in private
- in public
- in pursuit of
- in question
- in reality
- in relation to
- in residence
- in response to
- in retrospect
- in return
- in secret
- in self-defense
- in silence
- in suspense
- in tears
- in terms of
- in the absence of
- in the event of
- in the interests of
- in the lead
- in the making
- in the name of
- in the wrong
- in theory
- in tune with
- in vain
- of the opinion
- on account of
- on behalf of
- on good terms
- on leave
- on occasion
- on purpose
- out of context
- out of the question
- to an extent
- to the satisfaction of
- under cover of
- under discussion
- with regard to
- within reason
- without fail
- without precedent
- without question

Commonly Confused Words

- To test yourself, fold this page back so that you can only see the first column (Confused Words). Do you know the correct usage of each one?

Confused Words	Rule	Examples
Accept / Except	accept: receive except: excluding	My publisher will <u>accept</u> my submissions, <u>except</u> when they are late.
Affect / Effect	affect: a verb effect: a noun	The biggest <u>effect</u> of the loud music was how it <u>affected</u> my concentration.
Allude / Elude	allude: refer to elude: escape from	I <u>alluded</u> to the way Ulysses <u>eluded</u> the Cyclops.
Beside / Besides	beside: next to besides: in addition to	<u>Besides</u> the girl in the red shirt, I am also cousins with the boy <u>beside</u> her.
Choose / Chose	choose: present tense chose: past tense	I <u>chose</u> poorly last Sunday; I will <u>choose</u> more wisely this time.
Complement Compliment	complement: accompany compliment: flattery	Everyone <u>complimented</u> how well my baritone solo <u>complemented</u> the piece.
Elicit / Illicit	elicit: evoke illicit: illegal	The police are always trying to <u>elicit</u> information about <u>illicit</u> activities.
Have / Of	have: verb of: connecting word(preposition)	I would <u>have</u>. **Not** I would <u>of</u>.
Less & Much Fewer & Many	less & much: can't be counted fewer & many: can be counted	We have <u>less</u> time or <u>fewer hours</u>. We have <u>much</u> work or <u>many</u> assignments.
Lie / Lay	lie: recline (present tense) lay: place (present tense)	<u>Lay</u> the towel on the beach before you <u>lie</u> down.
Lose / Loose	lose: a loss loose: not tight	Your belt is so <u>loose</u> you may <u>lose</u> your pants.
Principal / Principle	principal: high-ranking person principle: belief	The school's <u>principal</u> wants the student to follow strict <u>principles</u>.
Than / Then	than: comparison then: time	I had more money <u>then</u> <u>than</u> I do now.
There / Their / They're	there: place their: possession they're: they are	Over <u>there</u> in <u>their</u> region, <u>they're</u> the friendliest people we met.
To / Too / Two	to: connecting word(preposition) too: comparison two: the number 2	Go <u>to</u> the café; buy <u>two</u> coffees that aren't <u>too</u> hot.
Weather / Whether	weather: climate whether: comparison / choice	<u>Whether</u> we go outside or not depends on the <u>weather</u>.
Your / You're	your: possession you're: you are	<u>You're</u> going to find <u>your</u> way.
All together / Altogether	all together: in a group altogether: thoroughly	We sang the last line of the song <u>all together</u>. <u>Altogether</u>, the show was a success.

Transition Words

- The SAT wants us to know which **Transition Word** to use when moving from one idea to the next.
- **Transition Words** come in many categories, but the main 5 categories on the SAT are:
    1. **Agreement**
    2. **Disagreement**
    3. **Result**
    4. **Example**
    5. **Conclusion**
- Fill in the chart below to familiarize yourself with the most common transition words.

Word	Category/synonym	Use in a sentence
Also		
Alternatively		
As Such		
Consequently		
Finally		
For Example		
Furthermore		
Hence		
However		
In Other Words		
In Contrast		
Likewise		
Moreover		
Nevertheless		
Previously		
Similarly		
Therefore		
Thus		
Whereby		

1

I sometimes make fun of Bieber. Therefore, I listen to his music all day.

2

Tried & True Tutoring is amazing. In contrast, Taylor Swift is even more amazing.

Word Choice Practice 1

Select from the following error types:
1. Concise Wording
2. Idioms
3. Commonly Confused Words
4. Transition Words

The following is adapted from William Shakespeare, *Henry V*.

WESTMORELAND: O that we now had here one ten-thousandth of those men in England **1** that do no work today!

HENRY V: **2** Who dat? My cousin, Westmorland? **3** Nuh-uh! If we are **4** going to take a long dirt nap,

1

A) NO CHANGE

B) what

C) which

D) who

Error Type: _____

2

A) NO CHANGE

B) Who wishes so?

C) Who's talking?

D) Which of ye scurvy landlubbers opened his mouth and signed his death warrant?

Error Type: _____

3

A) NO CHANGE

B) No, my fair cousin.

C) No, silly!

D) No no NO **NO!**

Error Type: _____

4

A) NO CHANGE

B) targeted by the reaper,

C) marked to die,

D) destined for a good old-fashioned whooping,

Error Type: _____

5 we will do so as a sacrifice for mother England, which we, having sworn and also vowed to defend her, must do honourably by our stocks and our troths to demonstrate our eternal devotion, forsooth! **6** By the same token, if we live, the **7** less men, the greater share of honour. **8** Similarly,

5

A) NO CHANGE

B) we will sacrifice for our country.

C) we will do it, by which I mean we will indeed pay the ultimate price and die not for ourselves but for England.

D) we'll give 'em the ol' one two first!

Error Type: _____

6

A) NO CHANGE

B) On the other hand,

C) Similarly,

D) In fact,

Error Type: _____

7

A) NO CHANGE

B) less men, the more

C) fewer men, the greater

D) fewer men, the more

Error Type: _____

8

A) NO CHANGE

B) Despite this,

C) However,

D) For example,

Error Type: _____

if we 9 win big with 200 men, our glory will be 10 many greater then had we accomplished 11 this feet with a thousand. 12 Westy, Westy, Westy:

A) NO CHANGE

B) conquer the blazes out of the French army

C) pwn France

D) gain victory over our enemies

Error Type: _____

A) NO CHANGE

B) many greater than

C) much greater then

D) much greater than

Error Type: _____

A) NO CHANGE

B) these feet

C) this feat

D) these feat

Error Type: _____

A) NO CHANGE

B) C'mon West!

C) Be possessed of faith, son of mine uncle:

D) Have faith, cousin:

Error Type: _____

13 <u>covet</u> not one man more. We 14 <u>little, we</u>

<u>happy little,</u> we band of brothers; for he today

15 <u>which</u> 16 <u>discards</u> his blood with me will be

my brother, shall be 17 <u>memorized.</u>

13

A) NO CHANGE

B) desire

C) wish

D) require

Error Type: _____

14

A) NO CHANGE

B) less, we happy less,

C) few, we happy few,

D) fewer, we happy fewer,

Error Type: _____

15

A) NO CHANGE

B) that

C) who

D) whom

Error Type: _____

16

A) NO CHANGE

B) sheds

C) drips

D) droppeth like it's hot

Error Type: _____

17

A) NO CHANGE

B) nostalgia

C) recalled

D) remembered

Error Type: _____

18 Therefore, 19 chaps in England now abed shall 20 consider themselves accursed they were not here 21 at the time anyone speaks who fought with us upon Saint Crispin's day!

A) NO CHANGE

B) Regardless,

C) However,

D) Instead,

Error Type: _____

A) NO CHANGE

B) dudes

C) blokes

D) gentlemen

Error Type: _____

A) NO CHANGE

B) ponder

C) cogitate

D) reflect upon

Error Type: _____

A) NO CHANGE

B) for the duration

C) when

D) if and only if

Error Type: _____

Word Choice Practice 2

Select from the following error types:
1. Concise Wording
2. Idioms
3. Commonly Confused Words
4. Transition Words

The following passage has been adapted from *The Adventures of Tom Sawyer* by Mark Twain, originally published in 1876.

Most of the adventures recorded in this book 1 did indeed befall; one or two were 2 things that happened to me, the rest those of boys who were schoolmates of mine. Huck Finn is 3 made from life; Tom Sawyer also, 4 on the other hand not

1

A) NO CHANGE
B) took place in reality;
C) for sure came to pass;
D) really occurred;

Error Type: _____

2

A) NO CHANGE
B) experiences of my own,
C) events that, let's just say, "actually" occurred,
D) occurrences of mine,

Error Type: _____

3

A) NO CHANGE
B) created
C) composed
D) drawn

Error Type: _____

4

A) NO CHANGE
B) instead
C) despite
D) but

Error Type: _____

from **5** <u>one fella</u>—he is a **6** <u>big ol' pot of stew</u>
of the characteristics of three boys whom I **7**
<u>identified</u>, **8** <u>however, he</u> belongs to the order

A) NO CHANGE

B) one single person alone

C) an individual

D) one muchacho

Error Type: _____

A) NO CHANGE

B) coming together

C) grouping

D) combination

Error Type: _____

A) NO CHANGE

B) experienced

C) understood

D) knew

Error Type: _____

A) NO CHANGE

B) and he

C) so he

D) by the same token he

Error Type: _____

of 9 <u>mixes.</u>

The 10 <u>real weird stuff</u> touched upon all 11 <u>effected</u> daily life among children in the West at the period of this story—12 <u>for example</u>, thirty or forty years ago. Although my

---

9

A) NO CHANGE
B) composites.
C) fine blends.
D) the phoenix.

Error Type: _____

10

A) NO CHANGE
B) curiousest phenomena
C) odd superstitions
D) witchcraft-like voodoo magic

Error Type: _____

11

A) NO CHANGE
B) were effected by
C) affected
D) had an affect on

Error Type: _____

12

A) NO CHANGE
B) which, in human years, would be
C) as luck would have it,
D) that is to say,

Error Type: _____

book is intended mainly for the 13 entertainment of boys and girls, 14 I have optimism it will not be 15 thrown on the ground, stepped on repeatedly, and later used as house-training paper for dogs by men and women 16 so far as that goes, for part of my

A) NO CHANGE
B) hobby
C) exciting
D) exuberance

Error Type: _____

A) NO CHANGE
B) I hope
C) I remain cautiously optimistic
D) fingers crossed

Error Type: _____

A) NO CHANGE
B) shunned
C) rescinded
D) ostracized

Error Type: _____

A) NO CHANGE
B) for a related reason,
C) with this in mind,
D) because of this,

Error Type: _____

WORD CHOICE PRACTICE 2

plan has been to try to <mark>17</mark> pleasantly remind adults of what they once were themselves, of how they felt and thought and talked, and of what <mark>18</mark> dumb things they used to do.

A) NO CHANGE

B) remind adults pleasantly of that which they themselves once were,

C) remind adults in a pleasing manner of what they themselves were once,

D) serve as a pleasant reminder to adults of their larval and pupal stages,

Error Type: _____

A) NO CHANGE

B) strange enterprises they sometimes engaged in.

C) shenanigans they oft perpetrated.

D) silly billies they were.

Error Type: _____

Blue Book Problem	My Answer	Correct Answer	Why did I miss?
P. 432 #1			
P. 432 #2			
P. 433 #5			
P. 435 #10			
P. 436 #12			
P. 440 #25			
P. 441 #28			
P. 442 #32			
P. 443 #34			
P. 443 #36			
P. 444 #38			
P. 444 #40			
P. 545 #9			
P. 545 #11			
P. 550 #25			
P. 556 #40			
P. 557 #44			

CORRECT OUT OF TOTAL: _____/17

NOTES:

Question Questions

- So far, you have learned the Grammar rules for the SAT Writing & Language Test, but you have not yet learned about **Question Questions** (Questions that look like an actual question!)
- This section will review:
  1. **Specific Goals** in a question
  2. **Sentence Placement** and paragraph structure
  3. **Adding/Deleting** sentences

Specific Goals

- Question questions sometimes ask you to accomplish a specific goal.
- The examples below are all real Question Questions that were taken from a Practice SAT.
- Read the questions and fill in the information below each one.

1

Which choice most clearly ends the passage with a restatement of the writer's primary claim?

Specific goal: _____

_____

What could you look for in the choices? _____

_____

2

Which choice gives a second supporting example what is most similar to the example already in the sentence?

Specific goal: _____

_____

What could you look for in the choices? _____

_____

3

Which choice best fits with the tone of the passage?

Specific goal: _____

_____

What could you look for in the choices? _____

_____

4

Which choice provides the most effective transition from the previous paragraph?

Specific goal: _____

_____

What could you look for in the choices? _____

_____

#sat_hack

#underline_your_goal

When you encounter a Question Question, first read it carefully and **underline the specific goal**. Keep the goal in mind while answering the question.

Sentence Placement

- The SAT might ask you to move a sentence to a different location within the passage (look for phrases in the answer choices like "before sentence 5" or "after sentence 1").
- On the SAT, paragraphs usually follow a specific structure:
  1. **Introductory sentence**
  2. **Detail**
  3. **Supporting detail**
  4. **Commentary (sometimes)**
  5. **Conclusion**
- When trying to identify a new location for a sentence, look at the sentence you are moving and the paragraph that surrounds it. Identify the parts of the paragraph to put them in the correct order.

#sat_hack
#matching_subjects

Look at the subject of the sentence you are moving. Can you match it to the subject of another sentence in the paragraph?

For example, this sentence:
"**The issue of littering** was very prominent in the most recent election."
…might be followed by this sentence:
"**This issue**, which has been a growing concern for the past several decades, needs to be resolved before it's too late."

Adding & Deleting Sentences

- In addition to moving sentences, the SAT might ask you whether or not you should add or delete a new sentence.
- To spot these questions, look for "**Should the writer make this addition here**?" followed by two "**Yes**" reasons and two "**No**" reasons in the answer choices.
- Added sentences should not only flow with the rest of the paragraph, but should support the main idea of the paragraph and passage as a whole.
- For example, if you are reading a brief passage that is a biography of the life of George Washington, you might add a sentence about his childhood, but probably would not add a sentence describing the beginning of the Civil War.

#sat_hack
#focus_on_the_reasons

For these **adding/deleting** Question Questions, focus on the reasons, rather than the "yes" or "no" part of the answer choices. Usually, there is a very distinct reason why or why not to add a sentence.

Question Questions Practice 1

For Question Questions Practice 1 and 2,
either a) **write the Specific Goal** or
b) choose from the following types of
Question Questions:
  1. Sentence Placement
  2. Adding and Deleting Sentences

The following passage has been adapted from *The Human Side of Animals* by Royal Dixon.

That 1 "if the only thing a man does is to sleep and eat, he's not better than an animal" is shown in no clearer way than by the games and play of animals. Recreation is as common among them as it is among our own children, 2 and it takes their minds off of the difficulties of the day. Young goats and lambs skip, jump, run races, throw flips in the air, and gambol; calves have interesting frolics; bears wrestle and tumble; puppies delight in acrobatic tussling. 3 But animal children grow up and stop playing to a certain extent as age advances, precisely as human children do; each settles down into a more practical condition of life.

1

Which Shakespeare quotation best establishes the paragraph's main point?

A) NO CHANGE

B) "the Earth has music for those who listen"

C) "one touch of Nature makes the whole world kin"

D) "as hounds, and greyhounds, mongrels, spaniels, curs… are 'clept all by the name of dogs: the valued file distinguishes the swift, the slow, the subtle…every one according to the gift which bounteous nature hath in him closed,"

Type of Question Question OR Specific Goal:

_____

2

Which choice best sets up the following examples?

A) NO CHANGE

B) and they seem always to play in groups.

C) and they are rarely self-conscious in their play.

D) and they seem always to be athletic and even skilled in their play.

Type of Question Question OR Specific Goal:

_____

3

The writer is considering deleting the underlined sentence.
Should the writer do this?

A) Yes, because it is false (as indicated by information elsewhere in the paragraph).

B) Yes, because it could be offensive to the elderly.

C) No, because it provides a valuable summary of the argument made in the previous two sentences.

D) No, because it supports the main topic of the paragraph and serves as a transition to a supporting point coming up in the next few sentences.

Type of Question Question OR Specific Goal:

_____

4 5 <u>The mother dog growls because her playful son has continuously tumbled over her while she was sleeping, or the cat-mother slaps her kitten because he plays with her tail. It is a display of</u> the same kind of emotion that prompts a human mother to rebuke her child in the nursery for making too much noise or for

At this point, the writer is considering adding the following sentence.

> They dislike having their games and play disturbed.

Should the writer make this addition here? For this question, assume the writer did NOT delete the previous sentence.

A) Yes, because it gives a specific example of the assertion made in the last sentence.

B) Yes, because it helps the reader connect with the animals written about in this passage.

C) No, because it does not adequately address a common counterargument to the passage's main claim.

D) No, because it is irrelevant to and distracts from the main argument of the passage.

Type of Question Question OR Specific Goal:

_____

Which choice most effectively combines the sentences at the underlined portion?

A) If the mother dog growls because her playful son has continuously tumbled over her while she was sleeping, or the cat-mother slaps her kitten because he plays with her tail, it is a display of

B) When the mother dog growls because her playful son has continuously tumbled over her while she was sleeping, a human mother does the same thing, just as when the cat-mother slaps her kitten because he plays with her tail, it is likewise a display of

C) The mother dog growls because her playful son has continuously tumbled over her while she was sleeping, or the cat-mother slaps her kitten because he plays with her tail, respectively, each showing through demonstration

D) Since the mother dog growls when her playful son has continuously tumbled over her while she was sleeping, or the cat-mother slaps her kitten when he plays with her tail, it is a display of

Type of Question Question OR Specific Goal:

_____

throwing toys out of the window. Animals, like ourselves, feel every sensation of joy, happiness, surprise, disappointment, love, hope, ambition, 6 and through their youthful games an entire index of their future may be obtained.

[1] This play has much to do with the development of the physical skills and mental attributes these animals will use throughout their lives. [2] Kittens begin to tumble and play before they are two 7 weeks old. They will roll and toss a ball, hunting it from the dark corners. [3] They will lie in silent wait for each other, suddenly springing upon an unsuspecting fellow-cat-baby's back, just as they will do later in life when seeking their prey. [4] I have seen them play with a catnip mouse for hours at a time, 8 probably because they have not yet grown to adulthood. [5] Brehm says that this is noticed in their earliest kittenhood, and that the mother cat encourages it in all ways possible,

6

Which choice provides the best transition to the next paragraph?

A) NO CHANGE

B) and every other emotion that humans feel.

C) several more that humans tend not to experience.

D) which is why the musical *Cats* was so successful.

Type of Question Question OR Specific Goal:

_____

7

Which choice most effectively combines the sentences at the underlined portion?

A) weeks old; for example: they will roll and toss a ball, hunting

B) weeks old, rolling and tossing a ball to hunt

C) weeks old, at which age they will begin rolling, which is to say tossing, a ball, then make a point of hunting

D) *weeks* old (amazing!), at which point they will roll and toss a ball, literally *hunting*

Type of Question Question OR Specific Goal:

_____

8

Which choice best ties this example to the paragraph's main argument?

A) NO CHANGE

B) just as the mother cat plays with a real mouse.

C) just as a human plays with a computer mouse.

D) and a mother cat plays with other toys.

Type of Question Question OR Specific Goal:

_____

even to becoming a child with her children from love of them, 9 <u>which is very sweet to watch.</u> [6] The mother cat begins the play by slowly moving her tail. [7] The kittens, while they may not understand what it means, are greatly excited by the movement. [8] Their eyes sparkle, their ears stand erect, and slowly one after another clutches after the moving tail. [9] 10 <u>Kittens, often unbelievably fluffy, can have such big, black eyes.</u> [10] Mama cat patiently and lovingly submits to all her kittens' treatment, as it is only play. [11] Gesner considered her tail as the indicator of her moods. 11

QUESTION QUESTIONS PRACTICE 1

9

The writer would like to use this example to relate the argument of this paragraph to that of the previous paragraph. Which choice most effectively accomplishes this goal?

A) NO CHANGE

B) and they also do some pretty human things.

C) which is something animals do better than humans.

D) as a human mother does in the nursery with her child.

Type of Question Question OR Specific Goal:

_____

10

Which choice adds specificity to the example while most effectively endearing the kittens to the reader?

A) NO CHANGE

B) Suddenly, one springs over the mother's back, another grabs at her feet, while a third playfully slaps her in the face with his tiny, soft, cushioned paw.

C) Out of nowhere, one pounces at the mother's face, often yanking out several whiskers.

D) If you can believe it, it's even cuter than… well than a kitten playing with a ball of yarn.

Type of Question Question OR Specific Goal:

_____

11

To make the paragraph most logical, sentence 11 should be placed

A) where it is now.

B) before sentence 5.

C) before sentence 6.

D) before sentence 7.

Type of Question Question OR Specific Goal:

_____

12 When we witness these abundant evidences of the need and prevalence of recreation in the animal world, we are confronted with one more argument for the existence of real mental and moral faculties among our four-footed friends.

Which choice most effectively uses a central argument from the passage to make a call for action?

A) NO CHANGE

B) When we see the lifespan of an animal displayed in their recreation, we are confronted with one question: could we use our four-footed friends to predict more than just their own futures?

C) When we see how human they are at play, we must ask ourselves why we don't treat our four-footed friends with more respect.

D) The importance of treating pets with dignity has never been more apparent; look into adopting a pet today.

Type of Question Question OR Specific Goal:

_____

Question Questions Practice 2

For Question Questions Practice 1 and 2,
either a) **write the Specific Goal** or
b) choose from the following types of
Question Questions:
1. Sentence Placement
2. Adding and Deleting Sentences

**The following passage is adapted from
Garth Brown, "Our Ram Sparky is a
Neurotic Mess."**

1 In a world full of rams, one stands out from
the flock. He has a shaggy beard, and this time
of year his thick winter coat is shedding out in
uneven clumps that drift across the pasture, like
thistle seeds come two months early. His burly
trunk coupled with twig legs makes him look
unbalanced. 2 He should run for office.

　　　[1] And like a politician he is a
blustering, 3 underhanded strategist,

1

Which choice most effectively, directly, and succinctly
establishes the central point of this passage?

A) NO CHANGE

B) Some animals act as you would expect, while others don't;
　　take our ram, Sparky.

C) Our ram Sparky is deeply strange.

D) Sparky is a ram.

Type of Question Question OR Specific Goal:

_____

2

Which choice provides the best transition from this paragraph to
the next?

A) NO CHANGE

B) He can filibuster with the best of politicians.

C) He has a proud nose and an uncomprehending gaze.

D) He has the proud, Roman nose and uncomprehending gaze of
　　a politician.

Type of Question Question OR Specific Goal:

_____

3

At this point the writer would like to demonstrate the ram's
strangeness by indicating his contradictory nature. Which choice
most effectively accomplishes this goal?

A) NO CHANGE

B) aggressive coward,

C) passionate bleater,

D) silly fool,

Type of Question Question OR Specific Goal:

_____

QUESTION QUESTIONS PRACTICE 2

131

4 who loves conflict so long as he is not a direct, active participant. [2] A couple months ago something, perhaps the unseasonable warmth, got the cows worked up, and they were running around, butting heads and pushing each other in circles. [3] Sparky could be found cantering around each 5 skirmish. It was as though he were cheering them on. As soon as one ended, he would race back and forth, looking for the next drama. [4] When I take Oban out to move the animals, Sparky will come to the fore, shaking his head and stamping his foot in a display of bravado, as if he's prepared to lay down his life in defense of his flock. [5] If I didn't know better I would have thought him quite brave. [6] But if the dog or I take so much as a single step in his direction he will take off, racing as far and as fast as he can, without a backward glance to check on the lambs and ewes. 6 7

4

Which choice most effectively sets up the examples that follow?

A) NO CHANGE
B) who charges despite his fear.
C) yet he sometimes appears to cheer on the other animals.
D) who spits in defiance at the slightest sound of danger.

Type of Question Question OR Specific Goal:

_____

5

Which choice most effectively combines these sentences at the underlined portion?

A) skirmish, by which action he seemed to be cheering them on, but no sooner had one skirmish ended than
B) skirmish, seemingly cheering them on, and when one ended,
C) skirmish, and in so doing appeared to the human eye to be cheering them on, but then when the proverbial bell rang,
D) skirmish like a cheerleader with only the pom-poms with which his body was naturally adorned, but when the time came for one skirmish to end,

Type of Question Question OR Specific Goal:

_____

6

At this point, the writer is considering adding the following sentence:

> It seems like he cares more about his own safety than that of the rest of the flock.

Should the writer make this addition here?
A) Yes, because it clarifies an example.
B) Yes, because it provides a valuable transition to the next paragraph.
C) No, because the information is clear enough from the previous example without being said.
D) No, because the information is irrelevant to the example and to the argument of the paragraph as a whole.

Type of Question Question OR Specific Goal:

_____

[8] Recently, he's dropped all pretenses of caring about them. He hung out with the other sheep so long as they were beside the cows, but since we've separated them he's made his true allegiances clear. Instead of ranging up the hill with the flock, he has opted to hang out with our bull and a couple steers, [9] two bachelors and two half bachelors that spend all day nibbling on clover and lying around.

7

To make the paragraph most logical, sentence 5 should be placed

A) where it is now.

B) before sentence 2.

C) before sentence 3.

D) before sentence 4.

Type of Question Question OR Specific Goal:

_____

Which choice most effectively provides a transition from the last paragraph to this one and establishes this paragraph's main idea? Assume the sentence in Question 6 was not added.

A) NO CHANGE

B) I always knew he didn't really care about them.

C) For a strange ram, he sure can run!

D) He is very loyal, just in a very, true to form, strange way.

Type of Question Question OR Specific Goal:

_____

The writer is considering deleting the underlined portion and ending the sentence by changing the previous comma to a period. Should the writer make this change?

A) Yes, because the underlined portion obscures the focus of the paragraph.

B) Yes, because the underlined portion gives away the ending.

C) No, because the underlined portion bespeaks the importance of companionship.

D) No, because the strangeness of the image described in the underlined portion links this paragraph to the central argument.

Type of Question Question OR Specific Goal:

_____

10 I just cannot believe how strange that ram is. **11** Though sometimes I don't know whether to laugh or cry, I do know one thing: he is clearly the biggest goofball on the farm.

10

At this point, the writer would like to support the main idea of the passage with one final example that didn't fit logically into any of the previous paragraphs. Which choice most effectively accomplishes these goals?

A) NO CHANGE

B) Last week I looked out the window and saw him sitting on his haunches, as if he were an oversized dog, obliviously staring at the chicken coop.

C) This morning, he snorted at me in warning, but I called his bluff and he backed down.

D) Sometimes he'll leave the rest of the flock to perform a surprisingly graceful dance with the pigs.

Type of Question Question OR Specific Goal:

_____

11

The writer would like to remind the reader of an argument from the passage as well as to hint that the writer is confused about how to feel towards the ram. Which choice best accomplishes these goals?

A) NO CHANGE

B) Clearly Sparky wishes to be seen as virile and unflappable, he's something else;

C) Whether I should laud his cosmopolitanism for preferring the company of cows or condemn his craven abandonment of his own kind,

D) Sparky may think he's pretty shifty—he's brave, he's afraid, he's a cheerleader, he's a cow—but I've got him pegged:

Type of Question Question OR Specific Goal:

_____

Blue Book Problem	My Answer	Correct Answer	Why did I miss?
P. 433 #4			
P. 434 #7			
P. 434 #9			
P. 435 #11			
P. 437 #15			
P. 437 #17			
P. 438 #18			
P. 438 #19			
P. 439 #22			
P. 440 #24			
P. 441 #26			
P. 442 #31			
P. 443 #37			
P. 444 #42			
P. 445 #43			
P. 542 #2			
P. 543 #3			
P. 543 #6			
P. 544 #7			
P. 546 #13			
P. 547 #17			
P. 548 #20			
P. 548 #22			
P. 549 #23			
P. 551 #30			
P. 552 #31			
P. 552 #32			

Blue Book Problem	My Answer	Correct Answer	Why did I miss?
P. 553 #33			
P. 554 #37			
P. 555 #39			
P. 556 #42			
P. 557 #43			
P. 655 #4			
P. 656 #8			
P. 657 #10			
P. 657 #11			
P. 659 #18			
P. 660 #20			
P. 662 #23			
P. 662 #25			
P. 663 #27			
P. 664 #31			
P. 664 #33			
P. 665 #37			

CORRECT OUT OF TOTAL: _____/44

NOTES:

Timed Assignments

- Assignment 1: Blue Book Pages 654-667
- Assignment 2: Blue Book Pages 772-786
- Assignment 3: Study Guide Simplified Pages 262-278
- Assignment 4: Study Guide Simplified Pages 322-336

Writing & Language Summary

1. **Overview**
   - Types of Questions: Grammar Questions and Question Questions
   - Grammar Guessing Strategy
2. **Punctuation**
   - Complete Sentences
   - Sentence Punctuation
   - Commas
   - Apostrophes
3. **Pronouns & Verbs**
   - Pronoun Number
   - Clear Pronouns
   - Subject vs. Object Pronouns
   - Subject-Verb Agreement
   - Verb Tense
4. **Writing Logically**
   - Redundancy
   - Parallelism
   - Faulty Comparisons
   - Misplaced Modifiers
5. **Word Choice**
   - Concise Wording
   - Idiomatic Phrases & Their Prepositions
   - Commonly Confused Words
   - Transition Words
6. **Question Questions**
   - Specific Goals
   - Sentence Placement
   - Adding and Deleting Sentences

Math
Test

Tried & True Tutoring

What is the Math Section?

Math Test –No Calculator
- Includes 20 questions
- Lasts 25 minutes

Both math sections require knowledge from basic math up to pre-calculus.

Math Test –Calculator
- Includes 38 questions
- Lasts 55 minutes

What's With The Grid-Ins?

- On each math test, there are Multiple-Choice Questions and Student Produced Response Questions (Grid-Ins).
- For the Grid-Ins, you have to calculate your own answer and bubble it into a box like the one below.
    - Math Test – No Calculator: #16-20 are Grid-Ins
    - Math Test – Calculator: #31-38 are Grid-Ins

#sat_hack

#never_put_off_grid_ins

Start with the Grid-Ins, so that if you run out of time, you are left with multiple choice questions. If you have 60 seconds left, wouldn't you rather be rushing on questions with answer choices?

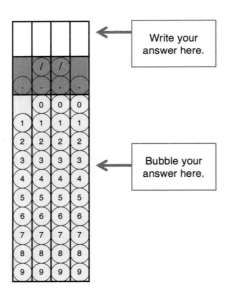

Write your answer here.

Bubble your answer here.

WATCH OUT!

- Be careful when gridding in fraction answers.

If you get:	1 ½
Grid in:	3/2 or 1.5
Not:	11/2

- Use the boxes below to see how this could be misinterpreted:

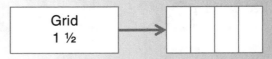

Grid 1 ½

Key Terms for SAT Math

Term	Definition/Example
Integer	Any whole number, positive or negative, **including zero**
Zero	An integer that is neither positive nor negative
Factor/Divisor	A number that goes evenly into a larger number (2 and 4 are factors of 16)
Multiple	A number that is the result of multiplying another number (16, 20, and 100 are multiples of 4)
Prime Number	A number that can only be divided evenly by itself and 1; 13 is prime because 13 and 1 are the only numbers that it can be divided by without having a remainder); 1 is not prime, and 2 is the only even prime number
Mean	Average
Median	The number in the middle of an ordered list of data (Note: If you have an even number of data in a list, the median is the average of the two in the middle)
Mode	The most frequently occurring number in a list
Range	The difference between the least and greatest values in a list of data (the range of 1 to 10 is 9)
Reciprocal	1 divided by a certain number; flipping a fraction (3 ➔ ⅓) and (3/4 ➔ 4/3)
Irrational Number	An unending decimal that does not repeat; cannot be expressed as a fraction/ratio; π and √3 are both irrational
Radical	A number with a root
Extraneous Solution	A solution that can be found algebraically but that does not make the statement true when you plug it back into the equation.

Review

Fill in the blank.

1. A number is _____ when it can only be divided by itself and 1.

2. Of the numbers 2, 5, 6, 8, 9, 9, 10: ___ is the mode and ___ is the median.

3. Zero is a(n) _____ but is not _____ or _____.

4. ___ is a multiple of 6.

5. ___ is a factor of 18.

6. If a number cannot be expressed as a fraction, it is _____.

7. The reciprocal of -7 is _____.

#sat_hack

#meaningful_flashcards

Making flash cards at home is a great way to memorize SAT terms. To make your flash cards more effective, put the term on one side and include your own example/definition on the other side!

SAT Math Tricks

- Keep in mind that on the SAT multiple-choice math questions, the answers are already on the page.
- There is no partial credit for showing your work; all that matters is that you bubble in the right answer.
- In this section, we will talk about three key SAT Hacks:
  - **Pick & Stick**
  - **Plug & Chug**
  - **Guess & Check**

Pick & Stick

- **Pick & Stick** works especially well when you are solving for a variable.
- All you need to do is **pick** one of the answer choices and **stick** it in for the variable in the problem.
- Try the solving the problems below by plugging in the answers:

1

If $3x = \frac{18}{y}$, which of the following could be (x, y)?

A) $(1, -2)$

B) $(0, 1)$

C) $(3, 2)$

D) $(4, 6)$

> Remember that (x, y) are coordinates. Plug the x-coordinate in for x and the y-coordinate in for y until the two sides are equal.

2

If $\sqrt{x + 5} - k = -3$, what is the value of x when $k = 7$?

A) -4

B) 5

C) 6

D) 7

> Be careful here, because you have two variables. Plug in the answer choices for $\boldsymbol{x}$, not k, which is already given in the problem.

#sat_hack

#answers_go_in_order

The multiple choice answer choices are always presented in order. Always test answer B or C first so you can quickly rule out answer choices that are too great or too small.

Example: In #2 above, if you determind that choice B is too small, you can automatically eliminate choice A.

Plug & Chug

- This strategy works on multiple-choice questions that have _____ in the question and in the answers.
- This strategy turns seemingly difficult algebra questions into simple middle school-level math questions.

1

Taylor Swift wants to buy a $135,000 diamond encrusted Shake Weight. Taylor earns $50,000 per concert performance, and pays $1/10^{th}$ of that income to her manager. How many times will she have to perform before she can "Shake It Off?"

> Here's a middle school-level word problem, which you can probably already solve.

2

Taylor Swift wants to buy a $135,000 diamond encrusted Shake Weight. Taylor earns x dollars per concert performance, and pays $x/10$ of that income to her manager. In terms of x, how many times will she have to perform before she can "Shake It Off?"

A) $\dfrac{135,000}{x}$

B) $\dfrac{135,000}{x - 10}$

C) $135,000x$

D) $\dfrac{150,000}{x}$

> Here's how the SAT would ask the same type of questions. What is different?
>
> _____ has been replaced with _____.
>
> STEPS:
> 1. Pick a value for x and circle it.
> $x =$ _____
> 2. Plug that value into the word problem and solve. Circle your answer: _____
> 3. Plug x into the answer choices to see which choice is the same is your answer.

3

If a and b are positive consecutive even integers, where $a > b$, which of the following is equal to $a^2 - b^2$?

A) $2b$

B) $2b + 2$

C) $2b + 4$

D) $4b + 4$

> RULES:
> 1. Choose a different value for each variable.
> 2. Choose values that satisfy the conditions.
> 3. Be careful with 0 or 1: they might not help you to eliminate answer choices.

Guess & Check

- This is a much broader strategy, which will work on multiple-choice questions – and Grid-Ins!
- To use Guess & Check, choose a value that could satisfy the answer, then solve the problem using that value. You may have to try a few times before you guess the correct number, so only use this strategy if there is no other way to solve the problem.
- Try using Guess & Check to solve the Grid-In problems below.

1

At Mindy's Lemonade Stand, a cup of lemonade costs 25¢ and a brownie costs 75¢. In the first hour, Mindy sells some brownies and some lemonade, and has made $3. What is one possible number of cups of lemonade that Mindy sold?

Try starting with 1 or 2.

If Mindy sold only 1 cup of lemonade, how much money came from brownie sales? Could that be evenly divided by 75¢?

Since the cost of a brownie is 3 times the cost of a cup of lemonade, is there a different number we could try guessing?
HINT: Try a multiple of 3.

2

The sum of four odd, consecutive integers is 176. What is the value of the smallest integer?

Remember that your answer is going the be the smallest of four "consecutive, odd integers", so try different combinations of numbers.

You might guess something slightly smaller than 50, since 50 is close to ¼ of 176.

$51 + 53 + 55 + 57 = 216$

This is too large. Try something smaller.

#sat_hack

#every_zebra_needs_one_friend

If you are stuck on **Plug and Chug** or **Guess and Check** problems, remember this anagram for different categories of values you should test:
Every ➔ **Extremes** (very high or low numbers)
Zebra ➔ **Zero**
Needs ➔ **Negatives**
One ➔ **Odds**
Friend ➔ **Fractions**

Math Tricks Practice 1

1

If $\frac{x}{y} = 6$, what is the value of $\frac{3y}{x}$?

A) $\frac{1}{2}$

B) 2

C) 1

D) 3

2

If $x - 2y = 16$, what is the value of $\frac{2^x}{4^y}$?

A) 4^{12}

B) 2^{16}

C) 8^4

D) The value cannot be determined

3

$$y > -x + a$$
$$y < x + b$$

In the xy-plane, if $(0,0)$ is a solution to the system of inequalities above, which of the following relationships between a and b must be true?

A) $a > b$

B) $a < b$

C) $a = b$

D) $|a| > |b|$

4

Fernando bought a basketball from a sports store that gave a 15 percent discount off its original price. The total amount he paid the cashier was d dollars, including a 9.5 percent sales tax on the discounted price. Which of the following represents the original price of the computer in terms of d?

A) $0.895d$

B) $\frac{d}{0.895}$

C) $(0.85)(1.095)d$

D) $\frac{d}{(0.85)(1.095)}$

5

$$A = \frac{B + 2C + 3D}{5}$$

According to the equation above, which of the following correctly gives the value of B in terms of A, C, and D?

A) $B = -5A + 2C + 3D$

B) $B = \frac{A - 2C - 3D}{5}$

C) $B = 5A - 2C - 3D$

D) $B = \frac{A + 2C + 3D}{5}$

6

The sales manager of a company awarded a total of $5000 in bonuses to the most productive salespeople. The bonuses were awarded in amounts of $250 or $750. If at least one $250 and at least one $750 bonus were awarded, what is one possible number of $250 bonuses awarded?

A) 1

B) 4

C) 6

D) 8

7

The expression $\dfrac{x^2 y^{-2}}{x^{-2} y^{\frac{1}{3}}}$, where $x > 1$ and $y > 1$, is

equivalent to which of the following?

A) $\dfrac{x^4}{x^2\sqrt[3]{y}}$ C) $\dfrac{x^4}{x^2\sqrt[3]{2y}}$

B) $\dfrac{x^4}{y^2\sqrt[3]{y}}$ D) $\dfrac{x^4\sqrt[3]{y}}{y^2}$

8

The expression $\dfrac{3x-4}{x+5}$ is equivalent to which of the following?

A) $3 - \dfrac{19}{x+5}$

B) $3 - \dfrac{19}{5}$

C) $3 - \dfrac{2}{x+5}$

D) $3 - \dfrac{2}{5}$

9

A farmer wants to plant flowers on his farm. He estimates that the project will take x hours to complete, where $x > 25$. The goal is for the estimate to be within 5 hours of the time it will actually take to complete the project. If the farmer meets his goal and it takes y hours to compete the project, which of the following inequalities represents the relationship between the estimated time and the actual completion time?

A) $x + y > 10$

B) $x + y < 10$

C) $-5 < y - x < 5$

D) $-5 > y - x < 5$

10

Trey wants to purchase a laptop before he attends his University in the fall. He found an amazing deal online which reduced the price by 30%. He decided to wait a day before purchasing it. The next day the price of the laptop had increased by 20%. If x represents the original price of the laptop, what is its current price?

A) $0.84x$

B) $0.1x$

C) $0.5x$

D) $0.75x$

Math Tricks Practice 2

1

$$\frac{2x - y}{x} = z$$

In the equation above, if x is negative and y is positive, which of the following must be true?

A) $z < 2$

B) $z > 2$

C) $z = 2$

D) $z < -2$

2

In the xy-plane, the point $(3,7)$ lies on the graph of the function f. If $f(x) = k + x^2$, where k is a constant, what is the vale of k?

A) -2

B) -6

C) 12

D) 30

3

Two different points on a number line are both 6 units from the point coordinate -5. The solution to which of the following equations gives the coordinates of both points?

A) $|x + 5| = 6$

B) $|x - 5| = 6$

C) $|x + 6| = 5$

D) $|x - 6| = 5$

4

A motor powers a model Harley motorcycle so that after starting from rest, the motorcycle travels x inches in t seconds, where $x = 36t\sqrt{t}$. Which of the following gives the average speed of the motorcycle, in inches per second, over the first t seconds after it starts?

A) $\frac{6}{\sqrt{t}}$

B) $6\sqrt{t}$

C) $36t$

D) $36\sqrt{t}$

5

A group of friends decided to divide the $1500 cost of a trip equally among themselves. When three of the friends decided not to go on the trip, those remaining still divided the $1500 cost equally, but each friend's share of cost increased by $25. How many friends were in the group originally?

A) 9

B) 12

C) 15

D) 18

6

Which of the following expressions is equivalent to $\dfrac{(2x^5-5x^4+7x^3+4x^2-10x+11)}{x^3+2}$?

A) $2x^2 - 5x + 7 + \dfrac{3}{x^3+2}$

B) $2x^2 - 5x + 7$

C) $2x^2 + 5x + 7 - \dfrac{20x-3}{x^3+2}$

D) $2x^2 - 5x + 7 - \dfrac{3}{x^3+2}$

7

The width of a rectangular dance floor is w feet. The length of the floor is 8 feet longer than its width. Which of the following expresses the perimeter, in feet, of the dance floor in terms of w?

A) $2w + 8$

B) $w^2 + 16$

C) $4w + 16$

D) $w^2 + 8$

8

$$y = x^2 - 8x + 15$$

The equation above represents a parabola in the xy-plane. Which of the following forms of the equation is equivalent to the one above?

A) $y - 15 = x^2 - 8x + 15 - 2y$

B) $y = (x - 3)(x - 5)$

C) $y = (x - 5)^2(x - 3)$

D) $x + 15 = y^2 - 8x$

9

Which of the following is equivalent to $4(x + 6) - 6$?

A) $2(2x + 10)$

B) $2(2x + 9)$

C) $4x + 19$

D) $4x - 20$

10

$$f(x) = x^3 - 4x$$
$$g(x) = x^2 + x - 6$$

Which of the following expressions is equivalent to $\dfrac{f(x)}{g(x)}$, for $x > 2$?

A) $\dfrac{x(x-2)}{x+3}$

B) $\dfrac{x(x+2)}{x+3}$

C) $\dfrac{1}{x+3}$

D) $\dfrac{x+2}{x+3}$

Blue Book Problem	My Answer	Correct Answer	Why did I miss?
P. 447 #2			
P. 448 #8			
P. 449 #10			
P. 450 #15			
P. 452 #16			
P. 455 #1			
P. 455 #3			
P. 460 #21			
P. 463 #29			
P. 562 #15			
P. 564 #16			
P. 573 #17			
P. 579 #31			

CORRECT OUT OF TOTAL: _____/12

NOTES:

Algebra FUN-damentals

- The SAT tests many Algebra skills. This section will review:
  - **Word problems** and how to attack them
  - **PEMDAS** and its traps on the SAT Math tests
  - **Function Notation**
  - **Algebraic manipulation** and what to do with Wordy Word Problems
  - **Absolute value equations and inequalities** and how to solve them

Translating Words Into Math

- While word problems can sometimes look overwhelming, remember that most of these can be translated into simple mathematic expressions and equations using the following rules:

If it says...	It means...
is, were, are, will be	=
more than, plus, combined, and increased by	+
less than, difference between, decreased by	−
of, double, triple, times, increased by a factor of	×
into, percent, shared between, per	÷

#sat_hack

#check_your_order

Remember that when something says *less than* it means you're subtracting it *from* something else.

Example ➔ **"Two less than five" translates into 5 − 2 *not* 2 − 5**

- Let's do some practice. Turn the following sentences into mathematical statements.

1

Three less than a number divided by two is four more than the number.

2

James picked six bags of a dozen oranges and then sold twenty-two oranges.

Please Excuse My Dear Aunt Sally!

- In middle school, you might have memorized the order of operations using the acronym PEMDAS
  - **P** = Parenthesis
  - **E** = Exponents
  - **M/D** = Multiplication/Division
    Remember: they go together because **dividing = multiplying by a reciprocal**. For example:
    $6 \div 2 = 6 \times \frac{1}{2}$
  - **A/S** = Addition/Subtraction
    Remember: these go together because **subtracting = adding a negative**. For example:
    $8 - 3 = 8 + (-3)$

#sat_hack

#squared_negatives

Be careful when you have negatives, exponents, and parentheses together. Is $-(4^2)$ the same thing as $(-4)^2$? What about -4^2?

No! This is because the (-) sign is really a (-1). When the (-) sign is outside the parentheses, simplify it last because **P**arentheses and **E**xponents come before **M**ultiplication.

1

Evaluate the following expression.

$$[-(3+4)^2 + (16 \div 4 - 2)] - 100$$

2

Which of the following is equivalent to $[\,(3-7)+16\,]^2$?

A) $(4+16)^2$

B) $-(4-16)^2$

C) $(16-4)^2$

D) -12^2

Function Notation

- On the SAT Math Test, you might see f(x)= or g(x)=.
- This is called Function Notation, and it is used to represent an equation with a variable.
- f(x) is another way of expressing y, which is the output.
  - Example: $f(x) = 3x^2 + 4x + 2$
- The term in parentheses, (x), is an input value, an x-coordinate on a graph.
- The whole expression equals the output, which is the y-coordinate that corresponds with that x-coordinate.

1

$$f(x) = (x+3)^2 - 2x + 7$$
$$g(x) = 3x + 1$$

For the functions f and g above, evaluate $f(g(-2))$.

1. First, you need to find $f(g(x))$. Plug $(3x+1)$ in for x in $f(x)$.

2. Plug (-2) in for x in your new expression and simplify.

Word Problems: Break It Down

- When you come across a long word problem, it's easy to get overwhelmed and not know where to start. The best approach is to tackle the word problem one bite-sized piece at a time.
- After each sentence, write down whatever mathematical statements you can. The first one has been done for you.

1

Last year, the varsity soccer team scored a total of 37 goals throughout its season, 13 of which were scored by graduating seniors. The remaining goals were shared evenly by the tenth and eleventh graders. Assuming that there were no freshmen on the team last year, how many goals were kicked by 11th graders?

Let's break it all down into smaller chunks.

Last year, the varsity soccer team scored a total of 37 goals throughout their season, 13 of which were scored by graduating seniors.

3. How many goals were NOT scored by seniors?
   $37 - 13 = 24$

The remaining goals were shared evenly by the tenth and eleventh graders.

4. "Shared evenly" means that we can divide the number of remaining goals by two.
   $24 \div 2 = 12$

Assuming that there were no freshmen on the team last year, how many goals were kicked by 11th graders?

5. Always double check what the question is. Here, you need the number of goals scored by juniors, which is 12.

2

The ASB at a large high school has a start of year fundraiser, where it needs to raise $1850 for the homecoming dance. At the fundraiser, the ASB sells short-sleeve and long-sleeve t-shirts for $18 and $24, respectively. There are 65 short-sleeved shirts that the ASB needs to sell at the start-of-year fundraiser because they won't sell in winter. If the remaining short-sleeve shirts sell out, how many long-sleeve shirts will the ASB need to sell to reach its goal?

_____ long-sleeve shirts

3

During the summer season, a national park has two popular trails that it sells permits to: the Dawn Mist trail, for $12 and the Glacier Peak trail, for $15. The park can sell 6300 permits per season, but since the Glacier Peak trail is much wider, it can allow twice as many Glacier Peak permits as Dawn Mist permits. How much revenue will the Glacier Peak trail bring in over one entire season if the national park sells out of permits?

$_____

Wordy Word Problems...

- Are a specific type of SAT word problem that display the following:
    1. an equation
    2. a word problem
- Appear to be long and overwhelming
- Simply ask you to "**express**", "**solve for**", "**find**", or "**isolate**" a variable "**in terms of the other variables.**"
    - This means: Isolate one variable by moving everything else to the other side using _____.
- Below are a few examples of Wordy Word Problems that you might see on the SAT:

1

$$\left[P + a\left(\frac{n}{V}\right)^2\right]\left(\frac{V}{n} - b\right) = RT$$

Van der Waal's Equation, shown above, expresses temperature, T, and the gas constant, R, in terms of pressure, P, and volume, V, for a specific gas. Give an equation that expresses pressure in terms of the other variables.

At first, this problem looks intimidating because there are many complicated variables. However, all it's asking us to do is isolate one variable: P (pressure). First, try dividing by $\frac{1}{\left(\frac{V}{n} - b\right)}$.

2

$$P = \frac{S}{S+A}$$

A tutoring company uses the formula above to calculate the percentage of SAT students, S, out of all the test prep students, S+A. Which of the following expresses the number of SAT students in terms of the other variables?

This equation might look simpler than #1, but there are some tricky steps involved. You might have to distribute or factor!

A) $S = \frac{PA}{P-1}$

B) $S = \frac{PA}{1-P}$

C) $S = \frac{A}{1-P}$

D) $S = \frac{A}{P-1}$

#sat_hack

#skip_ahead

When you encounter a Wordy Word Problem and see a scary-looking formula, skip to the end and find out what they are asking. There's a good chance you won't need much of the information to solve the problem!

Absolute Value

- Absolute value bars look like this | | and they represent a distance (right or left) from 0. For example:
  - 7 is seven units to the right of 0, so |7| is 7
  - -7 is seven units to the left of 0, so |-7| is also 7
- **One way of thinking about absolute value is to imagine the odometer of your car. If you drive 100 miles forward, then put it into reverse and drive those same 100 miles backward, you have still driven 200 miles, even though you are right back where you started.**

Let's practice. Follow these steps:

1

Find all possible values of x for the equation below.

$$(|x - 3| + 7) \div 2 = 6$$

Step 1: Start by isolating | x – 3 |
$$|x - 3| = 5$$
Step 2: x – 3 could either be 5 or -5, so create two equations.
x – 3 = 5 and x – 3 = -5
Step 3: Solve each equation for x.

Remember that even though absolute value cannot be negative, your solution might be.

$x = $ _____ or _____

2

Find all possible values of x for the inequality below.

$$(|x - 3| + 7) \div 2 < 6$$

Be careful when you are presented with an inequality that has absolute value. Step 2 is a little different.

Step 2: x – 3 could either be less than 5 or greater than -5, so create two inequalities with opposite signs.
x – 3 ≤ 5 and x – 3 ≥ -5

$x < $ _____ or $x > $ _____

3

Find all possible values of n for the equation below.

$$\frac{|n| + 6}{3} = 4$$

$n = $ _____ or _____

4

Find all possible values of n for the equation below.

$$\frac{8}{|2n|} \leq 4$$

$n \leq $ _____ or $n \geq $ _____

ALGEBRA FUN-DAMENTALS

Algebra FUN-Damentals Practice 1

1

If $\frac{(x-4)}{2} = b$ and $b = 7$ what is the value of x?

A) 0

B) 7

C) 10

D) 18

2

For $i = \sqrt{-1}$ what is the sum $(10 + 4i) - (-8 + 5i)$?

A) $18 - i$

B) $18 + i$

C) $2 - 9i$

D) $2 + 9i$

3

Scott sent m text messages each hour for 7 hours and Kim sent p text messages each hour for 3 hours. Which of the following represents the total number of texts Kim and Scott sent?

A) $21mp$

B) $7m + 3p$

C) $7 + m + 3 + p$

D) $m + p$

4

If $12 + 3x$ is 5 more than 13, what is $10x$?

A) 5

B) 10

C) 20

D) 40

5

$$(x^2y - 3y^2 + 5xy^2 + 3z + 6x^2yz^3) - (x^2y - 3y^2 + 6xy^2 + 10x^2z + 6x^2yz^3)$$

Which of the following is equal to the expression above?

A) $-xy^2 + 3z + 10x^2z$

B) $2x^2y - 6y^2 - 11xy^2 + 3z + 10x^2z + 12x^2yz^3$

C) $-6y^2 + 3z + 10x^2z + 12x^2yz^3$

D) $-6y^2 + xy^2 + 3z + 10x^2z$

6

$$7x(2x + 3) + 5(3x + 14) = ax^2 + bx + c$$

In the equation above a, b, and c are constants. If the equation is true for all values of x, what is the value of b?

A) 12

B) 24

C) 36

D) 48

7

If h hours and 45 minutes is equal to 885 minutes, what is the value of h?

A) 4

B) 7

C) 12

D) 14

8

If $\frac{3}{10}x + \frac{5}{10}x = \frac{3}{5} + \frac{9}{5}$ what is the value of x?

A) 1

B) 2

C) 3

D) 4

9

A function f satisfies $f(2) = 4$ and $f(4) = 6$. A function g satisfies $g(3) = 4$ and $g(5) = 7$. What is the value of $f(g(3))$?

A) 4

B) 6

C) 7

D) 8

10

$$\text{Formula 1: } X = \frac{\sqrt{ab}}{60}$$

$$\text{Formula 2: } X = \frac{5+b}{30}$$

Given the two formulas above, which of the following expressions is equivalent to $\sqrt{ab}$?

A) $\frac{5+b}{2}$

B) $\frac{5+b}{1800}$

C) $2(5 + b)$

D) $\frac{(5+b)^2}{2}$

Algebra FUN-Damentals Practice 2

1

$$S = \frac{F}{U + F}$$

A company uses the formula above to calculate a seller's rating, S, based on the number of favorable reviews, F, and unfavorable reviews U. Which of the following expresses the number of unfavorable reviews in terms of the other variables?

A) $U = \frac{F}{S} - F$

B) $U = S - F$

C) $U = \frac{S}{F} - F$

D) $U = \frac{S}{F} + F$

2

When 5 times the number x is added to 16, the result is 41. What number results when 3 times x is added to 7?

A) -7

B) 15

C) 22

D) 37

3

If $5a = 15$, what is the value of $3a - 12$?

A) -6

B) -3

C) 0

D) 4

4

Which of the following is equal to 0 for at least one value of x?

A) $|x - 1| - 1$

B) $|x + 1| + 1$

C) $|1 - x| + 1$

D) $|x - 1| + 1$

5

$$f(x) = \frac{3}{2}x + k$$

In the function above k is constant. If $f(4) = 15$. What is the value of $f(-2)$?

A) -2

B) 0

C) 5

D) 6

6

If $f(x) = -4x + 7$, what is $f(-2x)$ equal to?

A) $-8x + 7$

B) $8x + 7$

C) $8x^2 - 7x$

D) $8x^2 - 14x$

7

If $\frac{x+y}{y} = \frac{4}{9}$ which of the following must also be true?

A) $\frac{x}{y} = \frac{-5}{9}$

B) $\frac{x}{y} = \frac{5}{9}$

C) $\frac{x-y}{y} = \frac{-13}{9}$

D) $\frac{x-2y}{y} = \frac{13}{9}$

8

If $5p - 9 \geq 1$, what is the least possible value of $5p + 2$?

A) 12

B) 10

C) 2

D) 1

9

$$(3954 + 117y^2) - 9(9y^2 - 110)$$

The expression above can be written in the form $ay^2 + b$, where a and b are constants. What is the value of $a + b$?

A) 3880

B) 4064

C) 4100

D) 4980

10

The score on a trivia game is obtained by subtracting the number of incorrect answers from twice the number of correct answers. If a player answered 60 questions and obtained a score of 90, how many questions did the player answer incorrectly?

A) 10

B) 20

C) 35

D) 50

Algebra FUN-Damentals Practice 3

1

The CEO of a company purchased a total of $6000 in gifts for the raffle at the annual company party. The gifts cost either $250 or $1000. If at least one $250 and at least one $1000 gift was purchased, what is a possible number of $250 gifts purchased?

A) 3

B) 4

C) 5

D) 6

2

A gift requires 20 centimeters of tape to be wrapped fully. What is the maximum number of gifts of this type that can be wrapped with 5 meters of tape?
(1 meter = 100 cm)

A) 4

B) 25

C) 30

D) 250

3

Gina spent 20% of her 8-hour workday in meetings. How many minutes of her workday did she spend in meetings?

A) 1.6

B) 16

C) 32

D) 96

4

$$12ax + 12b + 6 = 150$$

Based on the equation above, what is the value of $ax + b$?

A) 3

B) 6

C) 12

D) 15

5

Let x and y be numbers such that $-y < x < y$. Which of the following must be true?

I. $|x| < y$

II. $x > 0$

III. $y > 0$

A) I only

B) III only

C) I and II only

D) I and III only

6

$$d = -15a^2 + ab + c$$

Which of the following gives b in terms of $a, c,$ and d?

A) $b = d + c - 15a$

B) $b = \frac{d-c+15}{a}$

C) $b = \frac{d+c}{a} - 15a$

D) $b = \frac{d-c}{a} + 15a$

7

Which of the following is equivalent to $3x + 9$?

A) $3(x + 9)$

B) $3(x + 5) - 6$

C) $3(x + 3) + 3$

D) $2(x + 2) + x + 4$

8

If $\frac{3}{x} = \frac{15}{x+20}$, what is the value of $\frac{x}{10}$?

A) 10

B) 5

C) 2

D) $\frac{1}{2}$

9

A software company is selling a new game in a standard edition and a collector's edition. The box of the standard edition has a volume of 30 cubic inches, and the box of the collector's edition has a volume of 50 cubic inches. The company receives an order for 125 copies of the game and the total volume of the order to be shipped is 2,380 cubic inches. Which of the following systems of equations can be used to determine the number of standard edition games, a, and collector's edition games, c, that were ordered?

A) $125 - a = c$
    $30a + 50c = 2380$

B) $125 - a = c$
    $30c + 50a = 2380$

C) $a - c = 125$
    $30a + 50c = 2380$

D) $a - c = 125$
    $30c + 50a = 2380$

Blue Book Problem	My Answer	Correct Answer	Why did I miss?
P. 447 #1			
P. 448 #5			
P. 449 #12			
P. 452 #17			
P. 455 #1			
P. 455 #3			
P. 456 #6			
P. 457 #8			
P. 457 #10			
P. 461 #22			
P. 465 #31			
P. 465 #32			
P. 467 #37			
P. 467 #38			
P. 559 #1			
P. 559 #4			
P. 560 #5			
P. 562 #13			
P. 574 #22			
P. 579 #33			

CORRECT OUT OF TOTAL: _____/22

NOTES:

Linear Equations

- The SAT's most common question category requires knowledge of linear equations. These are equations that express a **direct**, **constant** relationship between two variables, usually *x* and *y*.
- A linear equation is any equation that has two variables to the first power (no exponents), and is graphed as a straight line
- You might remember **slope-intercept form** from Pre-Algebra:

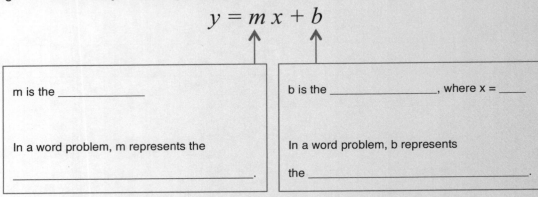

$$y = m\,x + b$$

m is the _____	b is the _____, where x = _____
In a word problem, m represents the _____.	In a word problem, b represents the _____.

What are x and y in slope-intercept form? _____

What Is A Linear Relationship?

- In a linear relationship, x and y always increase or decrease at a **constant rate** (the slope)
- Can you identify which relationships below are linear?

1

x	-1	0	1	2
f(x)	4	6	8	10

Circle one: **linear / nonlinear**

2

x	2	4	6	8
f(x)	6	18	38	66

Circle one: **linear / nonlinear**

3

When you drink a cup of coffee, the amount of caffeine in your bloodstream is halved approximately every 4 hours.

The relationship between <u>time passed (x)</u> and <u>caffeine in your bloodstream (y)</u> is…
(linear / nonlinear)

4

A student earns $16 per hour of work, 25% of which he saves towards the down payment for a car.

The relationship between <u>hours worked (x)</u> and <u>dollars saved (y)</u> is…
linear / nonlinear

Writing Linear Equations in Slope-Intercept Form

- The y = mx + b equation is a good starting point for many linear equations questions.
  1. **Find the slope (m) using the slope formula** ⟶
  2. **Plug in one of the given points for x and y**
  3. **Solve for b**
- Use these steps to work through the problems below.

$$m = \frac{y_2 - y_1}{x_2 - x_1}$$

How would you graph y = 2? It's a horizontal line going through (0, 2)! ⟶

What would the graph of x = -3 look like? Draw it in on the x-y plane.

1

The chart below gives points on a line. Where does the line cross the x-axis?

x	-3	2	6	11
f(x)	16	1	-11	-26

First, find m and b to write your linear equation (y = m x + b).

Now you can find the x-intercept, which is where y = 0.

2

Between ages 1 and 2, a child usually gains weight at a constant rate. If a child weighs 10.2 kg at fourteen months old and 11kg at eighteen months old, how much will it weigh at its 2-year checkup?

What two points are given? What point are you looking for?

3

A line crosses through the origin and (-4, 3). For which value of x does f(x) = 9?

4

What is the equation of a horizontal line passing through (2,3)?

What is the equation of a vertical line passing through the same point?

#sat_hack

#finding_intercepts

The SAT may ask you where a line crosses either axis (like #1 above).

When you see **"crosses the y-axis"**: plug in x = 0
When you see **"crosses the x-axis"**: plug in y = 0

LINEAR EQUATIONS

Finding Distance: Pythagorean Theorem

- To find the distance between two points, you can use the distance formula, given below.

$$d = \sqrt{(x_2 - x_1)^2 + (y_2 - y_1)^2}$$

- The _____ distance formula comes from the _____ Pythagorean theorem, a^2 _____ $+ b^2 = c^2$

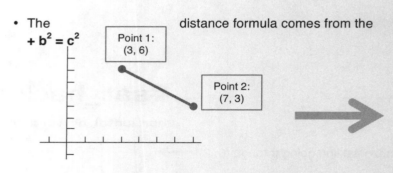

Point 1: (3, 6)

Point 2: (7, 3)

a is the "rise" $(y_2 - y_1)$

c is the distance (the hypotenuse)

b is the "run" $(x_2 - x_1)$

Remembering formulas can be overwhelming and can result in errors. The fewer formulas you have to memorize, the more easily you'll cruise through this math test. Remembering concepts is much more effective when it comes to SAT math.

Let's plug it all in to $a^2 + b^2 = c^2$
$$(3 - 6)^2 + (7 - 3)^2 = d^2$$

Now, solve for d.

1

Find the distance between (0,2) and (5,9).

2

Find the distance between (-3, 5) and (2, -7)

3

The diameter of a circle has endpoints P and Q at the origin and at (-5, -12) respectively. What is the length of the radius of the circle?

4

In Palmdale, the streets that run North to South are numbered and the streets that run East to West are lettered. The city blocks are all 100 feet on every side. If Matthew's house on the corner of 6th Street at and G Street, and his friend's house is on the corner of 9th Street and C street, how many feet apart are their houses?

Finding Midpoint: Using Averages

- To find the midpoint of two points on a one-dimensional number line, just average the two points.

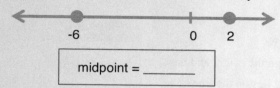

-6   0   2

midpoint = _____

- It gets a little trickier when you are working with x and y coordinates.
  1. To find the x-coordinate of the midpoint, average the two given x-coordinates
  2. To find the y-coordiante of the midpoint, average the two given y-coordinates

$$(x_{mid}, \ y_{mid}) = (\frac{x_1 \ + \ x_2}{2}, \ \frac{y_1 \ + \ y_2}{2})$$

#sat_hack

#reverse_midpoint

Sometimes, the SAT will ask you to find a missing point given a second point and the midpoint between the two. For these questions, you can still use the formula: just plug in what you are given and solve for what's not given.

1

What is the midpoint of a line segment with ends at (2,4) and (-3, 5)?

2

A circle has a center at the origin and a diameter $\overline{ST}$. Point S lies on the circle at (4,6). What are the coordinates of point T?

MATH LINEAR EQUATIONS

165

Linear Equations Practice 1

1

A line in the xy-plane passes through the origin and has a slope of $\frac{1}{5}$. Which of the following lies on the line?

A) (0,5)

B) (1,5)

C) (5,5)

D) (15,3)

2

The graph of a line in the xy-plane has a slope of 3 and contains the points $(1, -3)$. The graph of a second line passes through the points $(2,4)$ and $(5,1)$. If the two lines intersect at the point (a, b), what is the value of $a + b$?

A) 0

B) 3

C) 6

D) 9

3

In the video game *Mathematician's Creed*, each player starts the game with k points and loses 3 points each time a task is not completed. If a player who gains no additional points and fails to complete 150 tasks has a score of 300 points, what is the value of k?

A) 250

B) 550

C) 750

D) 1250

4

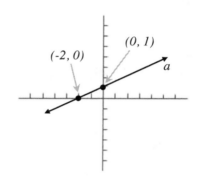

In the xy-plane above, line a is parallel to line b (not shown). Line b contain the points $(0, -1)$ and $(p, 0)$. What is the value of p?

A) -2

B) 1

C) 2

D) 3

5

Which of the following graphs is the correct graph of the following equation $2x + y = 1$ in the xy-plane?

A)

B)

C)

D)

6

$$s = 15t + 25$$

Linda made an initial deposit to a savings account. Each week thereafter she deposited a fixed amount to the account. The equation above models the amount s, in dollars, that Linda has deposited after t weekly deposits. According to the model, how many dollars was Linda's initial deposit?

A) 0

B) 15

C) 25

D) 40

7

In an xy-plane, $ABCD$ is square and point E is the center of the square. The coordinates of points C and E are $(2,2)$ and $(0,10)$, respectively. Which of the following is an equation of the line that passes through B and D?

A) $y = -4x + 10$

B) $y = \frac{1}{4}x + 10$

C) $y = 4x + 6$

D) $y = -\frac{1}{4}x + 6$

8

In the xy-plane, the line determined by the points $(4, k)$ and $(k, 16)$ passes through the origin. Which of the following could be the value of k?

A) -4

B) -8

C) 4

D) 16

9

x	$f(x)$
1	7
3	13
5	19

Some values of the linear function are shown in the table above. Which of the following defines f?

A) $f(x) = 3x + 4$

B) $f(x) = 4x + 3$

C) $f(x) = 2x + 9$

D) $f(x) = 7x$

10

The average number of students per classroom at Homestead High School from 2000 to 2010 can be modeled by the equation $y = 0.7x + 34.3$, where x represents the number of years since 2000, and y represents the average number of students per classroom. Which of the following best describes the meaning of the number 0.7 in the equation?

A) The total number of students at the school in 2000

B) The estimated increase in the average number of students per classroom each year

C) The average number of students per classroom in 2000

D) The estimated difference between average number of students per classroom in 2000 and in 2010

Linear Equations Practice 2

1

The line $y = kx + 7$ where k is a constant, is graphed in the xy-plane. If the line contains the point (a, b), where $a \neq 0$ and $b \neq 0$, what is the slope of the line in terms of a and b?

A) $\frac{b-7}{a}$

B) $\frac{a-7}{b}$

C) $\frac{7-b}{a}$

D) $\frac{7-a}{b}$

2

Which of the following equations represents a line that is parallel to the line with equation $y = -5x + 6$?

A) $y = \frac{1}{5}x + 12$

B) $x + 5y = 1$

C) $10x + 2y = 18$

D) $5x - y = 4$

3

$$-3x + 2y = 10$$

In the xy-plane, the graph of which of the following equations is perpendicular to the graph of the equation above?

A) $y = \frac{2}{3}x + 12$

B) $2x + y = 1$

C) $10x + 2y = 18$

D) $-2x = 3y - 24$

4

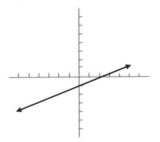

The graph of linear function f is shown in the xy-plane above. The slope of the graph of the linear function g is 6 times the slope of the graph of f. If the graph of g passes through the point $(0, -6)$, What is the value of $g(7)$?

A) 12

B) -8

C) 4

D) 15

5

While preparing to run a marathon, Henry created a training schedule in which the distance of his longest run every week increased by a constant amount. If Henry's training schedule requires that his longest run in week 8 is a distance of 10 miles and his longest run in week 20 is a distance of 28 miles, which of the following best describes how the distance Henry runs changes between week 4 and week 16 of his training schedule?

A) Henry increases the distance of his longest run by 0.5 miles each week

B) Henry increases the distance of his longest run by 3 miles each week

C) Henry increases the distance of his longest run by 2 miles every 3 weeks

D) Henry increases the distance of his longest run by 1.5 miles each week

6

A gym charges a one-time membership fee of $450 plus d dollars for each month. If a member pays $1,230 for the first 12 months, including the membership, what is the value of d?

A) 102.5

B) 65

C) 45.25

D) 135

7

The line with the equation $\frac{4}{7}x + \frac{1}{2}y = 1$ is graphed in the xy-plane. What is the x-intercept of the line?

A) 1

B) 0.6

C) 1.75

D) 2

8

The graph of the line in the xy-plane passes through the point $(1,6)$ and crosses the x-axis at point $(3,0)$. The line crosses the y-axis at the point $(0,p)$. What is the value of p?

A) 12

B) 8

C) -3

D) 9

9

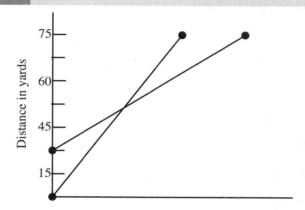

The graph above shows the positions of Mary and Lisa during a race. Mary and Lisa each ran at a constant rate, and Mary was given a head start to shorten the distance she needed to run. Lisa finished the race in 10 seconds, and Mary finished the race in 15 seconds. According to the graph, Mary was given a head start of how many yards?

A) 15

B) 25

C) 30

D) 35

10

x	1	2	3	4
y	$\dfrac{15}{6}$	$\dfrac{41}{6}$	$\dfrac{67}{6}$	$\dfrac{93}{6}$

Which of the following equations relates y to x for the values in the table above?

A) $y = \frac{13}{3}x - \frac{11}{6}$

B) $y = 3\left(\frac{11}{6}\right)^x$

C) $y = \frac{11}{6}x + 26$

D) $y = 3\left(\frac{13}{6}\right)^x$

Blue Book Problem	My answer	Correct answer	Why did I miss?
P. 447 #3			
P. 448 #6			
P. 449 #9			
P. 458 #12			
P. 462 #25			
P. 466 #35			
P. 560 #6			
P. 560 #8			
P. 569 #8			
P. 576 #26			

CORRECT OUT OF TOTAL: _____/10

NOTES:

Systems of Equations

- The SAT will test your knowledge of Systems of Equations, or problems where you are given multiple equations with multiple variables.
- The solution to a system is where two graphs intersect.
- You can solve systems using three methods: **substitution**, **elimination**, or **graphing**. See the examples below, and follow the steps to work through them.

1

At what point do the following equations intersect?

$$2y + 6 = 4x + 4$$
$$3x + y = 9$$

1. $y = 9 - 3x$

2. $2(9 - 3x) + 6 = 4x + 4$

3. $x = $ ___

4. The lines intersect at (____, ____)

Substitution

1. Isolate either of the variables. We will start with y because it doesn't have a coefficient.

2. Plug our y-expression (what y equals: $9 - 3x$) in for the y in the other equation.

3. Now, since we have only one variable (x) in our equation, we can solve it.

4. Take your x-value and plug it into either equation, then solve for y.

2

$$4x + 2y = 10$$
$$2x - y = -3$$

The equations above intersect at a point with coordinates (c, d).
What is the value of c?

Elimination

A common SAT test-writing tactic is to assign different letters to (x, y) coordinates to confuse you. Here, c and d are just referring to (x, y) coordinates.

Since #2 is asking us to solve for c, which is x, we need to manipulate one of the equations so that the y-terms cancel.

#sat_hack
#test_vocab

Remember that the "solution" is where the graphs cross.

When you see the term "no solution", it means that the lines never intersect. Lines that never intersect are parallel, and the equations have the same slope.

When you see the term "infinite solutions", it means that the lines are the same line. For example, $2x - y = -3$ and $4x - 2y = -6$ are the same line, because the second equation is just the first one multiplied by a factor of 2.

Systems of Equations in Word Problems

- Some SAT questions may require you to write a system before you can solve it.
- Back in Algebra FUN-damentals, we practiced turning word problems into bite-sized math pieces. You'll need that skill for the problems below.

1

At a basketball coach's last game ever, the team sells bobble heads and cardboard cutouts of him so that they can buy him a retirement gift. They sell a total of 67 items and raise $678. If a bobble head cost $6 and a cardboard cutout cost $18, how many of bobble heads did they sell?

Step 1: Decide what variables you will use.

Step 2: Write two equations. One equation should express the total dollars, and the other should express the total items sold.

Step 3: Remember which variable you are solving for. To avoid wasting time solving for the number of cutouts, put everything in terms of the **number of bobble heads.**

2

Big Benny's Burger Stand sells cheeseburgers and fries. A family orders five cheeseburgers and 3 orders of fries, and pays $17.20. The next person orders 2 cheeseburger and four orders of fries, and pays $12.20. How much does a cheeseburger cost?

3

The area of a patio is 108 square feet, and has a perimeter of 42 feet. What is the length of the patio's longest side?

#sat_hack
#when_to_use_what

Use **substitution** if you have one variable already isolated or easy to isolate.

Use **elimination** if the variables "line up" when you stack the two equations.

If you are really stuck, try **graphing** the equations (in your graphing calculator if possible) for a hint.

Systems of Equations Practice 1

1

$$x - y = 5$$
$$2x + y = 4$$

Which ordered pair (x, y) satisfies the system of equations shown above?

A) $(-3, -2)$

B) $(3, -2)$

C) $(1, 9)$

D) $(10, 5)$

2

If the system of inequalities listed below is graphed in an xy-plane, which quadrant contains **no solutions** to the system?

$$y \geq 2x - 4$$
$$y < -\frac{2}{5}x - 2$$

A) Quadrant I

B) Quadrant II

C) Quadrant III

D) There are solutions in all quadrants

3

$$x + 2y = 5$$
$$2x - 3y = 3$$

Which ordered pair (x, y) satisfies the system of equations shown above?

A) $(1, 2)$

B) $(5, 0)$

C) $(4, 1)$

D) $(3, 1)$

4

$$y = \frac{x}{3} - 2$$
$$2x - 3y = 3$$

Which ordered pair (x, y) satisfies the system of equations shown above?

A) $(-3, -3)$

B) $(-1, -\frac{1}{3})$

C) $(1, 3)$

D) $(3, 1)$

5

$$y \geq 2x - 3$$
$$y \leq \frac{5}{4}x + \frac{5}{2}$$
$$y > -3$$

If the system of inequalities above is graphed in an xy-plane, which one the following is a possible solution to the system?

A) $(-2, 2)$

B) $(3, 7)$

C) $(0, 1)$

D) $(-1, 4)$

6

$$2x + 4y = 5$$
$$3x - 3y = 3$$

For the solution (x, y) to the system of equations above, what is the value of $x - y$?

A) 0

B) 1

C) $\frac{3}{2}$

D) 2

7

If $a - b = 16$ and $\frac{b}{2} = 22$, what is the value of $a + b$?

A) 44

B) 50

C) 60

D) 104

8

$$y = x^2$$
$$2y - 6x = 4(x + 7)$$

If (x, y) is a solution of the system of equations above and $x > 0$, what is the value of xy?

A) 8

B) 49

C) 14

D) 343

9

Kobe Bryant is going to hire at least 15 staff members for a project called Space Jam 3. The staff members will be made up of Loony Toons, who will be paid $470 per week, and retired basketball players, who will be paid $940 per week. His budget for paying the staff members is no more than $12,350 per week. He must hire at least 4 Loony Toons and at least 2 retired basketball players. Which of the following systems of inequalities represents the conditions described if x is the number of Loony Toons and y is the number of retired basketball players?

A) $470x + 940y \geq 12,350$
$x + y \leq 15$
$x \geq 4$
$y \geq 2$

B) $470x + 940y \leq 12,350$
$x + y \geq 15$
$x \geq 4$
$y \geq 2$

C) $470x + 940y \geq 12,350$
$x + y \geq 15$
$x \leq 4$
$y \leq 2$

D) $470x + 940y \leq 12,350$
$x + y \leq 15$
$x \leq 4$
$y \leq 2$

10

A shipping service restricts the dimensions of the boxes it will ship for a certain type of service. The restriction states that for boxes shaped like rectangular prisms, the sum of the perimeter of the base of the box and the height of the box cannot exceed 150 inches. The perimeter of the base is determined using the width and length of the box. If a box has a height of 60 inches and its length is 3.5 times the width, which inequality shows the allowable width x, in inches, of the box?

A) $0 < x \leq 10$

B) $0 < x \leq 90$

C) $0 < x \leq 15\frac{1}{2}$

D) $0 < x \leq 150$

Systems of Equations Practice 2

1

An online bookstore sells novels and magazines. Each novel sells for $7, and each magazine sells for $3. If Leyla purchased a total of 15 novels and magazines that have a combined selling price of $61, how many novels did she purchase?

A) 2

B) 4

C) 6

D) 11

2

$$3x - 4y = -12$$

$$4x - 3y = -9$$

For the solution (x, y) to the system of equations above, what is the value of $x - y$?

A) 0

B) 3

C) −3

D) −7

3

$$y = 2x - 3$$

$$y - 1 = 4x$$

Which ordered pair (x, y) satisfies the system of equations shown above?

A) $(-1, -5)$

B) $(-\frac{2}{3}, -\frac{5}{3})$

C) $(0, -3)$

D) $(-2, -7)$

4

Casey has two summer jobs. She works as a barista at Starbucks, which pays $10.50 per hour, and she works as a dog walker for Waggin' Tails, which pays $15 per hour. She can Work no more than 17 hours per week, but she wants to earn at least $310 per week. Which of the following inequalities represents this situation in terms of x and y, where x is the number of hours she works as a barista and y is the number of hours she works as a dog walker?

A) $10.5x + 15y \geq 310$
$x + y \leq 17$

B) $10.5x + 15y \geq 310$
$x + y \geq 17$

C) $10.5x + 15y \leq 310$
$x + y \geq 17$

D) $10.5x + 15y \leq 310$
$x + y \leq 17$

5

$$kx - 5y = 4$$
$$3x - 4y = 7$$

In the system of equations above, k is a constant and x and y are variables. For what value of k will the system of equations have no solution?

A) $-\frac{14}{5}$

B) $\frac{12}{5}$

C) $\frac{15}{4}$

D) $-\frac{4}{7}$

6

At Monster Burger's food truck, each hamburger has 150 more calories than each order of fries. If 3 hamburgers and 5 orders of fries have a total of 2530 calories, how many calories does a hamburger have?

A) 180

B) 260

C) 410

D) 1230

7

$$3x + b = 5x - 7$$
$$3y + c = 5y - 7$$

In the equation above, b and c are constants. If b is c minus $\frac{1}{4}$, which of the following is true?

A) y is x plus $\frac{1}{8}$.

B) y is x minus $\frac{1}{4}$.

C) y is x minus $\frac{1}{8}$.

D) y is x plus $\frac{1}{4}$.

8

The sum of four numbers is 900. One of the numbers, y, is 50% more than the sum of the other 3 numbers. What is the value of y?

A) 225

B) 540

C) 460

D) 375

9

$$S(P) = \frac{1}{4}P + 60$$
$$D(P) = 280 - P$$

The quantity of a product supplied and the quantity of the product demanded in an economic market are functions of the price of the product. The functions above are the estimated supply and demand functions for a certain product. The function $S(P)$ gives the quantity of the product supplied to the market when the price is P dollars, and the function $D(P)$ gives the quantity of the product demanded by the market when the price is P dollars. At what price will the quantity of the product supplied to the market equal the quantity of the product demanded by the market?

A) $176

B) $220

C) $145

D) $167

10

$$y \le -15x + 4500$$
$$y \le 5x$$

In the xy-plane, if a point with the coordinates (a, b) lies in the solution set of the system of inequalities above, what is the maximum possible value of b?

A) 1,225

B) 750

C) 2,250

D) 1,125

Blue Book Problem	My answer	Correct answer	Why did I miss?
P. 453 #20			
P. 457 #9			
P. 465 #32			
P. 560 #6			
P. 561 #9			
P. 565 #19			
P. 573 #18			
P. 575 #24			
P. 577 #30			
P. 580 #36			

CORRECT OUT OF TOTAL: _____/10

NOTES:

Quadratic Equations. . .

- are equations where x is to the second power.
  - Example: $y = 3x^2 + 2x + 6$
- are equations that are graphed as a _____.

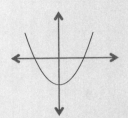

This is the graph of a Quadratic Equation.

- are usually represented by the **Standard Quadratic Form:**

$$y = ax^2 + bx + c$$

Quadratics: What is a solution?

- Many SAT questions will ask you to solve these quadratics. We will practice a few ways to do this on the next page, but first we need to understand what the "solution" really is.
- The solution to a quadratic is where it crosses the x-axis, or where y = 0.
- A quadratic can have two, one, or zero real solutions, shown below:

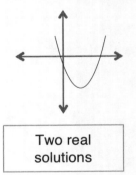

Two real solutions

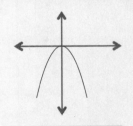

One real solution

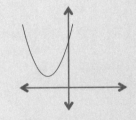

No real solutions

#sat_hack

#test_vocab

The SAT might refer to the solutions as **roots**, **zeros**, **x-intercepts**, or even simply **x's**. Just remember that the solution to a quadratic is where y = 0, and where the parabola crosses the horizontal axis.

A parabola has "no real solutions" if its solution contains i ($\sqrt{-1}$).

FOIL, Factoring, & the Quadratic Formula

- The solution to a quadratic is where it crosses the x-axis, or where y = 0.
- Finding this will require the following:
    1. **FOIL** (first, outer, inner, last)
    2. **Factoring** – the opposite of **FOIL**
    3. **Quadratic Formula** – requires a quadratic to be in **standard form**

$$x = \frac{-b \pm \sqrt{b^2 - 4ac}}{2a}$$

- Let's practice these skills.

1

Expand these expressions (FOIL):

A) $(x - 3)(x + 4)$

B) $(x + 2)(x - 2)$

C) $(x^2 - 4x + 5)(x + 3)$

2

Factor these expressions:

A) $x^2 - 5x + 6$

B) $x^2 + 9$

C) $2x^2 - 4x - 16$

3

Use the Quadratic Formula to solve for *x*.

$$0 = 3x^2 + 2x - 8$$

4

Use the Quadratic Formula to solve for *x*.

$$y = 2x^2 - 2x - 10$$

QUADRATIC EQUATIONS

179

The Vertex: A Maximum or Minimum

- The vertex of a parabola is the highest or lowest point on the graph, and tells you two other things:
  1. The maximum or minimum y-value
  2. The axis of symmetry (a vertical line running through the x-coordinate of the vertex)

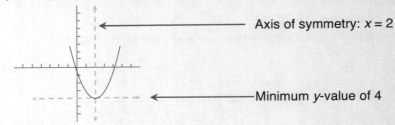

Axis of symmetry: $x = 2$

Minimum y-value of 4

- Vertex form looks like this:

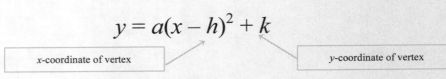

$$y = a(x - h)^2 + k$$

x-coordinate of vertex y-coordinate of vertex

- There are two ways to put a quadratic equation into vertex form:
  1. Use $x = -b/2a$
  2. Complete the square
- See the examples below for step-by-step examples of each process.

1

Put the following quadratic into vertex form by completing the square.

$$y = x^2 - 4x + 5$$

a) $y - 5 = x^2 - 4x$

b) $y - 5 + \underline{\quad} = x^2 - 4x + \underline{\quad}$

c) $y = (x - 2)^2 + 1$

Step 1: move the constant (c) to y's side of the equation, so that you are only working with the x^2 and x terms.

Step 2: take the coefficient of the x-term (b), divide it in half, and square it. Add the result to both sides.

Step 3: Factor the "x" side, and move your new c back home.

2

Find the vertex form of the equation below, using $x = -b/2a$.

$$y = x^2 - 6x + 8$$

$$x = \frac{-[\ ]}{2[\ ]}$$

To find the x-coordinate of the vertex, use $-b/2a$.

Once you have found the x-coordinate, plug it in to the original equation for x and solve for y.

QUADRATIC EQUATIONS

Quadratic Equations Practice 1

1

$$g(x) = ax^2 - 24$$

For the function g defined above, a is a constant and $g(4) = 8$. What is the value $g(-3)$?

A) -42

B) -6

C) 8

D) -15

2

If $(ax + 3)(bx + 5) = 12x^2 + cx + 15$ for all values of x, and $a + b = 8$, what are the two possible values for c?

A) 3 and 5

B) 6 and 8

C) 28 and 36

D) 42 and 52

3

If $x > 4$ which of the following is equivalent to $\dfrac{1}{\frac{1}{x+4}+\frac{1}{x+3}}$?

A) $\dfrac{x^2+7x+12}{2x+7}$

B) $x^2 + 7x + 12$

C) $\dfrac{2x+7}{x^2+7x+12}$

D) $2x + 7$

4

$$x^2 - 8x + 15 = y$$

The equation above represents a parabola in the xy-plane. Which of the following equivalent forms of the equation displays the x-intercepts of the parabola as constants or coefficients?

A) $y - 15 = x^2 - 8x$

B) $y = x(x - 8) + 15$

C) $y + 1 = (x - 4)^2$

D) $y = (x - 3)(x - 5)$

5

In the xy-plane, the point (2,8) lies on the graph of the function
$f(x) = 2x^2 - bx + 12$. What is the value of b?

A) 2

B) 6

C) 7

D) 14

6

If $c > 0$ and $c^2 - 25 = 0$, what is the value of c?

A) -3

B) -5

C) 25

D) 5

7

$$4a^4 + 20a^2b^2 + 25b^4$$

Which of the following is equivalent to the expression shown above?

A) $(4a^2 + 5b^2)^2$

B) $(4a + 5b)^4$

C) $(2a^2 + 5b^2)^2$

D) $(2a + 5b)^4$

8

$$y = x^2 - 2x - 8$$

Which of the following is an equivalent form of the equation of the graph shown in the xy-plane above from which the coordinates of vertex A can be identified as constants in the equation?

A) $y = (x + 4)(x + 2)$

B) $y = (x - 4)(x + 2)$

C) $y = x(x - 2) - 8$

D) $y = (x - 1)^2 - 9$

9

What is the sum of all the values of x that satisfy $2x^2 + 12x - 28 = 0$?

A) $-3 + \sqrt{23}$

B) -6

C) 0

D) 6

10

$$h = -6.9x^2 + 21x$$

The equation above expresses the approximate height h, of a ball x seconds after it is launched vertically upward from the ground with an initial velocity of 15 meters per second. After approximately how many seconds with the ball hit the ground?

A) 3.0

B) 4.5

C) 5.0

D) 7.0

Quadratic Equations Practice 2

1

In the xy-plane, the parabola with the equation $y = (x - 5)^2$ intersects the line with equation $y = 64$ at two points, A and B. What is the length of $\overline{AB}$?

A) 8

B) 10

C) 13

D) 16

2

$$y = a(x - 4)(x + 8)$$

In the quadratic equation above, a is a nonzero constant. The graph of the equation in the xy-plane is a parabola with vertex (c, d). Which of the following is equal to d?

A) $-6a$

B) $-8a$

C) $-12a$

D) $-36a$

3

In the xy-plane, the point $(2,8)$ lies on the graph of the function $f(x) = 2x^2 + bx - 20$. What is the value of $f(4)$?

A) 16

B) 28

C) 36

D) 52

4

x	$f(x)$
0	4
1	2
2	0
3	-2

The function f is defined by the polynomial. Some values of x and $f(x)$ are shown in the table above. Which of the following must be a factor of $f(x)$?

A) x

B) $x - 2$

C) $x - 3$

D) $x - 4$

5

$$\frac{4x + 5}{(x + 3)^2} - \frac{4}{(x + 3)}$$

The expression above is equivalent to $\frac{a}{(x+3)^2}$, where a is a positive constant and $x \neq -3$. What is the value of a?

A) 2

B) -7

C) $8x - 7$

D) $4x + 1$

6

What are the solutions to $4x^2 - 6x - 14 = 0$?

A) $\dfrac{3\pm\sqrt{65}}{4}$

B) $\dfrac{-3\pm\sqrt{65}}{8}$

C) $\dfrac{3\pm2\sqrt{65}}{4}$

D) $\dfrac{-3\pm\sqrt{65}}{2}$

7

What are the solutions to $\dfrac{1}{6}x^2 + \dfrac{4}{3}x - \dfrac{2}{3} = 0$?

A) $-4 \pm 4\sqrt{5}$

B) $-4 \pm 4\sqrt{3}$

C) $-4 \pm 2\sqrt{5}$

D) $-4 \pm 2\sqrt{3}$

8

$$2(3x + 1)(2x + 3)$$

Which of the following is equivalent to the expression above?

A) $40x$

B) $12x^2 + 6$

C) $12x^2 + 22x + 6$

D) $12x^2 + 11x + 3$

9

In the xy-plane, the graph of the function f has x-intercepts at -4, -2, and 2. Which of the following could define f?

A) $(x) = (x - 2)(x + 2)(x + 4)$

B) $f(x) = (x - 2)^2(x + 4)$

C) $f(x) = (x + 2)^2(x + 4)$

D) $f(x) = (x - 2)(x + 2)(x - 4)$

10

If $a^2 + b^2 = c$ and $3ab = d$, which of the following is equivalent to $9c + 6d$?

A) $(a + 3b)^2$

B) $(3a + 3b)^2$

C) $(6a + b)^2$

D) $(9a + 6)^2$

Blue Book Problem	My answer	Correct answer	Why did I miss?
P. 450 #13			
P. 456 #7			
P. 465 #33			
P. 561 #10			
P. 561 #12			
P. 562 #14			
P. 571 #13			

CORRECT OUT OF TOTAL: _____/7

NOTES:

Geometry: Shapes, Lines & Angles

- While the SAT tests 5 geometry concepts, this can be tricky since most students have not practiced many of these concepts for a few years. This section will review:
  1. **Parallel lines and angle pairs**
  2. **Triangles, quadrilaterals, and other polygons**
  3. **Circles**
  4. **Rectangular solids, cylinders, cones, and spheres**
  5. **Composite shapes**

Parallel Lines

- In **Geometry** you may have learned the names of many different types of angles and angle pairs.
- You will not need to know those terms on the SAT.
- However, you will need to be able to find the measures of all of the angles in the figure below.

1

Lines *A* and *B* in the figure at the right are parallel. Find the following:

l = _____   *m* = _____

n = _____   *o* = _____

p = _____   *q* = _____

r = _____

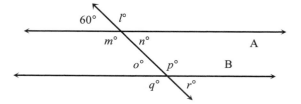

2

Lines P and Q in the figure at the right are parallel. Which of the following groups of angles MUST add to 180 degrees?

A) *a + b + e*

B) *a + d + f*

C) *b + d + f*

D) *c + e + f*

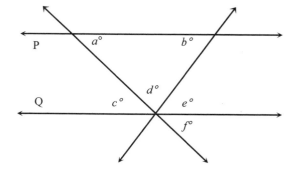

#sat_hack

#draw_it

When you are presented with a diagram, mark it up with any given information (angle measures, side lengths, parallel/congruent lines).

If the SAT describes a diagram but doesn't actually show it, draw it yourself and label your drawing. It's much easier than trying to visualize it mentally.

5 Types of Triangles

- **5 Types of Triangles** appear on the SAT.
- Familiarity with the following **5 Types of Triangles** is useful.
- Below, draw each type of triangle in the boxes on the left, and then draw a line connecting it to its description on the right.

Equilateral

1. • A

- One angle measures 90°
- Usually requires the Pythagorean Theorem (___ + ___ = ___)
- Label a, b, and c in your drawing

Isosceles

2. • B

- All sides have the same length, and all angles measure 60°.
- Has two hidden 30-60-90 triangles.

Right

• C

- Two of the sides have the same length
- Two of the angles have the same measure
- Can be either an acute, an obtuse, or a right triangle

3.

45-45-90

• D

- The sides of this triangle are always in a this ratio (from shortest to longest):
  - x
  - x√3
  - 2x (hypotenuse)
- Label the angles and ratio on your drawing

4.

30-60-90

• E

5.

- The sides of this triangle are always in this ratio (from shortest to longest)
  - x
  - x
  - x√2
- Label the angles and ratio on your drawing

#sat_hack
#pythagorean_triples

There are three special side ratios to remember. When you spot them, you don't have to use the Pythagorean Theorem.
- 3-4-5
- 5-12-13
- 8-15-17

These ratios may be doubled or even tripled (3-4-5 = 6-8-10 = 12-16-20). Remember the longest side is always the hypotenuse.

3 Triangles Rules

- In addition to the **5 Types of Triangles**, there are also **3 Triangle Rules** that you must be familiar with.

1. Area of a Triangle

$$Area = \frac{base \cdot height}{2}$$

- The height is always perpendicular to the base. Don't confuse the height with a side of the triangle.

1

Find the area of the triangle.

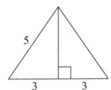

5

3   3

2

Find the area of the triangle.

3√2

3

#sat_hack

#height_of_equilaterals

Since there are two 30-60-90 triangles hidden in an equilateral triangle, the height of an equilateral triangle is $\frac{1}{2}s\sqrt{3}$ (s = measure of one side).

If an equilateral triangle has sides of 6 inches, what is its height?

2. Similar Triangles

- Have the same shape but different sizes
- Have congruent angles and proportional sides
- **Be careful**: sometimes the SAT will give you two similar triangles, but one is flipped or rotated.

3. Third Side Rule

- Any side of any triangle must be smaller than the sum of the other two sides.
- Any side of any triangle must be larger than the difference of the other two sides.

3

△ABC is similar to △DEF. Find x and y.

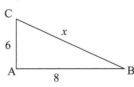

C
6
x
A   8   B

E
5   y
F 3 D

x=_____

y=_____

4

The missing side of this triangle must be greater than_____
and less than _____.

Not drawn to scale

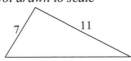

7   11

Quadrilaterals and Other Polygons

There are 2 important polygon rules to remember:
1. For each additional side of a polygon, the sum of its interior angles increases by 180°. So when a polygon goes from 3-sides (a triangle) to 4-sides (a quadrilateral) its interior angle total increases from 180° to _____°.
2. The exterior angles of a polygon always add to 360°. If you forget the first rule, this can be a helpful way to calculate the sum of its interior angles (exterior angle + interior angle = 180°)

#sat_hack
#diagonals_of_squares

If you need to find the diagonal of a square, remember that this is a line that cuts a square into a 45-45-90 triangle. For a square with sides s, its diagonal would be the hypotenuse of this triangle, or $s\sqrt{2}$.

$s = 3$ $d =$ _____

Solids: Volume and Surface Area

*   While the SAT will provide you with the formulas for solid shapes, you should still memorize these formulas and understand how and when to use them.

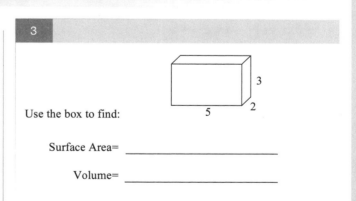

2

Use the cube to find:

Surface Area= _____

Volume= _____

3

Use the box to find:

Surface Area= _____

Volume= _____

#sat_hack
#real_life_geometry

There may be complicated word problems on the SAT with real life situations. If there isn't already an illustration, the best plan is to draw it out. The most complicated of these problems are usually as simple as finding volume or surface area.

GEOMETRY

Circles

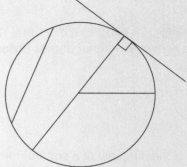

- To solve SAT **Circle Problems**, you must be familiar with the following **Circle Terminology**. Use the following terms to label the parts of the figure:
  - **Circumference**
  - **Diameter**
  - **Radius**
  - **Chord**
  - **Arc**
  - **Tangent**
  - **Sector**

- Here are two more circle formulas that you will need to be familiar with:

  - **Circumference:** _____

  - **Circle Area:** _____

- The SAT will not provide you with the **Circle Formula**. Make sure to memorize this:

$$(x - h)^2 + (y - k)^2 = r^2$$

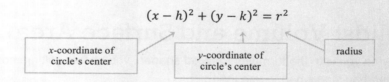

x-coordinate of circle's center | y-coordinate of circle's center | radius

#sat_hack

#arcs_n_sectors

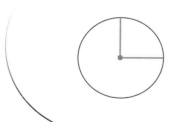

There will be questions on the SAT that ask about sector area and arc length. To solve these questions, find the fraction of circle you are working with by dividing the angle of the arc/sector by 360°.

If the angle measure of the sector here is 45°, what fraction of the whole circle is it?

1

Using the figure to the right, find the following:

Circle Area: _____   Sector Area: _____

Circumference: _____   Arc Length: _____

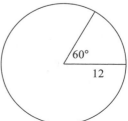

Geometry Practice 1

1

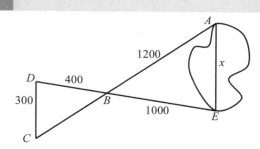

Zoey 101 wants to find a length, x, in feet, across a lake as represented in the sketch above. The lengths represented by $AB, EB, BD,$ and CD on the sketch were determined to be 1200 feet, 1000 feet, 400 feet, and 300 feet, respectively. Segments AC and DE intersect at B, and $\angle AEB$ and $\angle CDB$ have the same measure. What is the value of x?

A) 500

B) 750

C) 800

D) 1450

2

$$nA = 360$$

The measure A, in degrees, of an exterior angle of a regular polygon is related to the number of sides, n, of the polygon by the formula above. If the measure of an exterior angle of a regular polygon is greater than 70°, what is the greatest number of sides it can have?

A) 5

B) 6

C) 7

D) 8

3

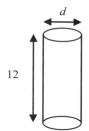

Pepsi Cola is trying to beat the world record for the biggest soda can. Their soda cans are the shape of the right cylinder shown above. If the height of the can needs to be 12 yards and the volume of the can is 300π cubic yards, what is the diameter of the base of the cylinder, in yards?

A) 5

B) 10

C) 15

D) 25

4

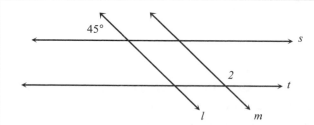

In the figure above, lines l and m are parallel and lines s and t are parallel. If the measure of $\angle 1$ is $\angle 45°$, what is the measure of $\angle 2$?

A) 45°

B) 35°

C) 135°

D) 145°

5

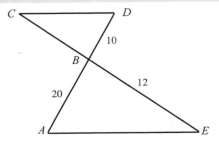

In the figure above, $\overline{AE} \parallel \overline{CD}$ and segment AD intersects segment CE at B. What is the length of segment CE?

A) 6

B) 12

C) 18

D) 20

6

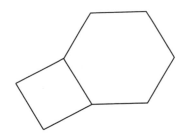

The figure above shows a regular hexagon with sides of length a and a square with sides of length a. If the area of the hexagon is $486\sqrt{3}$ square inches, what is the perimeter, in square inches, of the square?

A) 72

B) 36

C) 81

D) 324

7

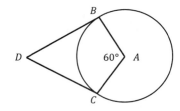

In the figure above, point A is the center of the circle, line segments BD and CD are tangent to the circle at points B and C, respectively, and the segments intersect at point D as shown. If the circumference of the circle is 132, what is the length of the minor arc $\overset{\frown}{BC}$?

A) 22

B) 44

C) 72

D) 120

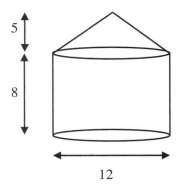

5

8

12

A Milk silo is built from two right circular cones and a right circular cylinder with internal measurements represented by the figure above. Of the following, which is closest to the volume of the milk silo in cubic feet?

A) 1392

B) 348

C) 4370.9

D) 1092.7

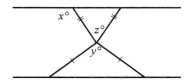

Two isosceles triangles are shown above. If $180 - z = 2y$ and $y = 80$, what is the value of x?

A) 80

B) 160

C) 100

D) 120

In a circle with the center O, central angle AOB has a measure of $\frac{7\pi}{4}$ radians. The area of the sector formed by central angle AOB is what fraction of the area of the circle?

A) 0.625

B) 0.875

C) 0.750

D) 0.500

Geometry Practice 2

1

In the triangle above the sine of $x°$ is 0.8. What is the cosine of $y°$?

A) 0.6

B) 0.4

C) 0.7

D) 0.8

2

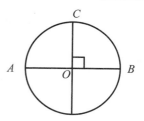

A circle with the center O has a circumference of 52. What is the length of minor $\widehat{AC}$?

A) 9

B) 13

C) 18

D) 36

3

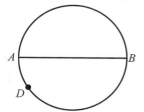

In the circle above, segment AB is a diameter. If the length of arc $\widehat{ADB}$ is 16π, what is the length of the radius of the circle?

A) 4

B) 8

C) 16

D) 32

4

The volume of right circular cylinder A is 24 cubic centimeters. What is the volume, in cubic centimeters, of a right circular cylinder with twice the radius and half the height of cylinder A?

A) 45°

B) 35°

C) 135°

D) 145°

In △ ABC above, what is the length of $\overline{AC}$?

A) $20\sqrt{2}$

B) 10

C) $10\sqrt{2}$

D) $10\sqrt{3}$

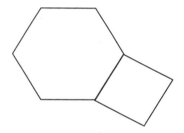

The figure above shows a regular hexagon with sides of length a and a square with sides of length a. If the area of the hexagon is $216\sqrt{3}$ square inches, what is the area, in square inches, of the square?

A) 48

B) 144

C) 256

D) 324

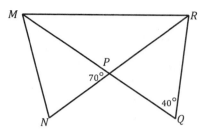

In the figure above, $\overline{MQ}$ and $\overline{NR}$ intersect at point P, $NP = QP$, and $MP = PR$. What is the measure, in degrees, of $\angle QMR$?

A) 25°

B) 55°

C) 35°

D) 65°

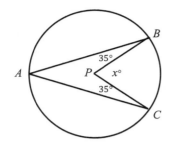

Point P is the center of the circle in the figure above. What is the value of x?

A) 70

B) 135

C) 175

D) 140

The surface area of a cube is $6(\frac{a}{2})^2$, where a is a positive constant. Which of the following gives the perimeter of one face of the cube?

A) $2a$

B) a

C) $\frac{a}{4}$

D) $\frac{a}{2}$

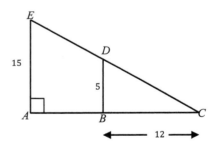

In the figure above, $\overline{BD}$ is parallel to $\overline{AE}$. What is the length of $\overline{CE}$?

A) 39

B) 45

C) 13

D) 25

Blue Book Problem	My Answer	Correct Answer	Why did I miss?
P. 452 #18			
P. 453 #19			
P. 461 #24			
P. 466 #36			
P. 561 #11			
P. 564 #18			
P. 565 #20			
P. 575 #23			
P. 575 #25			
P. 576 #27			
P. 579 #34			

CORRECT OUT OF TOTAL: _____/11

NOTES:

Ratios, Fractions, and Proportions

- The SAT asks questions about **fractions** and **ratios**.
- **Ratios** and **fractions** both show a relationship between two numbers.
- A **fraction** shows the relationship between a _____ and the _____, and a **ratio** shows the relationship between a _____ and another _____.
- A fraction is usually shown as a number over another number $\left(\frac{x}{y}\right)$ and a ratio is usually shown as $x : y$.
- Be careful, though: sometimes ratios can be disguised as fractions.

1

In a bowl full of berries, there are 8 raspberries, 12 blackberries, and 13 blueberries.

What is the fraction of raspberries? _____

What is the ratio of raspberries to blackberries? _____

2

In a certain SAT class, there are three times as many girls as there are boys.

What fraction of the class is made up of girls? _____

What fraction of the class is made up of boys? _____

3

The chemical symbol for ammonia is shown below.

$$NH_3$$

The ratio of nitrogen atoms to hydrogen atoms in ammonia is 1:3. When there are 1.2×10^4 nitrogen atoms, how many hydrogen atoms will there be? (When using scientific notation, $1 \times 10^1 = 10$).

4

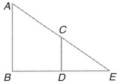

In the figure above, the ratio of triangle ABE to triangle CDE is 2:1. If line segment AC is 5 units long, and line segment BD is 4 units long, what is the measure of line segment AB?

#sat_hack

#reduced_ratios

If you often get stuck on ratio questions, just remember that a ratio is a fraction reduced to its simplest form. A ratio of 3:2 may not mean that there is 3 of something and 2 of something else. A ratio simply gives the relationship between two numbers.

Direct and Indirect (Inverse) Variation

- There are two types of relationships, or variation between sets of x and y values.
- **Direct variation** means that as one variable increases, the other also increases.
-

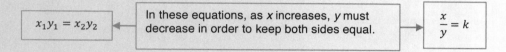

$$\frac{x_1}{y_1} = \frac{x_2}{y_2}$$ In these equations, x and y increase at the same rate. As x increases, y also increases. → $xy = k$

- **Indirect (inverse) variation**, means that as one variable increases, the other decreases.

$$x_1 y_1 = x_2 y_2$$ In these equations, as x increases, y must decrease in order to keep both sides equal. → $\dfrac{x}{y} = k$

- Below are some example problems.

1

People are sharing a pizza. If more people want to share, each person gets fewer slices.

The relationship between <u>people</u> and <u>slices each varies</u> (**directly / inversely**).

2

A truck driver has to travel a certain distance. If he drives faster, his travel time decreases.

The relationship between speed and <u>travel time</u> varies (**directly / inversely**).

3

A sunflower's height increases the more it is watered.

The relationship between <u>water</u> and <u>height</u> varies (**directly / inversely**).

4

As students study more hours for the SAT, their scores increase.

The relationship between <u>hours studied</u> and <u>score</u> varies (**directly / inversely**).

#sat_hack
#relationships_and_slopes

Remember when we learned about linear equations and relationships?
- If the numbers vary directly at a constant rate, we have a linear equation with a **positive slope**.
- If the numbers vary indirectly at a constant rate, we have a linear equation with a **negative slope**.

Percentage & Percent Change

- The easiest way to find a **Percentage** is to use this fraction:

| number of "the thing" you are looking for | → | $\dfrac{n}{t} \cdot 100$ | ← | the total |

- **Percent Change** tells us how much something increased or decreased. The easiest way to find **Percent Change** is to use this fraction:

| the amount of change: increase or decrease | → | $\dfrac{c}{o} \cdot 100$ | ← | the original |

#sat_hack

#everyday_percentages

Don't panic when you see a percentage problem – you probably do these more often than you think without even realizing it. When you get a test back, how do you calculate the percentage? Probably: (number correct ÷ total points) × 100.

What about when you are shopping or eating at a restaurant? How do you quickly figure out a 20% discount or tip?

1

Ivan is driving cross country. On Monday, he drive 441 miles. On Tuesday, he drove 367 miles. On Wednesday, he drove 472 miles. If the drive is 2800 miles altogether, approximately <u>what percent of his drive has he completed by Wednesday night</u>?

  a) 12%

  b) 46%

  c) 68%

  d) 72%

1. After you have carefully read the whole problem, underline what exactly it is asking. Here, this has already been done for you.
2. Set up a fraction. What is that part that we are finding, and what is the total?
3. Before you pull out your calculator, look at the answer choices. Are there any you can eliminate right away?

2

There are 500 students in each class at Woodlake High School. Last year, 12% of the senior class was on the honor roll. There are 15 more students on the honor roll this year than last year. What percent of this year's senior class is on the honor roll?

1. First, you need to find out how many students were on the honor roll last year.
2. Take this number, and add 15.
3. Find out what percent this new number is out of the total 500 students.

Ratios, Fractions & Proportions Practice Set 1

1

1 decagram = 10 grams

1,000 milligrams = 1 gram

A pharmacy lab stores one type of medicine in 10-decagram containers. Based on the information given above, how many 1-milligram doses are there in one 10-decagram container?

A) 0.1

B) 0.001

C) 10,000

D) 100,000

2

The distance traveled by Earth in one orbit around the sun is about 640,000,000 miles. Earth makes one complete orbit around the Sun in one year. Which of the following is closest to the average speed of Earth, in miles per hour, as it orbits the sun?

A) 65,000

B) 73,000

C) 176,000

D) 211,000

3

A quality control manager at a factory selects 8 light bulbs at random for inspection out of every 500 light bulbs produced. At this rate, how many light bulbs will be inspected if the factory produces 32,000 light bulbs?

A) 632

B) 600

C) 512

D) 545

4

Poison Ivy is studying the production of apples by two types of apple trees. The two types of breeds she is interested in give the eater itchy intestines. She noticed that Type A trees produced 30 percent more apples than Type B trees did. Based on Poison Ivy's observation, if Type A trees produced 195 apples, how many apples did the Type B trees produce?

A) 135

B) 150

C) 145

D) 160

5

Jimmy Neutron bought a laptop computer at a store that gave him 35 percent discount off its original price. The total amount he paid to the cashier was m dollars, including a 7 percent sales tax on the discounted price. Which of the following represents the original price of the computer in terms of m?

A) $\dfrac{m}{0.72}$

B) $0.72m$

C) $\dfrac{m}{(1.07)(0.65)}$

D) $(1.07)(0.65)m$

6

Baxter walks 32 meters in 15.8 seconds. If he walks at the same rate, which of the following is **closest** to the distance he will walk in an hour and 10 minutes?

A) 5250 meters

B) 6,600 meters

C) 7,300 meters

D) 8,500 meters

7

Graphene, which is used in the manufacture of integrated circuits, is so thin that a sheet weighing one ounce can cover up to 6 football fields. If a football field has an area of approximately $2\frac{2}{3}$ acres, about how many acres could 42 ounces of grapheme cover?

A) 670

B) 110

C) 160

D) 840

8

A rectangle was altered by increasing its length by 20 percent and decreasing its width by m percent. If these alterations decreased the area of the rectangle by 10 percent, what is the value of m?

A) 15

B) 25

C) 50

D) 75

9

The amount of money a Cirque de Soleil performer earns is directly proportional to the number of people attending the performance. The performer earns $560 at a performance where 7 people attend.
No matter how many people attend, the performer uses 62% of the money earned to pay the costs involved in putting on the performance. The rest of the money earned is the performer's profit. What is the profit the performer makes at a performance where 12 people attend?

A) $347.20

B) $212.80

C) $364.80

D) $595.20

10

Year	Number of CDs (in millions)
1998	510
1999	715
2000	640
2001	523
2002	499
2003	437
2004	329

According to the table above, the number of compact discs sold in 1999 is what fraction of the number sold in 2003?

A) 1.64

B) 0.61

C) 0.20

D) 0.12

Ratios, Fractions & Proportions Practice 2

1

In a study of whale eating habits, 160 male whales and 70 female whales have been tagged. If 60 more female whales are tagged, how many more male whales must be tagged so that $\frac{3}{5}$ of the total number of whales in the study are male?

A) 35

B) 45

C) 55

D) 65

2

Tony drives an average of 200 miles each week. His car can travel an average of 23 miles per gallon of gasoline. Tony would like to reduce his weekly expenditure on gasoline by $4. Assuming gasoline costs $3 per gallon, which equation can Tony use to determine how many fewer average miles, m, he should drive each week?

A) $\frac{23}{3}m = 200$

B) $\frac{23}{3}m = 4$

C) $\frac{3}{23}m = 200$

D) $\frac{3}{23}m = 4$

3

Jordi surveyed a random sample of the senior class of his high school to determine whether the Spring Festival should be held in March or May. Of the 70 students surveyed, 32% preferred May. Based on this information, about how many students in the entire 330-person class would be expected to prefer having the Spring Festival in May?

A) 23

B) 83

C) 106

D) 260

4

The weight of an object on Venus is approximately $\frac{7}{8}$ of its weight on Earth. The weight of an object on Jupiter is approximately $\frac{15}{8}$ of its weight on Earth. If an object weights 100 pounds on Earth, approximately how many more pounds does it weigh on Jupiter than it weighs on Venus?

A) 87.5

B) 100

C) 187.5

D) 275

5

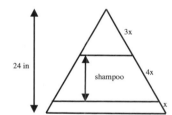

Kiana has a triangular shelf system that attaches to her showerhead. The total height of the system is 24 inches, and there are three parallel shelves as shown above. What is the maximum height, in inches, of a shampoo bottle that can stand upright on the middle shelf?

A) 9

B) 12

C) 21

D) 24

6

A school district is forming a committee to discuss plans for the construction of a new high school. Of those invited to join the committee, 12% are parents of students, 38% are teachers from the current high school, 25% are school and district administrators, and the remaining 8 individuals are students. Approximately how many more teachers were invited to join the committee than school and district administrators?

A) 2

B) 4

C) 6

D) 10

7

A gear ratio $r:s$ is the ratio of the number of teeth of two connected gears. The ratio of the number of revolutions per minute (rpm) of two gear wheels is $s:r$. In an antique clock, Gear A is turned by a motor. The turning of Gear A causes Gears B and C to turn as well. Gears A, B, and C have 20, 60, and 10 teeth respectively. If Gear A is rotated by motor at a rate of 100 rpm, what is the number of revolutions per minute for Gear C?

A) 150

B) 100

C) 200

D) 170

8

A customer's monthly water bill was $82.53. Due to a rate increase, her monthly bill is now $92.76. To the nearest tenth of a percent, by what percent did the amount of the customer's water bill increase?

A) 10.2%

B) 11.7%

C) 12.4%

D) 13.6%

9

Year	Subscriptions sold
2012	4300
2013	4880

The manager of an online news service received the report above on the number of subscriptions sold by the service. The manager estimated that the percent increase from 2012 to 2013 would be double the percent increase from 2013 to 2014. How many subscriptions did the manager expect would be sold in 2014?

A) 4,750

B) 4,510

C) 5,209

D) 6,530

10

Macronutrient	Food calories	Kilojoules
Protein	7.0	22.3
Fat	12.0	38.3
Carbohydrate	7.0	22.3

The table above gives the typical amounts of energy per gram, expressed in both food calories and kilojoules, of the three macronutrients in food. If m food calories is equivalent to k kilojoules, of the following, which best represents the relationship between m and k?

A) $k = 0.32m$

B) $m = 3.2k$

C) $k = 3.2m$

D) $m = 0.32k$

Blue Book Problem	My Answer	Correct Answer	Why did I miss?
P. 455 #2			
P. 456 #4			
P. 456 #5			
P. 456 #11			
P. 459 #15			
P. 459 #16			
P. 459 #17			
P. 460 #20			
P. 461 #23			
P. 567 #2			
P. 568 #5			
P. 569 #9			
P. 570 #10			
P. 570 #11			
P. 573 #19			
P. 577 #29			

CORRECT OUT OF TOTAL: _____/16

NOTES:

Statistics

- The SAT will require knowledge of 5 statistics concepts. This section will review:
  - **Average (mean), median, and mode, and range**
  - **Standard deviation**
  - **Probability**
  - **Collecting/interpreting data**
  - **Critical reasoning**

Mean, Median, Mode, and Range

- To find the **mean**, or average, of a set of numbers, use this formula:

$$\text{mean} = \frac{\text{sum of all data}}{\text{number of entries}}$$

- The **median** is the number in the middle of an ordered list of data. If there is an even number of data, take the average of the two numbers in the middle. The median of the data below is _____.

6, 8, <u>9</u>, <u>12</u>, 15, 19

- The **mode** of a set of data is the number that occurs the most. If no numbers occur more than once, then there is no mode.
- The **range** is the difference between the highest and lowest values in a set of data.
- While these concepts seem simple, the SAT will probably ask them in complex or confusing ways. Try the practice problems below.

1

In Mr. Mallaley's math class, the average on the most recent test was 75.5%, but Marni still has to take this test. If the class has 35 students total, what must Marni score in order to bring the class average up to 76%?

For this problem, use ANT:
average • number = total

75.5 • 34 = 2,567
This is the whole class's scores added together. Marni's test (x) will be the 35th score.

$$\frac{(2,567 + x)}{35} = 76$$

2

A product online is rated out of 4 stars. The number of ratings is shown in the chart below. What is the median rating?

Rating	1	2	3	4	5
Number per rating	16	23	24	2	1

At first glance, this might seem overly simple: the rating in the middle is 3, so isn't that the median?

NO. This is a typical SAT trick problem. There are a total of 66 ratings, which means that the median will be the average of the 33rd and 34th ratings, which were both 2-star.

What is Standard Deviation?

- The SAT may ask you about **standard deviation**, which is a value that tells how much a set of data varies from the average.
- You won't need to calculate standard deviation, but you will need to know how to compare two sets of data and find the greater standard deviation.
- To do this, look at the tables below representing low temperatures for City A and City B in February:

CITY A	
Low Temperature	Number of Days
32	1
33	1
34	8
35	9
36	7
37	1
38	1

CITY B	
Low Temperature	Number of Days
32	4
33	3
34	6
35	5
36	6
37	2
38	2

- In both cities, the range of temperatures was the same, and the averages are both approximately 35.
- However, in City A, there were only 4 days where the temperature was more than 1 degree away from the average.
- In City B, there were 11 days where the temperature was more than 1 degree away from the average.
- Therefore, the standard deviation was greater in City B.

Statistics

- On questions about probability, remember that probability is just a fraction of what you are looking for over thetotal possibilities.
- Example: In Mary's sock drawer, there are 14 black socks, 8 red socks, and 6 white socks all mixed up. What is the probability that the first sock she pulls out is red?

$$\frac{\text{number we are looking for}}{\text{total}} = \frac{\text{number of red socks}}{\text{total number of socks}} = \frac{8}{14 + 8 + 6} = \frac{8}{28}$$

The SAT may also ask the probability of **two events both occurring**. To do this, find the probability of each event occurring, as a fraction, and multiply those fractions together.

- Example: What is the probability that Mary pulls out two red socks in a row?
- The probability of the first sock being red is still the same as before, but now we need the probability of the second sock also being red.
- Once we pull the first red sock, there will be 7 red socks and 27 total socks.

$$\frac{8}{28} \times \frac{7}{27} = \frac{56}{756} \times \frac{2}{27}$$

Interpreting Charts & Graphs

- There are 4 types of **Charts & Graphs** that typically appear on the SAT:
  1. **Line Graphs**
  2. **Bar Graphs**
  3. **Circle Graphs** (Pie Charts)
  4. **Scatter Plots**
- Let's take a look at some examples.

Line Graphs

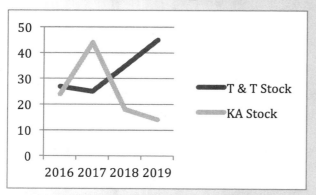

- This **Line Graph** compares the performance of two stocks over several years.

Bar Graphs

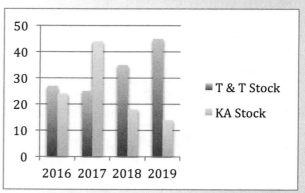

- This **Bar Graph** displays that same stock data.

1

What is the approximate difference in dollars between the highest and lowest values of a share of T & T stock?

2

Between what two years was the percent decrease in the value of KA Stock the greatest?

Circle Graphs

- Circle Graphs usually show a **Percentage** or **Proportional** breakdown.

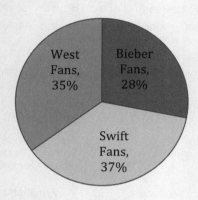

- This **Circle Graph** uses data from an internet survey of 17-year olds to determine their favorite artists.

Scatter Plot

- A **Scatter Plot** displays the relationship between two variables. There are a number of key terms to be familiar with when looking at **Scatter Plots**.
  - **Line of Best Fit** – a line that is drawn through the middle of the data points (dots), can be used for making predictions
  - **Positive Correlation** – as one variable increases the other also increases, or as one variable decreases the other also decreases; this is when the **Line of Best Fit** has a **Positive Slope**
  - **Negative Correlation** – as one variable increases the other decreases, or as one variable decreases the other increases; this is when the **Line of Best Fit** has a **Negative Slope**
  - **No Correlation** – when there is no clear connection between the variables. The data points appear to be scattered in a totally random way.
  - **Causation** – when a change in one variable affects change in the other variable. Just because we find a **Correlation**, does not necessarily mean there is **Causation**.

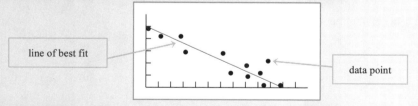

- This **Scatter Plot** shows a _____ **Correlation**.

#sat_hack

#slope_and_correlation

Positive slope = **positive** correlation = **direct** variation = x⬆ y⬆

Negative slope = **negative** correlation = **indirect** variation = x⬆ y⬇

Using Critical Reasoning

- The SAT asks questions that don't require actual calculations, but instead require reasoning skills to interpret data and draw conclusions.
- In general, you should not assume cause and effect. Be wary of drawing too-specific conclusions.
- You should also be able to spot biases: note the description of how and where data is collected on these problems.

1

In order to find out the average number of children per household in a certain neighborhood, a researcher goes to the playground to collect data.

Why might this method of research collection produce a bias?

_____

_____

2

A phone survey calling to single-family homes is conducted at 9am on Tuesday, and it finds that out of the people surveyed, only 8% responded that they had full-time jobs.

Why might this method of research collection produce a bias?

_____

_____

3

The Center for Disease Control and Prevention conducted a study on Americans infected with HIV. This study found a positive correlation between people with the virus and people who have used intravenous drugs. What conclusion can be drawn from this study?

A) Intravenous drug users will contract HIV at some point.

B) People with HIV use intravenous drugs more than people without HIV.

C) There is an association between intravenous drugs and HIV.

D) There is an association between intravenous drugs and HIV in Americans.

This is a typical reasoning problem. You don't have to do any math; you just have to be able to understand the information presented and draw a conclusion.

The answer can't be **A** – this is because there is an implied cause and effect that shouldn't be assumed.

B is more on the right track, but it switches up the cause and effect.

C is almost right, but the study was only done on Americans, which is why **D** is correct.

#sat_hack

#jumping_to_conclusions

For many of these reasoning questions it is best to stick to one rule of thumb: don't ever assume anything. Go with the choice that is most broad and supported by the evidence given – just like you would on the Reading Test.

Statistics & Data Practice 1

1

Gender	Age Under 25	Age 25 or older	Total
Male	15	5	20
Female	12	8	20
Total	27	13	40

The table above shows the distribution of age and gender for 40 people who entered an eating competition. If the winner will be selected at random, what is the probability that the winner will be either a female under the age of 25 or a male age 25 or older?

A) $\frac{20}{40}$

B) $\frac{12}{40}$

C) $\frac{23}{40}$

D) $\frac{17}{40}$

2

An online store receives customer satisfaction ratings between 0 and 100, inclusive. In the first 15 ratings the store received, the average (arithmetic mean) of the ratings was 65. What is the least value the store can receive for the 16th rating and still be able to have an average of at least 76 for the first 25 ratings?

A) 25

B) 50

C) 75

D) 100

3

A survey was taken of the value of homes on Gullah Gullah Island, and it was found that the mean home value was $1,268,000 and the median was $999,000. Which of the following situations could explain the difference between the mean and the median home values in the country?

A) There are few homes that are valued much less than the rest.

B) There are few homes that are valued much more than the rest.

C) Many homes have values between values between $999,000 and $1,268,000.

D) The homes have values that are close to each other.

4

	None	1 to 8	8+	Total
Group A	14	52	34	100
Group B	39	36	25	100
Total	53	88	59	200

The data in the table above was produced by a researcher studying the number of Instagram posts college students post per month. Group A consisted of 100 females and Group B consisted of 100 males. If a person is chosen at random from those who posted at least once, what is the probability that the person belonged to group A?

A) $\frac{52}{100}$

B) $\frac{86}{147}$

C) $\frac{86}{200}$

D) $\frac{147}{200}$

5	8	8	12
12	12	15	15
16	17	17	23

The table above lists the lengths, to the nearest inch, of tentacles of the poisonous blue-ring octopi. A random sample of 15 was recorded. The outlier measurement of 23 is an error. Of the mean, median, and range of values listed, which will change the most if the 23-inch measurement is removed from the data?

A) Range

B) Mean

C) Median

D) They will all change by the same amount.

Villains	Age (years)	Villains	Age (years)
Penguin	32	The Joker	34
The Riddler	34	Mr. Freeze	42
Fish Moony	39	Scarecrow	37
Bane	52	Harley Quinn	27
Poison Ivy	25	Dr. Strange	62
Two-face	48	Killer Croc	45

The table above lists the ages of the villains in Gotham City. According to the table, what is the mean age, in years, of these villains? (Round your answer to the nearest whole number.)

A) 34

B) 36

C) 38

D) 40

7

A researcher conducted a survey to determine whether people in a certain large town prefer watching the San Jose Sharks game live or on the television. Last Wednesday, he attended a Sharks game and asked 215 people of which 25 people refused to respond. Which of the following factors makes it least likely that a reliable conclusion can be drawn about the sports-watching preferences of all the people in the town?

A) Sample size

B) Population size

C) Where the survey was given

D) The number of people who refused to respond

Number of pets	Pitch Pine High School	Tulip Poplar High School
0	62	50
1	50	46
2	68	88
3	20	16

A researcher chose 200 students at random from each of the two schools and asked each student how many pets he or she has. The results are shown above. There are a total of 2,400 students at Pitch Pine High School and 3,600 students at Tulip Poplar High School. Based on the survey data, which of the following most accurately compares the expected total number of students with 3 pets at the two schools?

A) The total number of students with 3 pets is expected to be equal at the two schools.

B) The total number of students with 3 pets at Pitch Pine High School is expected to be 48 more than at Tulip Poplar High School.

C) The total number of students with 3 pets at Tulip Poplar is expected to be 4 less Pitch Pine High School.

D) The total number of students with 3 pets at Tulip Poplar is expected to be 48 more than Pitch Pine High School.

Number of pets	Pitch Pine High School	Tulip Poplar High School
0	62	50
1	50	46
2	68	88
3	20	16

A researcher chose 200 students at random from each of the two schools and asked each student how many pets he or she has. The results are shown below. What is the median number of pets for all the students surveyed?

A) 0

B) 1

C) 2

D) 3

	Passed	Did not pass
Took review course	67	28
Did not take review course	58	47

Results of the Part I Boards of Medical School Students

The table above summarizes the results of the 200 medical school students who took the part I board exam. If one of the surveyed students who passed the exam is chosen at random for an interview, what is the probability that the person chosen did take the review course?

A) $\frac{67}{125}$

B) $\frac{67}{200}$

C) $\frac{95}{200}$

D) $\frac{67}{95}$

Statistics & Data Practice 2

1

State	18-24 (Age)	25-44 (Age)	45 to 64 (Age)	65 to 74 (Age)	Total
CA	2,710	3,045	7,290	4,301	17,346
AZ	1,430	3,713	14,671	3,240	23,054
OR	4,230	5,145	16,742	2,190	28,307
WA	3,148	4,570	12,345	5,914	25,977
Total	11,518	16,473	51,048	15,645	94,684

The table above shows the number of registered voters in 2016, in thousands, in four states and four age groups. Based on the table, if a registered voter who is 25 to 64 years old in 2016 is chosen at random, which of the following is closest to the probability that the registered voter was from Oregon?

A) 0.23

B) 0.76

C) 0.55

D) 0.32

2

The mean score of 15 players in a basketball game was 25.6 points. If the highest individual score is removed, the mean score of the remaining 14 players becomes 24 points. What was the highest score?

A) 24

B) 32

C) 36

D) 48

3

If x is the average (arithmetic mean) of y and 12, z is the average of $2y$ and 8, and t is the average of $3y$ and 24, what is the average of x, z, and t in terms of y?

A) $y + \frac{44}{3}$

B) $y + 44$

C) $y + \frac{22}{3}$

D) $y + 6$

4

City A		City B	
(°F)	Frequency	(°F)	Frequency
70	4	70	2
69	3	69	3
68	5	68	1
67	3	67	10
66	4	66	3

The table above gives the distribution of high temperatures in degrees Fahrenheit (°F) for City A and City B over the same 19 days in April. Which of the following is true about the data shown for these 19 days?

A) The standard deviation of temperature in City A is larger.

B) The standard deviation of temperature in City B is larger.

C) The standard deviation of temperature in City A is the same as that of City B.

D) The standard deviation of temperature in these cities cannot be calculated with the data provided.

5

Gender	Number one passion		Total
	Singing	Acting	
Male	230	316	546
Female	310	154	464
Total	540	470	1010

In a survey, 1010 male and female celebrities indicated their number one passion. The results are in the table above. If one of the celebrities is selected at random, which of the following is closest to the probability that the selected celebrity is a male whose indicated passion is singing?

A) 0.53

B) 0.23

C) 0.57

D) 0.15

6

Jordan is preparing for a 15k race. His goal is to run an average of at least 120 miles per week for 4 weeks. He ran 80 miles the first week, 140 the second week, and 160 the third week. Which inequality can be used to represent the number of miles, x, Jordan could run on the 4th week to meet his goal?

A) $\frac{80+140+160}{3} + x \geq 120$

B) $80 + 140 + 160 \geq x(120)$

C) $80 + 140 + 160 + x \geq 4(120)$

D) $\frac{80}{4} + \frac{140}{4} + \frac{160}{4} + x \geq 120$

7

I.   Of all the adults in the city, 65 percent are satisfied with their cars.

II. If another 10,000 adults are selected at random from the city were surveyed, 65 percent of them would report they are satisfied with their car.

III. If 10,000 adults selected at random from a different city were surveyed, 65 percent of them would report they are satisfied with their car.

A car dealership recently surveyed 10,000 adults who were selected at random from a large city and asked each of the adults, "Are you satisfied with the car you're driving?" Of those surveyed, 65 percent responded that they were satisfied with their car. Based on the results of the survey, which of the following statements must be true?

A) I and II only

B) I and III only

C) I, II, and III

D) None

Grade	Frequency
63	5
67	4
72	3
75	4
80	3
85	4
88	5
93	1
95	3

An AP Physics teacher has recorded her students' grades in the table above. Based on this information, what was the median of the grades?

A) 75

B) 77.5

C) 80

D) 85

9

A study was done on the weights of different types of isopod crustacean of the family armadillidiidae more commonly known as "roly-poly." A random sample of roly-polies was caught in a park and marked in order to ensure that none were weighed more than once. The sample contained 250 Brown roly-polies of which 20% weighed more than 2 grams. Which of the following conclusions is best supported by the sample data?

A) The majority of all the roly-polies weigh less than 2 grams.

B) The average weight of all the roly-polies in the park is approximately 2 grams.

C) Approximately 20% of all the roly-polies in the park weigh more than 2 grams.

D) Approximately 20% of all Brown roly-polies in the park weigh more than 2 grams.

	Masses (kilograms)				
Gwen	x	4.1	1.4	2.6	2.2
Blake	1.6	2.5	1.7	4.3	3

Gwen and Blake each collected 5 fruits from their garden and the masses of the fruits are recorded in the table. The mean of the masses of the fruits Gwen collected is 0.1 kilogram greater than the mean of the masses of the fruits Blake collected. What is the value of x?

A) 4.2

B) 3.3

C) 2.6

D) 1.9

Statistics & Data Practice 3

1

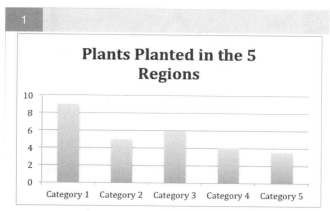

The number of trees planted by the same farmer in different regions of his farm is shown in the graph above. If the total number of plants is 2,750, what is an appropriate label for the vertical axis of the graph?

A) Number of plants planted (in tens)

B) Number of plants planted (in hundreds)

C) Number of plants planted (in thousands)

D) Number of plants planted (in tens of thousands)

2

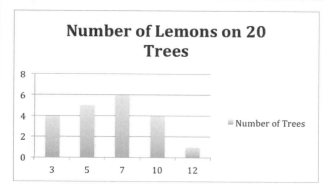

Based on the histogram above, of the following, which is the closest to the average (arithmetic mean) number of lemons produced per tree?

A) 5.55

B) 5.75

C) 6.55

D) 6.75

3

Number of hours Ryan plans to read the novel per day	5
Number of parts in the novel	7
Number of chapters in the novel	15
Number of words Ryan reads per minute	160
Number of pages in the novel	1,472
Number of words in novel	465,276

Ryan is planning to read a novel. The table above shows information about the novel, Ryan's reading speed, and the amount of time he plans to spend reading the novel each day. If Ryan reads at the rates given in the table, which of the following is closest to the number of days it would take Ryan to read the entire novel?

A) 5

B) 23

C) 10

D) 46

4

Miles Traveled by Air Passengers in Country X

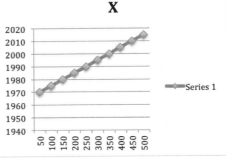

According to the line of best fit in the scatterplot above, which of the following best approximates the year in which the number of miles traveled by air passengers in Country X was estimated to be 350 million?

A) 1999

B) 2005

C) 2007

D) 2003

5

Annual Music Album Sales

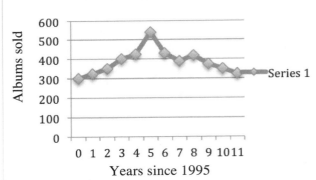

The graph above shows the total number of music album sales, in millions, each year from 1995 through 2005. Based on the graph, which of the following best describes the general trend in music album sales from 1995 through 2005?

A) Sales generally increased each year since 1995

B) Sales generally decreased each year since 1995

C) Sales generally remained steady from 1995 through 2005

D) Sales increased until 2000 and then generally decreased

		Course			
		Trigonometry	Calculus 1	Calculus 2	Total
Gender	Female	70	132	53	255
	Male	67	108	40	215
	Total	137	240	93	470

A group of eleventh-grade students responded to a survey that asked which math course they were currently enrolled in. The survey data were broken down as shown in the table above. Which of the following categories accounts for approximately 28 percent of all the survey respondents?

A) Females taking Calculus 1

B) Males taking Calculus 1

C) Females taking Trigonometry

D) Males taking Trigonometry

Source	Percent of those surveyed
Barnes and Noble	10%
Amazon	32%
University Bookstore	26%
Chegg.com	15%
Ecampus.com	5%
Valorebooks.com	12%

The table above shows the summary of 800 responses to a survey question. Based on the table, how many students surveyed buy most of their textbooks from either their University bookstore or Amazon?

A) 220

B) 580

C) 336

D) 464

Species of tree	Growth factor
Jacaranda	6
Privet	4.5
Holly	2
Palm	3
Sequoia	7.5

One method of calculating the approximate age, in years of a tree of a particular species is to multiply the diameter of the tree, in inches, by a constant called the growth factor for that species. The table above gives the growth factors for five species of trees. What is the approximate age of a Privet tree with a diameter of 8 inches?

A) 24

B) 60

C) 36

D) 48

Segment of drive	Distance (miles)	Average driving speed with no traffic delay (mph)
From home to freeway entrance	1.2	25
From freeway entrance to freeway exit	8.75	55
From freeway exit to gym	0.55	20

If Demi starts her drive at 7:00 a.m., she can drive at her average driving speed with no traffic delay for each segment of the drive. If she starts her drive at 7:30 a.m., the travel time from the freeway entrance to the freeway exit increases by 25% due to slower traffic, but the travel time for each of the other two segments of her drive does not change. Based on the table, how many more minutes does Demi take to arrive at her gym if she stats her drive at 7:30 a.m. than if she starts her drive at 7:00 a.m.? (Round your answer to the nearest whole number)

A) 2

B) 4

C) 6

D) 8

Blue Book Problem	My Answer	Correct Answer	Why did I miss?
P. 458 #13			
P. 458 #14			
P. 459 #18			
P. 460 #19			
P. 572 #15			
P. 574 #20			
P. 579 #32			
P. 580 #35			

CORRECT OUT OF TOTAL: _____/8

NOTES:

Exponents

- When you raise a number or variable to an exponent, you are multiplying that number by itself the exponent's number of times.
  - Example: $x^2 = x \cdot x$ base $\longrightarrow x^2 \longleftarrow$ exponent

- In this chapter, we will review:
  - **Exponents**
  - **Complex numbers**
  - **Exponential growth and decay**
  - **Geometric sequences**

Exponent Rules

- To solve **Exponent Questions** on the SAT, we must be familiar with three **Exponent Rules**.
  1. When variables are multiplied, you _____ the exponents.

    - Example: $x^2 \cdot x^3 = $ _____

  2. When variables are divided, you _____ the exponents.

    - Example: $\frac{x^6}{x^2} = $ _____

  3. When variables are raised by multiple powers, you _____ the exponents.

    - Example: $(x^2)^3 = $ _____

- Fill in this chart to review some other **Exponent Facts** that you should be familiar with.

$x^{\frac{1}{2}}$	
$x^{\frac{3}{4}}$	
x^{-2}	
$x^{-\frac{3}{4}}$	
x^0	

#sat_hack

#exponent_rules

Be careful when combining like terms by adding and subtracting. You **cannot** combine terms if they have different exponents.

Example: $x + x^2 \neq x^3$

Exponents

- An important skill for the SAT is knowing how to make the bases of exponential numbers the same.
  - For example, in the equation $3^x = 9^2$, we can't solve for x until we make the two sides the same base.
  - If we change it to $3^x = (3^2)^2$, now we know that **x = 2 • 2**, or **x = 4**
- Practice using the problems below.

1

Find the value of x in the expression below.

$$3^x + 3^x + 3^x = 27^4$$

Hint #1: On the left side of the equation, the same thing is added together 3 times, so it's being multiplied by 3.

Hint #2: 27 is 3 • 3 • 3. Can you change all the bases to 3?

2

Find the value of x in the expression below.

$$\frac{4^{2x}}{2^2} = 32^2$$

3

Find the value of x in the expression below.

$$81^x = \frac{9^2}{3^4}$$

Exponential Growth & Decay

- The SAT tests us on two main types of **Exponential Functions**. These are equations where there is a variable in the **Exponent**.
  - **Exponential Growth** – something that is growing (such as bacterial growth or compounded investments), rate (*r*) will be positive
  - **Exponential Decay** – something that is decaying (such as radioactive decay), rate (r) will be negative.

- Use this equation:

Rate, percent, enter a decimal

Amount at the "end" → $A = P(1 + r)^t$

Time

Principal; amount at the "beginning,"

4

Justin Bieber invests his entire life savings, $20, in a bank account that pays 6% interest. To the nearest cent, how much will Justin have in his account after 25 years?

5

Taylor Swift was exposed to a substance with a radioactive half-life of 12 years. If she started with 8 grams, how many grams of radioactive material will she have left after 16 years?

Complex Numbers & *i*

- A complex number is a polynomial containing *i*, and usually takes the form *a + bi*.
- *i* is the square root of -1. Fill in the chart below:

i^1	
i^2	
i^3	
i^4	
i^5	

- You can't take the square root of a negative. For example:
  - (6)(6) = 36
  - (-6)(-6) = 36
  - Since the square of any positive or negative number is a positive number, there is no such thing as a negative square root.
- Simplified expressions cannot have *i* in the denominator. When you see *i* in the denominator, your first step should be to remove it.
- You can do this by multiplying by the **conjugate** – the complex number with the opposite sign.
  - Example: the conjugate of (*a + bi*) is (*a – bi*)
  - You don't need to remember this term, but you do need to know when to use it.
- Try the examples below.

1

Which of the following is equivalent to $(4 - i)(6 + i)$?

A) $10 + i$

B) $25 + 2i$

C) $25 - 2i$

D) $25 + 10i$

2

The complex number below is simplified to the form *a + bi*. What is the value of *ab*?

$$\frac{4 + 6i}{2 - i}$$

#sat_hack

#FOILing_i

When FOILing two complex numbers, treat *i* like any variable. If you start with plugging in $\sqrt{-1}$, you will end up with too many radicals and overcomplicate the problem.

Exponents, Roots & i Practice 1

1

If $y = 7\sqrt{3}$ and $2y = \sqrt{3x}$, what is the value of x?

A) 14

B) 49

C) 196

D) 588

2

If $\frac{x^{a^2}}{x^{b^2}} = x^{36}$, $x > 1$, and $a + b = 12$, what is the value of $a - b$?

A) 3

B) 4

C) 6

D) 9

3

A radioactive substance decays at an annual rate of 26 percent. If the initial amount of the substance is 415 grams, which of the following functions f models the remaining amount of the substance, in grams, t years later?

A) $f(t) = 415\,(0.74)^t$

B) $f(t) = 415\,(0.26)^t$

C) $f(t) = 0.74\,(415)^t$

D) $f(t) = 0.26\,(415)^t$

4

Ty Dollarsign opened a bank account that earns 5 percent interest compounded annually. His initial deposit was $200, and he uses the expression 200(x)^t$ to find the value of the account after t years. What is the value of the x in the expression?

A) 1.5

B) 1.05

C) 1.005

D) 0.95

5

Ty Dollarsign opened a bank account that earns 5 percent interest compounded annually. His initial deposit was $200, and he uses the expression 200(x)^t$ to find the value of the account after t years.
Ty Dollarsign's friend Wiz found an account that earns 5.5 percent interest compounded annually. Wiz made an initial deposit of $200 into his account at the same time Ty Dollarsign made a deposit of $200 into his account. After 10 years, how much more money will Wiz's initial deposit have earned than Ty's initial deposit? (Round your answer to the nearest cent.)

A) $1.00

B) $6.16

C) $12.33

D) $15.85

6

Which of the following is equal to $a^{-\frac{4}{5}}$, for all values of a?

A) $\frac{1}{\sqrt[4]{a^5}}$

B) $\frac{1}{\sqrt[5]{a^4}}$

C) $-\sqrt[5]{a^4}$

D) $-\sqrt[4]{a^5}$

$$\frac{3-7i}{2+6i}$$

If the expression above is written in the form of $a + bi$, where a and b are real numbers, what is the value of a? (Note: $i = \sqrt{-1}$)

A) $\frac{1}{10}$

B) $\frac{6}{5}$

C) $-\frac{4}{5}$

D) $-\frac{9}{10}$

$$\sqrt{x+a} = x - 3$$

If $a = -3$, what is the solution set of the equation above?

A) {3,4}

B) {3}

C) {4,6}

D) {3,6}

$$\sqrt{x-a} = x - 5$$

If $a = 3$, what is the solution set of the equation above?

A) {4,7}

B) {4}

C) {7}

D) There is no solution set for the equation above.

10

$$1{,}000 \left(1 + \frac{x}{1{,}200}\right)^{12}$$

The expression above gives the amount of money, in dollars, generated in a year by a $1,000 deposit in a bank account that pays an annual interest rate of $x\%$ compounded monthly. Which of the following expressions shows how much additional money is generated at an interest rate of 10% than at an interest rate of 5%?

A) $1{,}000 \left(1 + \frac{10-5}{1{,}200}\right)^{12}$

B) $1{,}000 \left(1 + \frac{10}{1{,}200}\right)^{12} - 1{,}000 \left(1 + \frac{5}{1{,}200}\right)^{12}$

C) $1{,}000 \left(1 + \frac{\frac{10}{5}}{1{,}200}\right)^{12}$

D) $\dfrac{1000\left(1+\frac{10}{1{,}200}\right)^{12}}{1000\left(1+\frac{5}{1{,}200}\right)^{12}}$

Exponents, Roots & i Practice 2

1

$$f(x) = -\left(\frac{1}{4}\right)^x + 1$$

The function f is defined by the equation above. Which of the following describes the graph of $y = -f(x)$ in the xy-plane?

A) an exponential increase function passing through (0,0)

B) an exponential decrease function passing through (0,0)

C) an exponential increase function passing through (0,-2)

D) an exponential decrease function passing through (0,-2)

2

If $\sqrt{x} + \sqrt{81} = \sqrt{225}$, what is the value of x?

A) 6

B) 36

C) 12

D) 144

3

If $x^{\frac{y}{4}} = 36$ for positive integers x and y, what is NOT a possible value of y?

A) 1

B) 2

C) 8

D) 16

4

The stock price of one share in a certain company is worth $400 today. A stock analyst believes that the stock will lose 13% of its value each week for the next three weeks. The analyst uses the equation $V = 400(r)^t$ to model the value, V, of the stock after t weeks. What value should the analyst use for r?

A) 1.13

B) 0.13

C) 0.39

D) 0.87

5

The stock price of one share in a certain company is worth $400 today. A stock analyst believes that the stock will lose 13% of its value each week for the next three weeks. The analyst uses the equation $V = 400(r)^t$ to model the value, V, of the stock after t weeks. To the nearest dollar, what does the analyst believe the value of the stock will be at the end of three weeks?

A) $124

B) $263

C) $348

D) $577

Which of the following is equal to $4^{10} + 4^{10} + 4^{10} + 4^{10} + 4^{11}$?

A) 2^{42}

B) 2^{51}

C) 2^{82}

D) 2^{23}

Which of the following complex numbers is equal to $(7 + 9i) - (4i^2 - 5i)$, for $i = \sqrt{-1}$?

A) $-3 + 4i$

B) $3 + 4i$

C) $11 + 14i$

D) $-11 + 14i$

$$\left(\frac{x^2 y^{-\frac{2}{3}}}{x^{-\frac{1}{2}} y^{-3}}\right)^{-\frac{1}{7}}$$

Which of the expressions below is equivalent to the expression above?

A) $\dfrac{\sqrt[5]{x^{14}}}{\sqrt{y^3}}$

B) $\dfrac{1}{\sqrt[5]{x^{14}}\sqrt{y^3}}$

C) $\dfrac{\sqrt[3]{y}}{\sqrt[14]{x^5}}$.

D) $\dfrac{1}{\sqrt[14]{x^5}\sqrt[3]{y}}$

9

If $4x - 2y = 15$, what is the value of $\frac{16^x}{4^y}$?

A) 2^{15}

B) 4^7

C) 8^5

D) 16^3

Kevin deposited x dollars in his investment account on January 1, 2007. The amount of money in the account tripled each year until Kevin had \$5,832 in his investment account on January 1, 2012. What was the value of x? (Round your answer to the nearest dollar)

A) \$24

B) \$72

C) \$389

D) \$486

EXPONENTS, ROOTS & i PRACTICE 2

Blue Book Problem	My Answer	Correct Answer	Why did I miss?
P. 448 #7			
P. 449 #11			
P. 450 #14			
P. 559 #3			
P. 574 #21			
P. 576 #28			

CORRECT OUT OF TOTAL: _____/6

NOTES:

Blue Book Timed Assignments

- **Math – No Calculator (25 minutes)**
  - Assignment 1: Blue Book Pages 668-675
  - Assignment 2: Blue Book Pages 789-796
  - Assignment 3: Study Guide Simplified Pages 280-285
  - Assignment 4: Study Guide Simplified Pages 338-343
- **Math – Calculator (55 minutes)**
  - Assignment 5: Blue Book Page 677-692
  - Assignment 6: Blue Book Pages 798-815
  - Assignment 7: Study Guide Simplified Pages 286-299
  - Assignment 8: Study Guide Simplified Pages 344-357

Math Summary

1. **Math Overview**
   - No-Calculator Test vs Calculator Test
   - Grid-Ins
   - Key Terms for SAT Math
2. **Math Tricks**
   - Pick & Stick
   - Plug & Chug
   - Guess & Check
3. **Algebra FUN-Damentals**
   - Translating Words Into Math
   - PEMDAS
   - Function Notation
   - Word Problems: Break It Down
   - Wordy Word Problems
   - Absolute Value
4. **Linear Equations**
   - What Is A Direct Relationship?
   - Writing Equations in Slope-Intercept Form
   - Finding Distance: Pythagorean Theorem
   - Finding Midpoint: Using Averages
5. **Systems of Equations**
   - Substitution
   - Elimination
   - Systems of Equations in Word Problems
6. **Quadratic Equations**
   - What Is A Solution?
   - FOIL, Factoring, & the Quadratic Formula
   - The Vertex: A Maximum or Minimum

7. **Geometry**
   - Parallel Lines
   - 5 Types of Triangles
   - 3 Triangle Rules: Area, Similar Triangles, and Third Side Rule
   - Quadrilaterals & Other Polygons
   - Solids: Volume and Surface Area
   - Circles
8. **Ratios and Percentages**
   - Ratios vs. Fractions
   - Direct and Indirect (Inverse) Variation
   - Percentage & Percent Change
9. **Statistics & Data**
   - Mean (Average) Median, Mode, and Range
   - Standard Deviation
   - Probability
   - Line Graphs
   - Bar Graphs
   - Pie Charts
   - Scatterplots
   - Using Critical Reasoning
10. **Exponents & i**
    - Bases & Exponents
    - Exponent Rules
    - Matching Bases
    - Exponential Growth & Decay
    - Complex Numbers and i

Essay
Test

Tried & True Tutoring

What is the SAT Essay?

- The SAT Essay is the optional fifth test of the SAT.
- You will have the option to register for the Essay when you enroll in the SAT.
- Not all colleges require you to take the essay, but many competitive colleges/universities do.
- We recommend taking it since it's a great way to demonstrate your writing and critical thinking skills.
- When you register for the SAT, the College Board offers a tool that helps you find out which schools require or recommend the essay.
- The essay score does not factor into your overall SAT score.

What does the SAT Essay involve?

- You will have _____ minutes to read and analyze another writer's work and write a clear, concise **Analytical Essay** in which you explain how the author builds his or her argument.
- Your essay will be read by two graders, who will each give your essay a score from 1-4 in three different areas:
  - **Reading:** Does your essay demonstrate that you read and understood the author's work?
  - **Analysis:** Have you effectively analyzed the author's argumentation and use of literary/rhetorical devices?
  - **Writing:** Does the quality of your writing (grammar, structure, vocabulary, etc.) demonstrate a clear message?
- These scores are added together to give you three area scores between 2-8.
  - For example, Reading 8, Analysis 8, Writing 8 would be a **perfect Essay score.**
- There is no overall Essay score.

#sat_hack

#essay_pacing

You only have **50 minutes**, so use your time wisely.
Part One – **deep reading** the whole passage should take you around **5 minutes**.
Part Two – **building your outline** should take you between **5-10 minutes**.
Part Three – **writing the essay** should take you about **30 minutes**.
Part Four – **proofreading** your essay should take you **5 minutes**.

Review

Fill in the blank.

1. True or False: You will be writing a persuasive essay. _____

2. What type of essay will you be writing? _____

3. How is the essay scored? _____

_____

_____

The Essay Assignment

- The SAT Essay assignment always looks the same; the only thing that will change is the passage and a few words in the prompt:

Directions

As you read the passage below, consider how *(the author)* uses

- evidence, such as facts or examples, to support claims.

- reasoning to develop ideas and to connect claims and evidence.

- stylistic or persuasive elements, such as word choice or appeals to emotion, to add power to the ideas expressed.

- The passage you will analyze will be here.

- It will be 650-850 words on a straightforward topic. It will probably be from an author who is not famous.

- Most of the recent SAT Essay passages are only a few decades old.

Write an essay in which you explain how *(the author)* builds an argument to persuade *(his/her)* audience that *(what the author is arguing)*. In your essay, analyze how *(the author)* uses one or more of the features listed in the box above (or features of your own choice) to strengthen the logic and persuasiveness of his argument. Be sure that the analysis focuses on the most relevant features of the passage.

Your essay should not explain whether you agree with *(the author's)* claims, but rather explain how *(the author)* builds an argument to persuade his audience.

Assignment

Note: The SAT **DOES NOT** want your opinion on the topic being discussed. The SAT wants your analysis of the writer's argument. **DO NOT** give your opinion.

Essay Rubric: Straight from the ETS

Reading	Analysis	Writing
• The response demonstrates thorough comprehension of the source text. • The response shows an understanding of the text's central ideas and of most important details and how they interrelate, demonstrating a comprehensive understanding of the text • The response is free of errors or interpretation with regard to the text • The response makes skillful use of textual evidence (quotations, paraphrases, or both), demonstrating a complete understanding of the source text.	• The response offers an insightful analysis of the source text and demonstrates a sophisticated understanding of the analytical task. • The response offers a thorough, well-considered evaluation of the author's use of evidence, reasoning, and/or stylistic and persuasive elements and/or features of the student's own choosing • The response contains relevant, sufficient, and strategically chosen support for claim(s) or point(s) made. • The response focuses consistently on those features of the text that are most relevant to addressing the task.	• The response is cohesive and demonstrates a highly effective use and command of language. • The response includes a precise central claim. • The response includes a skillful introduction and conclusion. The response demonstrates a deliberate and higly effective progression of ideas both within paragraphs and throughout the essay. • The response has a wide variety in sentence structures. The response demonstrates a consistent use of precise word choice. The response maintains a formal style and objective tone. • The response shows a strong command of the conventions of standard written English and is free or virtually free of errors.

How To Get A Perfect Score

- The rubric above represents what the ETS considers to be the perfect essay.
- Getting a perfect score may not be as hard as it seems. The rubric tells you exactly what to do.
- We have broken down the rubric over the next few sections so that you can construct your essay accordingly.

Part One: Reading

- This section focuses on how to get all 4 points from both graders.
- As you read, you will need to identify two important pieces of information:
  - The context – answer the 5W Questions (Who, What, When, Where, Why)
  - Which persuasive elements the author used to build their argument.

What The Directions Say:

- The box at the top of the prompt contains the "directions"
- These directions contain the specifics of what exactly you need to look for **as you read**.

> As you read the passage below, consider how *(the author)* uses
>
> - evidence, such as facts or examples, to support claims.
>
> - reasoning to develop ideas and to connect claims and evidence.
>
> - stylistic or persuasive elements, such as word choice or appeals to emotion, to add power to the ideas expressed.

What These Directions Mean:

- There are many persuasive devices that writers use to build their arguments.
- These devices fall into three categories: **evidence**, **reasoning**, and **stylistic/emotional devices**
- You must familiarize yourself with these devices so that you can **identify** them while Deep Reading
- You must also know how these devices work so you can explain **why** the author is using them.
- These three charts on the next few pages contain many of the persuasive devices (organized by category) that you are likely to find in SAT reading passages.

What To Look For: Evidence

What the directions say: "evidence, such as facts or examples, to support claims."		
Type of Persuasive Device:	**What to look for in the passage:**	**Why it works and how it could relate back to the argument:**
Statistics	• Percentages • Numbers	• Makes the author more credible in order to gain the reader's trust
Results from a survey or other research	• "According to a [survey, poll, experiment] conducted by…"	• Strengthens the argument • Grabs the reader's attention
Facts	• Concrete details • Not opinions	• Bolsters the author's clout and credibility
Quotes from other experts	• "According to [expert]…" • "[Expert] states that…"	• Highlights an issue to grab/maintain the reader's attention • Appeals to the reader's sense of authority

What To Look For: Reasoning

What the directions say: "stylistic or persuasive elements, such as word choice or appeals to emotion, to add power to the ideas expressed."		
Type of Persuasive Device:	**What to look for in the passage:**	**Why it works and how it could relate back to the argument:**
Cause and effect	• If _____, then _____ • Can be past, present, or future	• Draws the author's arguments together
Deductive reasoning	• Connecting a claim to a generally accepted rule or belief	• Appeals to the reader's logic • Makes the argument make sense
Inductive reasoning	• Taking many facts/arguments and connecting them together to draw a conclusion • Be careful that it is not a generalization	**Be careful of these Logical Fallacies:**
Comparative reasoning	• Connecting something the author knows the reader believes to another claim they are trying to make	• **Red herring** – introducing an irrelevant point to distract the reader's attention from the main issue
Pros and Cons	• Discussing both sides • Using facts to strengthen or favor one side (the "pros")	• **Slippery Slope** – saying that one issue will lead to a much more extreme issue; "snowball effect"

What To Look For: Stylistic (Emotional) Devices

What the directions say: "reasoning to develop ideas and to connect claims and evidence."		
Type of Persuasive Device:	**What to look for in the passage:**	**Why it works and how it could relate back to the argument:**
Diction	• Sensory language (Think 5 senses) • Words that paint a picture	• These words are vivid and invoke feeling
Rhetorical Questioning	• Question mark • Questions that have an extremely obvious (implied) answer, a very abstract answer, or no answer at all	• Can usually invoke a logical or emotional cognitive response • Can drive the reader to draw an implied conclusion
Anecdotes	• Recounting a personal experience	• Are often relatable and connect the reader to the author
Repetition	• Emphasizing or repeating certain words or phrases	• Strengthens a point by
Irony	• Sarcasm • Humor • Saying the opposite of what he/she actually means	• Can emphasize something the reader knows to be true by contradicting or denying it
Contrast	• Comparing two very different things in order to emphasize a specific trait in either • Similes or metaphors	• Can cause the reader to favor one thing over another ("Organic vegetables contain less hormones than those that are conventionally grown." • Can be used to paint a picture or elicit an emotional response

Sample Prompt

As you read the passage below, consider how Patrick Henry uses

- evidence, such as facts or examples, to support claims.

- reasoning to develop ideas and to connect claims and evidence.

- stylistic or persuasive elements, such as word choice or appeals to emotion, to add power to the ideas expressed.

Adapted from former governor of Virginia Patrick Henry, *Give Me Liberty or Give Me Death*, a speech delivered March 20, 1775 at the Second Virginia Convention in Richmond, Virginia.

1   Has Great Britain any enemy, in this quarter of the world, to call for all this accumulation of navies and armies? No, sir, she has none. They are meant for us; they can be meant for no other. They are sent over to bind and rivet upon us those chains which the British ministry have been so long forging. And what have we to oppose to them? Shall we try argument? Sir, we have been trying that for the last ten years. Have we anything new to offer upon the subject? Nothing. We have held the subject up in every light of which it is capable; but it has been all in vain. Shall we resort to entreaty and humble supplication? What terms shall we find which have not been already exhausted? Let us not, I beseech you, sir, deceive ourselves. Sir, we have done everything that could be done, to avert the storm which is now coming on. We have petitioned; we have remonstrated; we have supplicated; we have prostrated ourselves before the throne, and have implored its interposition to arrest the tyrannical hands of the ministry and Parliament. Our petitions have been slighted; our remonstrances have produced additional violence and insult; our supplications have been disregarded; and we have been spurned, with contempt, from the foot of the throne. In vain, after these things, may we indulge the fond hope of peace and reconciliation. There is no longer any room for hope. If we wish to be free²if we mean to preserve inviolate those inestimable privileges for which we have been so long contending²if we mean not basely to abandon the noble struggle in which we have been so long engaged, and which we have pledged ourselves never to abandon until the glorious object of our contest shall be obtained, we must fight! I repeat it, sir, we must fight! An appeal to arms and to the God of Hosts is all that is left us!

2   They tell us, sir, that we are weak; unable to cope with so formidable an adversary. But when shall we be stronger? Will it be the next week, or the next year? Will it be when we are totally disarmed, and when a British guard shall be stationed in every house? Shall we gather strength by irresolution and inaction?

3   Shall we acquire the means of effectual resistance, by lying supinely on our backs, and hugging the delusive phantom of hope, until our enemies shall have bound us hand and foot? Sir, we are not weak if we make a proper use of those means which the God of nature hath placed in our power. Three millions of people, armed in the holy cause of liberty, and in such a country as that which we possess, are invincible by any force which our enemy can send against us. Besides, sir, we shall not fight our battles alone. There is a just God who presides over the destinies of nations; and who will raise up friends to fight our battles for us. The battle, sir, is not to the strong alone; it is to the vigilant, the active, the brave. Besides, sir, we have no election. If we were base enough to desire it, it is now too late to retire from the contest. There is no retreat but in submission and slavery! Our chains are forged! Their clanking may be heard on the plains of Boston! The war is inevitable and let it come! I repeat it, sir, let it come.

4   It is in vain, sir, to extenuate the matter. Gentlemen may cry, Peace, Peace, but there is no peace. The war is actually begun! The next gale that sweeps from the north will bring to our ears the clash of resounding arms! Our brethren are already in the field! Why stand we here idle? What is it that gentlemen wish? What would they have? Is life so dear, or peace so sweet, as to be purchased at the price of chains and slavery? Forbid it, Almighty God! I know not what course others may take; but as for me, give me liberty or give me death!

Write an essay in which you explain how Patrick Henry builds an argument to persuade his audience that the American Colonies should declare war against Great Britain. In your essay, analyze how Henry uses one or more of the features listed in the box above (or features of your own choice) to strengthen the logic and persuasiveness of his argument. Be sure that the analysis focuses on the most relevant features of the passage.

Your essay should not explain whether you agree with Henry's claims, but rather explain how Henry builds an argument to persuade his audience.

As you read, look for examples of each:

	Line Numbers	Device used	Context (Why was it used?)
Evidence			

	Line Numbers	Device Used	Context (Why was it used?)
Reasoning			

	Line Numbers	Device Used	Context (Why was it used?)
Stylistic/Emotional			

Understanding Context

- When you are finished reading, answer the following **5W Questions**:

  Who wrote it? (Was it someone significant?)

  _____

  _____

  _____

  What is it about? (The general topic – are there multiple opposing views?)

  _____

  _____

  _____

  When was it written? (Was there anything historical occurring at the time that makes this debate

  significant?)

  _____

  _____

  _____

  Where was it written? (Where was it published? Was it a speech? Consider the intended audience.)

  _____

  _____

  _____

  Why was it written? (What was the author's argument trying to prove?)

  _____

  _____

  _____

Extra Practice: Make Flash Cards

- On the SAT, you won't have these steps to follow, so you will need to remember them.
- Before your next class or tutoring session, make 15 flash cards.
  - 5 of them will be the **5W Questions**
  - The other 10 will have a **persuasive device** on one side, and a **definition** and an **example** on the other side. Choose 10 from the charts on pages 235 and 236, or choose other persuasive devices that you have learned in your English classes.
- These flash cards will help you remember the devices so that you can recognize them more quickly on the essay test.

Part Two: Analysis

- Now that you have read the passage and made yourself some notes, you can begin to build your body paragraphs.
- Each of your body paragraphs will accomplish four things:
    1. State which device you are about to analyze. You could use the following sentence structures:
        - **"The author used** (device**) in order to** (its effect)."
        - **"The author** (does this – effect) **by using** (device)."
    2. Cite the device using a paraphrase or quote.
        - You must include **at least one paraphrase or quote in every single body paragraph,** or you will not get a perfect Analysis score.
    3. Explain how the technique contributes to the author's argument, and restate that argument (this also scores you reading points because it's making it even clearer that you understood the passage). You could use the following sentence starters:
        - **"This use of** (device) **contributes to the author's argument that** (what the author is arguing) **because…"**
        - **"This** (device) **is particularly effective in strengthening the author's argument that** (what the author is arguing) **because it accomplishes…"**
    4. Elaborate on **what effect this persuasive device has on the reader,** and conclude with how this effectively persuades the reader.
- Use the chart below to organize your body paragraphs. The first body paragraph has already been done as an example/.

Analysis: Body Paragraphs

Body Paragraph 1	Body Paragraph 2	Body Paragraph 3
1. State the device. Emotional device: a metaphor comparing the colonists' situation to slavery	1. **State** the device.	1. **State** the device.
2. Cite the device. Third paragraph: "Our chains are forged! Their clanking may be heard on the plains of Boston!"	2. **Cite** the device.	2. **Cite** the device.
3. Explain how it contributes to the author's argument. Henry is arguing that the colonists should fight for freedom from England, so Henry uses a metaphor to paint the colonists as slaves to the monarchy.	3. **Explain how it contributes** to the author's argument.	3. **Explain how it contributes** to the author's argument.
4. Explain its effect on the reader. This has a powerful effect on the reader since slavery was a divisive issues at the time; whether for or against, most people at the time had strong emotional opinions about slavery.	4. Explain its **effect on the reader.**	4. Explain its **effect on the reader.**

Constructing Your Body Paragraphs

- Now that you have organized your thoughts in the chart above, you will need to put then into cohesive paragraphs.
- The first body paragraph has been completed for you as an example of how to transfer your notes into a clear, succinct paragraph.

First Body Paragraph

(1) Patrick Henry uses a **metaphor**, comparing the colonists' predicament to slavery, in order to evoke an emotional response from his audience. (2) In the third paragragh, he exclaims **"Our chains have been forged! Their clanking may be heard on the plains of Boston!"** (3) As Henry is trying to persuade his fellow colonists to follow him into war with Britain, this metaphor plays a particularly important role in his argument, because it **provokes the colonists to see themselves as slaves to the Monarchy**. (4) This surely triggered an **emotional response**, since even at the time of the American Revolution slavery was a divisive issue. (5) Whether the colonists listening to Henry's speech were abolitionists or slaveholders, the idea of being a slave to the Monarchy was likely to be rejected by American colonists alike. (6) Henry uses this metaphor to effectively convince his audience that fighting for freedom is the only option.

The first two sentences explain what the literary device is, what it's used for, and cite the device by including a direct quote.

The third sentence identifies how the device functions within the author's argument.

The fourth and fifth sentences explain what effect this device has on the reader (or in this case, on the audience).

The sixth (final) sentence concludes by restating the author's argument and why it works.

- Use the lines on the next page to write your body paragraphs, using your notes from the chart on page 240 and following the one above as an example.

ESSAY ANALYSIS

Part Three: Writing

1. The rubric on page 234 does not prescribe a structure that your essay must follow, but most high-scoring essays follow the same general structure:
   1. Your **Intro Paragraph** should contain the following (in no specific order, but it still needs to "flow"):
      a. **Context** – this sentence should try to answer all **5W's** (who, what, when, where, and why). Some students like to make this the first sentence to gain the reader's interest.

      _____

      _____

      b. **Thesis** – this sentence should restate the author's argument and what they appealed to (Credibility, emotion, and/or logic).

      _____

      _____

      c. **Plan of Attack** – this sentence should **briefly sum up** your entire essay (which 3 elements will your body paragraphs be addressing?)

      _____

      _____

   2. Your **3 Body Paragraphs** should be 5-8 sentences and should contain the following, in this order (you already filled this information out in the chart on page 240):
      a. Identify and cite the rhetorical device.
      b. Explain how it contributes to the author's argument.
      c. Explain its effect on the reader.
   3. Finally, your conclusion should include, but not be limited to:
      a. **A strong, brief restatement of the author's argument and which three rhetorical devices were used.**

      _____

      _____

#sat_hack

#writing_score_8

All of the grammar and writing rules that you learned for the Writing and Language test apply on the SAT essay.

You will not be graded on your spelling unless it affects the grammar (using the wrong their/there/they're)

You will also not be graded on handwriting, but neatly-written essays often score higher because they are easier to read.

Timed Assignments

Essay Summary

1. **Overview**
   - Optional 5th Test
   - 50 minutes to write an analytical essay
   - Scoring: Reading, Writing, Analysis
   - ETS Rubric
2. **Part One: Reading**
   - Interpreting the DIrections
   - Evidence
   - Reasoning
   - Stylistic/Emotional Devices
   - Sample Prompt
3. **Part Two: Analysis**
   - Body Paragraph: 4 Parts:
     a. State the device
     b. Cite the device
     c. Explain how it contributes to the argument
     d. Explain its effect on the reader
   - Body Paragraphs: Practice
4. **Part Three: Writing**
   - Intro Paragraph
   - 3 Body Paragraphs
   - Conclusion

Sample Exam A

Tried & True Tutoring

Reading Test
65 Minutes, 52 Questions

DIRECTIONS

Each passage or pair of passages below is followed by a number of questions. After reading each passage or pair, choose the best answer to each question based on what is stated or implied in the passage or passages and in any accompanying graphics (such as a table or graph).

Questions 1 - 10 are based on the following passage.

This passage is adapted from Sir Arthur Conan Doyle, *The Adventures of Sherlock Holmes: A Scandal in Bohemia*. Originally published in 1891.

One night—it was on the twentieth of March, 1888—I was returning from a journey to a patient (for I had now returned to civil practice),
Line
5 when my way led me through Baker Street. As I passed the well-remembered door, which must always be associated in my mind with my wooing and with the dark incidents of the Study in Scarlet, I was seized with a keen desire to see Holmes again, and to know how he was
10 employing his extraordinary powers. His rooms were brilliantly lit, and, even as I looked up, I saw his tall, spare figure pass twice in a dark silhouette against the blind. He was pacing the room swiftly, eagerly, with his head sunk upon his chest and his hands clasped behind him. To
15 me, who knew his every mood and habit, his attitude and manner told their own story. He was at work again. He had risen out of his drug-created dreams and was hot upon the scent of
20 some new problem. I rang the bell and was shown up to the chamber which had formerly been in part my own.

His manner was not effusive. It seldom was; but he was glad, I think, to see me. With hardly a
25 word spoken, but with a kindly eye, he waved me to an armchair, threw across his case of cigars,

and indicated a spirit case and a gasogene in the corner. Then he stood before the fire and looked me over in his singular introspective fashion.
30 "Wedlock suits you," he remarked. "I think, Watson, that you have put on seven and a half pounds since I saw you."

"Seven!" I answered.

"Indeed, I should have thought a little more.
35 Just a trifle more, I fancy, Watson. And in practice again, I observe. You did not tell me that you intended to go into harness."

"Then, how do you know?"

"I see it, I deduce it. How do I know that
40 you have been getting yourself very muddy lately, and that you have a most clumsy and careless servant girl?"

"My dear Holmes," said I, "this is too much. You would certainly have been burned,
45 had you lived a few centuries ago. It is true that I had a country walk on Thursday and came home in a dreadful mess, but as I have changed my clothes I can't imagine how you deduce it. As to Mary Jane, she is incorrigible, and my wife has
50 given her notice, but there, again, I fail to see how you work it out."

He chuckled to himself and rubbed his long, nervous hands together.

"It is simplicity itself," said he; "my eyes
55 tell me that on the inside of your left shoe, just where the firelight strikes it, the leather is scored by six almost parallel cuts. Obviously they have been caused by someone who has very carelessly scraped round the edges of the sole in order to
60 remove crusted mud from it. Hence, you see, my double deduction that you had been out in vile

CONTINUE ➤

246

double deduction that you had been out in vile weather, and that you had a particularly malignant boot-slitting specimen of a London
65 maid. As to your practice, if a gentleman walks into my rooms smelling of iodoform, with a black mark of nitrate of silver upon his right forefinger, and a bulge on the right side of his top-hat to show where he has secreted his stethoscope, I
70 must be dull, indeed, if I do not pronounce him to be an active member of the medical profession."

I could not help laughing at the ease with which he explained his process of deduction. "When I hear you give your reasons," I remarked,
75 "the thing always appears to me to be so ridiculously simple that I could easily do it myself, though at each successive instance of your reasoning I am baffled until you explain your process. And yet I believe that my eyes are
80 as good as yours."

1

Over the course of the passage, the main focus shifts from

A) a walk through London to an argument between friends.

B) nostalgic wandering to an unplanned visit between friends.

C) an introduction to the environment in which the scene takes place to a productive business meeting.

D) a nighttime stroll to a friend making deductions about a case.

2

Which of the following can most reasonably be inferred about Baker Street and the Study in Scarlet?

A) They both have something to do with wooing.

B) They both have something to do with extraordinary powers.

C) They both have something to do with Holmes.

D) The narrator has worked at both of them.

3

What function does the section in the first paragraph beginning with "His rooms" and ending with "some new problem" (lines 10-20) serve in the passage as a whole?

A) It demonstrates the narrator's powers of reasoning which will be overshadowed by those of Holmes.

B) It gives information about Holmes that the narrator will disprove later in the passage.

C) It indicates a business partnership between the narrator and Holmes to give context to their conversation.

D) It hints at Holmes's health issues which have brought the narrator to his door.

4

As used in line 23, "effusive" most nearly means

A) kind.

B) dour.

C) happy.

D) exuberant.

5

Holmes's purpose in asking the narrator a question in the seventh paragraph (lines 39-42) is most likely to

A) accuse the narrator of making poor choices.

B) set up an example to support a claim he has made.

C) hint that he has been keeping a very close eye on the narrator.

D) answer the narrator's question as directly as possible.

6

The narrator hints that Holmes's ability to reason is

A) like witchcraft.

B) offensive.

C) incorrigible.

D) not to be trusted.

7

Which choice provides the best evidence for the answer to the previous question?

A) Lines 43-48 ("My dear... deduce it")

B) Lines 48-51 ("As to Mary Jane... work it out")

C) Lines 72-73 ("I could not... deduction")

D) Lines 74-80 ("When I hear... good as yours")

8

Which of the following can most reasonably be inferred about Holmes from the passage?

A) He has studied at a prestigious university.

B) He sees everyone as equals.

C) He does not get many visitors.

D) He views his powers of deduction as common sense.

9

Which choice provides the best evidence for the answer to the previous question?

A) Lines 30-37 ("Wedlock... harness")

B) Lines 52-53 ("He chuckled...together")

C) Lines 60-65 ("Hence... London maid")

D) Lines 65-71 ("As to your... medical profession")

10

As used in line 70, "pronounce" most nearly means

A) enunciate.

B) declaim.

C) declare.

D) exclaim.

CONTINUE

Questions 11-20 are based on the following passages.

Passage 1 is adapted from Clarence Darrow, *Crime: Its Cause and Treatment*. Originally published in 1922. Passage 2 is adapted from Arthur Train, *Courts and Criminals*. Originally published in 1912.

Passage 1

The acorn will inevitably produce the oak tree and it will grow true to its pattern. All seeds and cells will do likewise. Still if the acorn
Line
5 is planted in good soil, where it is properly nourished and in a spot where it is sufficiently sheltered, the tree will be more likely to become large and symmetrical, than if it is planted in poor soil or in an exposed spot.

In one sense heredity is the seed, and
10 environment the soil. The whole structure and pattern and inherent tendencies and potentiality are in the seed and cannot be changed. The child has nothing to do with its early environment during the period when impressions sink the
15 deepest and when habits are formed. It is then that the meaning of facts is interpreted. At this time the child is fashioned by the teachings and environment in which it is placed. As the child receives its first impressions, and all along
20 through its development, it is forming habits from those about it. These habits come to be strong, dominating forces in its life. Very few people, if any, can trace definite views of conduct or thought to their conscious effort, but these are
25 born of their structure and the environment that formed their habits after birth.

The fact that an individual's political and religious faith depends almost entirely on his place of birth and early youth, shows the strength
30 of environment in forming and shaping opinions and beliefs.

Endless discussions have been devoted to the relative importance of heredity and environment in human conduct. This is a fruitless
35 task. In a sense, each one is of supreme importance in the outcome of a life. It is obvious that some structures are so perfect that almost no environment will overcome them. Instances of
40 strong men developing out of poor environment are not rare. Many of these may be subject to doubt as to whether the heredity caused the strength, for the smallest particle of luck at some special or vital time may make all the difference

45 possible in the outcome of a life. While some heredities withstand a poor environment, others are so poor that, no matter how good the environment, the man will fail. No heredity will overcome the hardest environment.

Passage 2

50 During this period 50,004 cases of felonious homicides of known causes were recorded. Of these homicides, 33,476 were due to quarrels and 4,799 to liquor, a total of 38,275 out of the 50,004 cases of known causes being
55 traceable in this, another seven years, to motives the most casual.

It would be stupid to allege that the reason men killed was because they had been stepped on or had been deprived of a glass of
60 beer. The cause lies deeper than that. It rests in the willingness or desire of the murderer to kill at all.

This, then, is the real reason why men
65 kill—because it is inherent in their state of mind, it is part of their mental and physical make-up—they are ready to kill, they want to kill, they are the kind of men who do kill. This is the result of their heredity, environment, educational and
70 religious training, or the absence of it. How many readers of this paper have ever experienced an actual desire to kill another human being? Probably not one hundredth of one per cent. They belong to the class of people who either never
75 have such an impulse, or at any rate have been taught to keep such impulses under control. Hence it is futile to try to explain that some men kill for a trifling sum of money, some because they feel insulted, others because of political or
80 labor disputes, or because they do not like their food. Any one of these may be the match that sets off the gunpowder, but the real cause of the killing is the fact that the gunpowder is there, lying around loose, and ready to be touched off.
85 What engenders this gunpowder state of mind would make a valuable sociological study, but it may well be that a seemingly inconsequential fact may so embitter a boy or man toward life or the human race in general that in time he "sees red"
90 and goes through the world looking for trouble. Any cause that makes for crime and depravity makes for murder as well. The little boy who is driven out of the tenement onto the street, and in turn off the street by a policeman, until, finding
95 no wholesome place to play, he joins a "gang" and begins an incipient career of crime, may end in the "death house."

11

Darrow discusses acorns in the first paragraph of Passage 1 primarily to

A) illustrate the importance of environment to the growing process.

B) emphasize the inevitability of heredity as the primary determinant of an organism's future.

C) instruct the reader as to how to live a more symmetrical life.

D) convince the reader that sometimes we should forgive people for committing crimes.

12

Which of the following does Darrow most strongly imply about a person's beliefs?

A) Beliefs are largely born into a person.

B) Beliefs color the way a person sees his or her environment.

C) Usually a person can take little to no credit for his or her beliefs.

D) A person's political beliefs are as important as his or her religious beliefs.

13

Which choice provides the best evidence for the answer to the previous question?

A) Lines 12-16 ("The child... interpreted")

B) Lines 18-22 ("As the child... its life")

C) Lines 22-26 ("Very few... after birth")

D) Lines 27-31 ("The fact... beliefs")

14

Based on information in Passage 1, how would Darrow most likely respond to Train's claims in lines 70-76 ("How many readers... impulses under control")?

A) Debating the importance of heredity over environment and vice versa is a fruitless task.

B) Without the influence of environment, no man would ever experience the urge to kill.

C) In rare cases a man's heredity could be such that he will not control his impulses regardless of teaching.

D) There are some heredities that no environment can overcome.

15

As used in line 78, "trifling" most nearly means

A) small.

B) owed.

C) massive.

D) ill-gained.

16

Which of the following does Train indicate about the "gunpowder state of mind" (lines 85)?

A) It is a result of environment.

B) Anyone might develop this state of mind.

C) Sociological studies suggest that not one hundredth of one percent experience it.

D) Maybe it could be caused by something that someone else would see as insignificant.

17

Which choice provides the best evidence for the answer to the previous question?

A) Lines 64-70 ("This, then… absence of it")

B) Lines 70-73 ("How many readers… one per cent")

C) Lines 81-84 ("Any one of these… touched off")

D) Lines 85-90 ("What engenders… for trouble")

18

As used in line 91, "depravity" most nearly means

A) deprivation.

B) moral corruption.

C) punishment.

D) ignorance.

19

Which choice best describes how each author argues someone turns to crime or murder?

A) Darrow indicates that heredity and environment each play a vital role; Train argues that the absence of educational and religious training causes people to kill.

B) Darrow argues that a person's environment while he or she is very young has great influence on whether or not he or she becomes a criminal; Train argues that the main difference between someone who kills and someone who does not is the desire to kill, which is or is not present as a result of heredity and environment.

C) Darrow argues that political and religious faith, determined largely by where one is born, allow people to overcome environment and that lack of such faith causes them to turn to crime; Train argues that some people, as a result of heredity and environment, "see red" and are ready to kill at the least provocation.

D) Darrow argues that heredity counts for a lot, but that some environments are such that they will corrupt anyone of any heredity; Train argues that people kill for motives which are "the most casual."

20

Based on Passage 1, Darrow would most likely say that someone who "sees red" (line 89)

A) probably spent his or her early years in a harsh environment.

B) would not commit a crime given the right environment.

C) will probably end up in the death house.

D) had poor heredity as well as a difficult environment.

Questions 21 - 30 are based on the following passage.

This passage is adapted from "New USGS assessment provides fresh insights into nation's brackish groundwater inventory" from the U.S. Geological Survey (USGS) website. The USGS is a branch of the Department of the Interior. Originally published 2017.

A new nationwide assessment by the U.S. Geological Survey suggests that the nation's brackish groundwater could help stretch limited freshwater supplies.

This study, the first of its kind in more than 50 years, found that the amount of brackish groundwater underlying the country is more than 800 times the amount currently used each year. With issues like drought, groundwater depletion, dwindling freshwater supplies, and demand for groundwater expected to continue to rise, understanding brackish groundwater supplies can help determine whether they can supplement or replace taxed freshwater sources in water-stressed areas.

"This assessment lays the foundation for building a deeper understanding of brackish groundwater resources and how they might be used to better ensure our water security," said Jennifer Stanton, a USGS hydrologist and lead author of this assessment.

In general, brackish groundwater is groundwater that has a dissolved-solids content greater than freshwater but less than seawater. It is defined for this assessment as having a dissolved-solids concentration ranging from 1,000 to 10,000 milligrams per liter.

This new assessment was authorized by the 2009 SECURE Water Act and builds on a 1965 study which, for more than five decades, has served as the primary source of information on the national distribution of brackish groundwater. By incorporating data from more than 380,000 sites, compared to about 1,000 for the 1965 study, the 2017 assessment provides more comprehensive, nationwide data on the quantity and quality of brackish groundwater across the country. This includes information like chemical composition of the water and well yields, which are necessary for understanding the potential—at the national and regional scales—for expanding brackish groundwater development and for informing decision and policy makers.

The assessment provides data for states and other public agencies interested in using brackish groundwater. It also supports the efforts of the U.S. Bureau of Reclamation to promote sustainable water treatment for brackish aquifers. "The use of brackish groundwater to augment water supply in the West has been analyzed as a potential adaptation strategy in a number of studies under Reclamation's Basin Studies Program," said Katharine Dahm, an engineer with the U.S. Bureau of Reclamation.

Advances in desalination technology and increases in demand for uses that don't need high-quality water, like mining, oil and gas development, and thermoelectric power generation, have led states like Texas and California to turn to brackish groundwater as an alternative to freshwater.

Data from the study released today indicate that brackish groundwater is present at some depth within 3,000 feet below ground beneath parts of every state except New Hampshire and Rhode Island. Using available data, a conservative estimate for the volume of brackish groundwater underlying the country is more than 35 times the amount of fresh groundwater currently used each year. Consequently, it is reasonable to consider brackish groundwater a substantial water resource available for use by the nation. In some parts of the country, freshwater has become more limited and brackish groundwater use has been increasing.

Despite the availability of this new information, there's still more to uncover on sustainable development of brackish groundwater. For many locations, data haven't been collected for depths greater than 500 feet. "Until recently, brackish groundwater has mostly been overlooked. It was difficult to find data for depths greater than 500 feet below ground in many parts of the country," said Stanton. "More work is needed to fully understand the resource. Although this assessment can't answer all of the questions related to sustainable use, it represents a starting point for identifying the gaps in our knowledge and for directing research to locations where further study would be most beneficial."

CONTINUE ➡

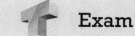

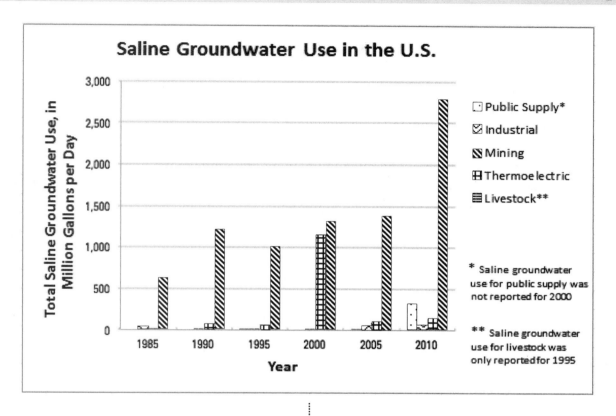

Saline Groundwater Use in the U.S.

Legend:
- Public Supply*
- Industrial
- Mining
- Thermoelectric
- Livestock**

* Saline groundwater use for public supply was not reported for 2000

** Saline groundwater use for livestock was only reported for 1995

Y-axis: Total Saline Groundwater Use, in Million Gallons per Day (0 to 3,000)

X-axis: Year (1985, 1990, 1995, 2000, 2005, 2010)

21

The primary purpose of the passage is to

A) explain research methods that led to conclusions regarding brackish water.

B) discuss findings that prove brackish water to be a good source of drinking water.

C) present promising findings about brackish water that will hopefully lead to more research.

D) provide a brief overview of the uses of different kinds of water.

22

The primary purpose of the passage is to

A) explain research methods that led to conclusions regarding brackish water.

B) discuss findings that prove brackish water to be a good source of drinking water.

C) present promising findings about brackish water that will hopefully lead to more research.

D) provide a brief overview of the uses of different kinds of water.

CONTINUE ▶

23

According to the passage, researchers in the study collected information primarily

A) from regional sites that study the chemical composition of water.

B) from a nationwide study conducted in 1965.

C) from hundreds of thousands of facilities in the US.

D) by collaborating with sites all over the world to retrieve data that, in some cases, goes all the way back to 1965.

24

Which choice provides the best evidence for the answer to the previous question?

A) Lines 22-27 ("In general... per liter")

B) Lines 33-38 ("By incorporating... country")

C) Lines 38-43 ("This includes... makers")

D) Lines 62-70 ("Data... year")

25

As used in line 49, "augment" most nearly means

A) magnify.

B) cleanse.

C) improve.

D) supplement.

26

According to the passage, where of the following would you be most likely to find brackish groundwater?

A) less than 3,000 feet below parts of Connecticut

B) 5,000 feet below New Hampshire

C) less than 3,000 feet below parts of Rhode Island

D) just below the surface of parts of California and Texas

27

As used in line 72, "substantial" most nearly means

A) essential.

B) ample.

C) significant.

D) invaluable.

28

According to information in the graph,

A) the use of saline groundwater in mining nearly doubled between 1985 and 2000.

B) saline groundwater use increased across all categories in every five-year period between 1985 and 2000.

C) about 1,000 gallons of saline groundwater was used for mining in 1995.

D) the supply of saline groundwater increased every five years between 1995 and 2010.

CONTINUE

29

According to information in the passage, the changes shown in the graph between 2005 and 2010 are partially responsible for

A) a decrease in the nation's overall supply of usable water.

B) some states seeing brackish groundwater as a substitute for freshwater.

C) funding for more studies into brackish groundwater in the near future.

D) the belief that supplies of brackish groundwater exists below the surface of nearly every state.

30

Which choice provides the best evidence for the answer to the previous question?

A) Lines 49-54 ("The use of… Bureau of Reclamation")

B) Lines 55-61 ("Advances in… to freshwater")

C) Lines 62-66 ("Data from… Rhode Island")

D) Lines 82-91 ("Until recently… most beneficial")

Questions 31-41 are based on the following passage.

This passage is adapted from Garth Brown, "Utopia, Lard, and Many Questions." Originally published in 2017.

I read a *New Yorker* article about a failed Utopian reality TV show with great interest. In it a group of strangers was confined to about 600 acres on a peninsula in western Scotland, with the intent of establishing a new society from the ground up, at least for a year. Boredom, bickering, factionalism and cheating ensued.

First, I had a good time appreciating all of the poor choices made in setting things up. There were the obvious, material mistakes, like picking a location for scenery rather than livability, and apparently not consulting anyone knowledgeable about the realities of subsistence farming. But the larger mistake (if indeed the creators actually wanted any sort of harmony to spontaneously emerge) was conceptual. A group of strangers trying to make a new society in a severely food-limited environment have little chance of success. In fact, I would venture that an abundant surplus of calories is a prerequisite to social order. How different might the results have been had they been given better tools and soil, access to enough land for consistent hunting, and facilities for managing the livestock?

But, speaking of animals, all these considerations are secondary to the most important question: what happened to the pigs?

Infuriatingly, the article mentions them once, then never again, and I'm not going to watch twelve hours of what sounds like extremely depressing television to find out their fate. Anyways, I feel reasonably confident in assuming the participants killed them almost immediately. Without fences to keep them in, pigs can get up to all sorts of destructive mischief, and though they could probably scrounge up a living for themselves if given free run, they'd be less efficient about it than sheep. Even if an allotment of feed was provided for the pigs, it would make far more sense to repurpose it as human food.

When the pigs were killed, whether it was quickly or sometime later, was every little morsel of fat saved and rendered? Did it yield enough lard to use as the primary cooking fat? This may seem like a small thing, but when Ed and I spent a year eating exclusively food we'd grown the biggest challenge of those first dark

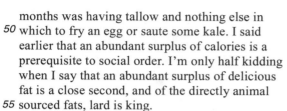

months was having tallow and nothing else in
50 which to fry an egg or saute some kale. I said
earlier that an abundant surplus of calories is a
prerequisite to social order. I'm only half kidding
when I say that an abundant surplus of delicious
fat is a close second, and of the directly animal
55 sourced fats, lard is king.

       You can use it to scramble eggs, fry
donuts, make a pie crust, or confit a pork
shoulder. It has a texture that evokes good butter
and a flavor that is at once savory and subtle
60 enough to use in scones or cookies. If you need to
feel virtuous, there are compelling suggestions
that lard derived from pastured hogs is
exceptionally high in vitamin D.

       It infuriates me that lard has so little
65 currency in our food system. Want to combat the
tropical deforestation and labor abuses associated
with palm and coconut oil cultivation? Replace
them with lard. Want a non-dairy source of fat
that is truly local? Lard is for you. Want to make
70 raising meat as environmentally sound as possible
by ensuring that every bit of each animal is used?
Lard.

       So, to summarize: lard is delicious and
probably critical to establishing a cohesive
75 society and you should all be eating it by the
spoonful; the next time someone wants to make a
show centered around subsistence they should
pay me a generous stipend to be a consultant; I'm
really leaning on questions as a rhetorical device
80 today.

Percent of Food Energy Contributed to the US Food Supply

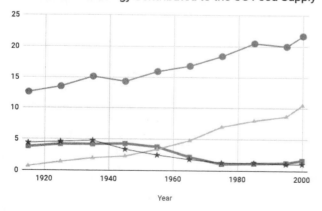

- ● All fats and oils
- ■ Lard and beef tallow
- ▲ Salad, cooking and other edible oils
- ★ Butter

31

Over the course of the passage, the primary focus shifts from

A) musings over food-supply issues in specific situations to a discussion of a related issue on a larger scale.

B) the poor choices made in setting up a TV show to the cooking mistakes made on the show.

C) analysis of a failed farming society to a demonstration of why society at large is failing.

D) a description of a what a utopian society requires to a discussion of what steps we can take to increase our chances of bringing about that utopian society.

32

As used in line 19, "venture" most nearly means

A) assert.

B) state without evidence.

C) make a bet.

D) agree wholeheartedly.

33

Which of the following does the author indicate as the worst mistake made in attempting to create a utopian society on TV?

A) a location chosen for the wrong reasons

B) a lack of access to food

C) failing to consult experts

D) the participants being strangers

CONTINUE ➤

34

Which choice provides the best evidence for the answer to the previous question?

A) Lines 6-7 ("Boredom, bickering… cheating ensued")

B) Lines 8-14 ("First, I had… subsistence farming")

C) Lines 16-21 ("A group of… social order")

D) Lines 21-27 ("How different… to the pigs")

35

Based on the passage, it is most likely that the author believes the participants on the TV show "killed [the pigs] almost immediately" (lines 33-34) primarily because

A) people who know very little about farming are likely to make decisions that would benefit them immediately even if these decisions might jeopardize their long-term success.

B) strangers are likely to make rash decisions when put together.

C) pigs can be a threat to human life when not properly contained.

D) it would be in their best interest to do so.

36

Based on his tone, which of the following attributes of lard is/are least important to the author?

A) its versatility in cooking

B) its texture and flavor

C) its vitamin D content

D) the environmental soundness of its use

37

As used in line 65, "currency" most nearly means

A) profit for its producers.

B) cost to consumers.

C) advantage.

D) prevalence.

38

The primary purpose of the eighth paragraph (lines 64-72) is to

A) convince the reader of the importance of making sustainable food choices.

B) give reasons for advocating a more widespread use of lard.

C) argue against the stigma of lard as unhealthy.

D) offer several alternatives to an infuriating problem.

39

Based on the graph, which of the following statements is true?

A) The number of grams of butter consumed in the US decreased from 1930 to 2000.

B) The percentage of food energy contributed by fat to the US food supply increased every decade between 1920 and 2000.

C) The volume of butter in the US in every decade from 1970 to 2000 was roughly the same as that of and lard and beef tallow over the same time period.

D) In 1940, all fats and oils contributed approximately 3 times as great a percentage of food energy as lard and beef tallow in the US.

CONTINUE ➡

40

Based on information in the passage, in which of the following ways would the author most likely reply to data shown in the graph?

A) "It may have been better for the environment if there had been an increase in lard's contribution to the food supply starting in the fifties rather than an increase in cooking and edible oils."

B) "The drop in butter's contribution to the food supply starting in the thirties represents a steady decline in the cohesiveness of US society."

C) "The consistent rise of fat in the US over these 85 years has alarming implications on national health."

D) "While the decrease in lard's contribution to the US food supply infuriates me, the rise in the contribution of overall fats clearly indicates that the US has been trending strongly towards becoming a utopia for nearly a century."

41

Which choice provides the best evidence for the answer to the previous question?

A) Lines 19-24 ("In fact, I... the livestock")

B) Lines 46-52 ("This may seem... social order")

C) Lines 52-63 ("I'm only half... vitamin D")

D) Lines 65-72 ("Want to combat... Lard")

Questions 42 - 52 are based on the following passage.

This passage is adapted from "Cold Mountain Streams Offer Climate Refuge" from the U.S. Geological Survey (USGS) website. The USGS is a branch of the Department of the Interior. Originally published 2016.

A new study offers hope for cold-water species in the face of climate change. The study, published today in the Proceedings of the
Line National Academy of Sciences, addresses a
5 longstanding paradox between predictions of widespread extinctions of cold-water species and a general lack of evidence for those extinctions despite decades of recent climate change.

The paper resulted from collaborative
10 research led by the U.S. Forest Service with partners including the U.S. Geological Survey, the National Ocean and Atmospheric Administration, University of Georgia and the Queensland University of Technology. The
15 research team drew information from huge stream-temperature and biological databases contributed by over 100 agencies and a USGS-run regional climate model to describe warming trends throughout 222,000 kilometers (138,000
20 miles) of streams in the northwestern United States.

The scientists found that over the last 40 years, stream temperatures warmed at the average rate of 0.10 degrees Celsius (0.18 degrees
25 Fahrenheit) per decade. This translates to thermal habitats shifting upstream at a rate of only 300-500 meters (0.18-0.31 miles) per decade in headwater mountain streams where many sensitive cold-water species currently live. The
30 authors are quick to point out that climate change is still detrimentally affecting the habitats of those species, but at a much slower rate than dozens of previous studies forecast. The results of this study indicate that many populations of cold-
35 water species will continue to persist this century and mountain landscapes will play an increasingly important role in that preservation.

CONTINUE

"The great irony is that the cold headwater streams that were believed to be most vulnerable to climate change appear to be the least vulnerable. Equally ironic is that we arrived at that insight simply by amassing, organizing and carefully analyzing large existing databases, rather than collecting new data that would have been far more expensive," said Dr. Daniel Isaak, lead author on the study with the U.S. Forest Service.

The results also indicate that resource managers will have sufficient time to complete extensive biological surveys of ecological communities in mountain streams so that conservation planning strategies can adequately address all species.

"One of the great complexities of restoring trout and salmon under a rapidly changing climate is understanding how this change plays out across the landscape. Dr. Isaak and his colleagues show that many mountain streams may be more resistant to temperature change than our models suggest and that is very good news. This provides us more time to effect the changes we need for long-term persistence of these populations," said Dr. Jack Williams, senior scientist for Trout Unlimited.

This study is complementary and builds upon the Cold-Water Climate Shield. This new study is unique as it describes current trends rather than relying on future model projections and addresses a broad scope of aquatic biodiversity in headwater streams (e.g., amphibians, sculpin and trout). In addition, the data density and geographic extent of this study is far greater than most previous studies because over 16,000 stream temperature sites were used with thousands of biological survey locations to provide precise information at scales relevant to land managers and conservationists.

42

This passage primarily serves to

A) describe the methods used in conducting a study.

B) summarize the findings of a study.

C) explain the details of an experiment.

D) draw new conclusions from an old study.

43

According to the passage, which of the following is true of cold-water species?

A) Scientists are offering them hope in the form of a way to face climate change.

B) We should strive to save them from extinction.

C) They don't appear to be dying off as quickly as scientists had predicted.

D) They are less affected by climate change than warm-water species.

44

Which of the following methods was used in collecting data for the study discussed in the passage?

A) executing a series of experiments

B) gathering existing information from many organizations

C) conducting geological surveys throughout the northwestern United States

D) sponsoring research by over 100 agencies

45

Which of the following can be most reasonably inferred from the passage?

A) Scientists had expected thermal habitats to shift upstream faster than 500 meters per decade in headwater mountain streams.

B) Scientists had expected thermal habitats to shift upstream more slowly than 300 meters per decade in headwater mountain streams.

C) Scientists expect stream temperatures to continue warming at an average rate of 0.10 degrees Celsius per decade.

D) Based on this study, funding will shift away from preserving cold-water species to more pressing matters.

CONTINUE →

46

Which of the following statements would opponents of funding climate-change research most likely use to support their position?

A) Lines 21-25 ("The scientists found... per decade")

B) Lines 32-33 ("but at a much... studies forecast")

C) Lines 54-57 ("One of the great... the landscape")

D) Lines 65-71 ("This new study... sculpin and trout")

47

Dr. Isaak most likely uses the words "irony" (line 38) and "ironic" (line 41) to

A) highlight the importance of the results and method of the study.

B) indicate his skepticism toward the study and its results.

C) emphasize what an unparalleled achievement the study was.

D) draw attention to the surprising nature of what he is saying.

48

As used in line 40, "vulnerable" most nearly means

A) ardent.

B) adaptive.

C) indomitable.

D) susceptible.

49

It can be most reasonably inferred that the author of the passage hopes that the findings of the study will lead to

A) further research that scientists had thought there might not be enough time for.

B) immediate action to save cold-water species.

C) a greater level of funding for conservation strategies that could adequately address all cold-water species.

D) the slowing and eventual stop of climate

50

Which choice provides the best evidence for the answer to the previous question?

A) Lines 29-37 ("The authors... that preservation")

B) Lines 48-53 ("The results... all species")

C) Lines 54-61 ("One of the... very good news")

D) Lines 61-63 ("This provides... these populations")

51

Which of the following advantages does the author indicate the study discussed in the passage has over other studies on the same subject?

A) The study discussed in the passage cost less money than other similar studies.

B) The study discussed in the passage returned definitive, positive results.

C) The study discussed in the passage dealt with present data rather than predictions of the future.

D) The study discussed in the passage gathered data from every region in the United States.

CONTINUE

52

Which choice provides the best evidence for the answer to the previous question?

A) Lines 14-21 ("The research team… United States")

B) Lines 54-64 ("One of the great… Trout Unlimited")

C) Lines 66-71 ("This new study… sculpin and trout")

D) Lines 71-77 ("In addition… and conservationists")

STOP
**If you finish before time is called, you may check your work on this section only.
Do not turn to any other section.**

Writing and Language Test
35 Minutes, 44 Questions

DIRECTIONS

Each passage or pair of passages below is followed by a number of questions. For some questions, you will consider how the passage might be revised to improve the expression of ideas. For other questions, you will consider how the passage might be edited to correct errors in sentence structure, usage, or punctuation. A passage or a question may be accompanied by one or more graphics (such as a table or graph) that you will consider as you make revising and editing decisions.

Some questions will direct you to an underlined portion of the passage. Other questions will direct you to a location in a passage or ask you to think about the passage as a whole.

After reading each passage, choose the answer to each question that most effectively improves the quality of writing in the passage or that makes the passage conform to the conventions of standard written English. Many questions include a "NO CHANGE" option. Choose that option if you think the best choice is to leave the relevant portion of the passage as it is.

Questions 1-11 are based on the following passage.

This passage is adapted from Jessica Riskin, "Frolicsome Engines: The Long Prehistory of Artificial Intelligence," originally published online on *The Public Domain Review* under a Creative Commons Attribution-ShareAlike 3.0.

How old are the fields of robotics and artificial intelligence? 1 It has a prehistory; a tradition of machines that imitate living and intelligent processes, stretching back centuries and, depending how you count, even millennia.

1

A) NO CHANGE

B) It has a prehistory, a tradition of machines that imitate living and intelligent processes, stretching

C) They have prehistories; traditions of machines that imitate living and intelligent processes, stretching

D) They have prehistories, traditions of machines that imitate living and intelligent processes, stretching

CONTINUE

The first-century-AD engineer Hero of Alexandria described lots of automata. **2** Many performed a variety of actions as water passed through them that was carried by elaborately intricate networks of siphons which activated these actions, especially figures of birds drinking, fluttering, and chirping. A late twelfth-century example of this kind is a peacock fountain for hand-washing, in which flowing water triggers little figures to offer the washer first a dish of perfumed soap powder, then a hand towel. Such hydraulic automata became **3** global on the grounds of palaces and wealthy estates. So-called "frolicsome engines" were to be found as early as the late thirteenth century at the French chateau of Hesdin, the account books of which mention mechanical monkeys and other animals. At the beginning of the 17th Century, Tomaso Francini built hydraulic grottoes devoted to the Greek pantheon and **4** their adventures. Mercury played a trumpet and Orpheus his lyre: Perseus freed Andromeda from her dragon.

2

A) NO CHANGE

B) Many were figures of birds with elaborate networks of siphons that activated various actions, such as drinking, fluttering, and chirping.

C) Many figures of birds drinking, fluttering, and chirping made up the bulk of these siphon-activated machines, which siphon networks were elaborately crafted.

D) Drinking, fluttering, and chirping, these machines with elaborate networks of siphons to activate with water their various actions were often birds.

3

A) NO CHANGE
B) widespread
C) boundless
D) ubiquitous

4

A) NO CHANGE

B) adventures: Mercury played a trumpet and Orpheus his lyre, Perseus

C) adventures, Mercury played a trumpet and Orpheus his lyre; Perseus

D) adventures: Mercury played a trumpet and Orpheus his lyre; Perseus

CONTINUE ➡

5 Mankind began to wonder what lessons could be learned from machines: perhaps they 6 might genuinely model the workings of nature. The French philosopher René Descartes made this case powerfully during the 1640s, arguing that the entire world was essentially machinery composed of moving parts and could be understood in just the way a clockmaker understands a clock. His work was foundational to modern science in general, and to modern physiology in particular.

With the sixteenth-century advent of the pinned cylinder—a barrel with pins or bars sticking out, such as in a music box—even 7 more, complex lifelike machines were possible.

5

Which choice most effectively provides a transition from the last paragraph and sets up the main point of this paragraph?

A) NO CHANGE

B) These machines were truly remarkable:

C) These machines helped inspire the idea that perhaps automata accomplished something deeper than merely entertaining tricks:

D) People flocked from miles around to see these machines;

6

A) NO CHANGE

B) could genuinely model the workings of nature.

C) could be said to genuinely model the workings of nature.

D) genuinely modeled the workings and doings of nature.

7

A) NO CHANGE

B) more complex, lifelike machines

C) more, complex, lifelike machines

D) more complex, lifelike, machines

CONTINUE

8 <u>Additionally</u>, people began to design automata that actually enacted the tasks they appeared to perform. The first simulative automata were designed by a Frenchman named Jacques Vaucanson. Two were musicians, a "Piper" and a "Flutist." 9 <u>Vaucanson's creation's</u> craftsmanship and engineering quickly became the talk of Europe. The flutist had lips that flexed, jointed fingers, and lungs made of bellows that gave three different blowing pressures. It was the first automaton musician actually to play an instrument, rather than being a music box with a decorative figure.

[1] How should we regard the Renaissance frolicsome engines, the android musicians and artists? [2] They can certainly be seen as the ancestors of modern robotics and artificial intelligence. [3] These automata were

8

A) NO CHANGE
B) Regardless,
C) Consequently,
D) However,

9

A) NO CHANGE
B) Vaucansons' creations'
C) Vaucansons' creation's
D) Vaucanson's creations'

CONTINUE

also expressions of a very different mode of understanding. [4] It is hard to imagine that our own conceptual frameworks will one day seem as remote and exotic as an Aristotelian account of Hero's siphons seems to us, but they surely will. [5] 10 Can knowing this perhaps help us to imagine how future generations will understand the "workings of nature"? 11

The writer would like to conclude with a sentence that flows logically from the rest of the passage, makes the reader think about the future, and lends value to the discussion of the history of robotics. Which choice best accomplishes these goals?

A) NO CHANGE

B) Considering the leaps and bounds we've taken in the fields of robotics and artificial intelligence, who knows what amazing machines we have in our future?

C) Perhaps knowing how far we've come will give us the confidence to move onward.

D) Maybe in a few generations, robots will help us to keep everyone on the planet well fed; that's a future worth fighting for.

11

To make the paragraph most logical, sentence 4 should be placed

A) where it is now.

B) before sentence 1.

C) before sentence 2.

D) before sentence 3.

Questions 12-22 are based on the following passage.

This passage is adapted from Garth Brown, "The Cows of Winter."

I don't think I'm particularly prone to anthropomorphizing livestock. **12** I do think they have states that vary, I doubt very much these are similar enough to the commonly understood meanings of the words "emotion" or "mood" to make these words useful. **13** Although not ascribing to cows the existential concerns particular to humans does not mean I don't worry about them. While **14** thats easy for me to question how much concern for the future they have or if their attachment to the other members of their herd **15** resemble affection, I am confident that they at least experience physical discomfort.

12

A) NO CHANGE

B) I do think they have states that vary; but

C) While I do think they have states that vary;

D) While I do think they have states that vary,

13

A) NO CHANGE

B) On the other hand,

C) However,

D) To wit:

14

A) NO CHANGE

B) it's

C) its

D) that's

15

A) NO CHANGE

B) resembles

C) might resemble

D) do resemble

CONTINUE

So, while I don't lie awake worrying about whether or not the cows like 16 me; I'm confident of their indifference, when the temperature is forecast to drop well below zero I can't help but imagine how I would feel if I were out in the cold without any blankets. 17 But inevitably, when I go outside the next morning,

16

A) NO CHANGE

B) me—I'm confident of their indifference—when the temperature is forecast to drop well below zero,

C) me (I'm confident of their indifference) when the temperature is forecast to drop well below zero

D) me, I'm confident of their indifference, the temperature is forecast to drop well below zero, it's then that

17

At this point, the writer is considering adding this sentence.

> On these nights, sleep can be
> slow to come.

Should the writer make this addition here?

A) Yes, because it provides a contrast to a statement made in the previous sentence that shows the writer's level of concern.

B) Yes, because it shows something the writer and the cows have in common.

C) No, because this paragraph is about the cattle, not the writer.

D) No, because it neither adequately summarizes the paragraph's central argument nor provides an example that supports it.

CONTINUE

18 they will all be standing around munching on hay, and I will be reminded again of how different not just their inner lives are, but also that, despite some commonalities, their physical experiences, even those within the same environment, drastically differ from my own.

    Unlike 19 there human brothers and sisters, the cow is a ruminant, which means that the largest of her four stomachs (or, more accurately, the largest of the four chambers that together make up her one stomach) is full of fermenting hay. If you've ever dug into a compost pile in the middle of winter only to find it 20 smoldering, you can appreciate how much heat fermentation can make. A well-fed cow has this reaction continuously occurring within her, which, when coupled with her subcutaneous fat and shaggy winter coat, keep her plenty warm in conditions in which my nose and fingers feel like they're going to fall off after twenty minutes.

18

Which choice best supports an assertion made at the end of the sentence and fits the way the writer has characterized the cattle earlier in the paragraph?

A) NO CHANGE

B) they will be running as fast as they can to keep warm,

C) they will rush to greet me as though it were sixty-eight degrees and sunny,

D) they will be going about their daily chores as well,

19

A) NO CHANGE

B) their

C) her

D) hers

20

A) NO CHANGE

B) boiling,

C) oppressive,

D) steaming,

CONTINUE

The calves born last spring have access to a barn, but sheet metal walls and an open door don't do much to keep out the cold. They do fine with this, and the cows, steers, and bull do fine with the natural windbreaks provided by [21] <u>plants, trees, and bushes</u> along the fenceline. [22] <u>I do fine too, knowing my cattle are safe and comfortable enough.</u>

21

A) NO CHANGE

B) trees, oaks, and spruce

C) large rocks, trees, and boulders

D) trees, bushes, and large rocks

22

The writer would like to conclude with an example that flows naturally from the examples before it and emphasizes the relationship the writer has with the cows, as established in the rest of the passage. Which choice best accomplishes these goals?

A) NO CHANGE

B) I do fine too, though I wouldn't without my house and fire and bed and quilts and long underwear.

C) I sure wouldn't if I were in their hoofs.

D) I do fine with my house and fire and bed and quilts and long underwear.

CONTINUE

Questions 23-33 are based on the following passage.

This passage is adapted from Deirdre Loughridge and Thomas Patteson, "Cat Pianos, Sound-Houses, and Other Imaginary Musical Instruments," originally published online on *The Public Domain Review* under a Creative Commons Attribution-ShareAlike 3.0.

Deprived of physical reality, 23 <u>one might suppose imaginary musical instruments to have no place in the cultural histories that a museum of musical instruments aims to preserve.</u> 24 <u>Yet,</u> in their own strange ways, imaginary musical instruments exist. No 25 <u>fewer than</u> instruments you hold in your hand, imaginary instruments act as interfaces between mind and world, limning the edges of what we may think and do.

23

A) NO CHANGE

B) you might suppose imaginary musical instruments to have no place in the cultural histories that a museum of musical instruments aims to preserve.

C) imaginary musical instruments, one, having no place in the cultural histories that a museum of musical instruments aims to preserve, might suppose.

D) imaginary musical instruments, one might suppose, have no place in the cultural histories that a museum of musical instruments aims to preserve.

24

A) NO CHANGE

B) Albeit,

C) Notwithstanding the foregoing,

D) On the other hand,

25

A) NO CHANGE

B) less than

C) smaller than

D) less then

CONTINUE

One such 26 device is a curious, nearly unknown instrument, called: the cat piano. The earliest known image of a set of cats arrayed as sound-producing elements 27 for activating by the fingers dates to the late sixteenth century, that is, over a hundred years before the invention of the piano. 28 The image comes from an emblem book, Johann Theodor de Bry's *Emblemata saecularia mira et iucunda uarietate saeculi huius mores ita exprimentia ut sodalitatum symbolis...* (1596), and shows a motley ensemble of animals and confused musicians with a subtitle alluding to an ancient king with the ears of a donkey.

26

A) NO CHANGE

B) device, is a curious, nearly unknown instrument called

C) device is a curious, nearly, unknown instrument, called

D) device is a curious, nearly unknown instrument called

27

A) NO CHANGE

B) to be activated

C) that one should have activated

D) that had been activated

28

The writer is considering deleting the following sentence. Should the writer make this change?

A) Yes, because the image was explained clearly enough in the previous sentence.

B) Yes, because it is irrelevant to the rest of the paragraph.

C) No, because it sets up the transition to the next paragraph.

D) No, because it provides information that will impress most readers.

CONTINUE ➡

From a comical image of cacophony, the cat piano underwent a series of unexpected functional transformations. By the 1650s, the device had come 29 <u>so far so</u> to be a legendary music therapy: supposedly, an Italian prince was cured of his melancholy by the device when he found its meowing cats, triggered by driving spikes through their tails, irresistibly funny.

The eighteenth-century Parisian Louis-Bertrand Castel invoked the instrument to prove his contention that what mattered in music was the combination of sounds, not sounds in their own right. The fact that one could make music from the individually 30 <u>weird yelps</u> of pained cats proved that "sounds on their own possess no beauty, and that all the beauties of music come not from sound, but from the melodic sequence and the harmonic combination of these sounds, multiplied and varied in proportion."

31 <u>The imagination is often figured as a site of infinite possibility, free</u> to create without regard to material 32 <u>constrictions</u>. The museum of imaginary musical instruments illuminates not only the intersection of reality and fantasy, but also the unknown history of the imagination.

29

A) NO CHANGE

B) so far

C) as far

D) as far as

30

A) NO CHANGE

B) homely wails

C) random calls

D) ugly cries

31

Which choice provides the best transition from the previous paragraph to this one?

A) NO CHANGE

B) The imagination is a mysterious instrument, free

C) The harmony of the imagination is also multiplied and varied, mysterious and free

D) The pained screams of the human imagination cry out for freedom

32

A) NO CHANGE

B) boundaries

C) bonds

D) limitations

CONTINUE ➡

33 It reveals numerous paths of inventive thought not taken, paths covered up by years of "progress," but which, when cleared off, might yet lead us back to something new.

A) NO CHANGE

B) Numerous paths, paths covered up by years of "progress," but which, in being cleared off, might yet lead us back to something new, paths of inventive thought which have not been taken are revealed by the museum.

C) It reveals numerous paths covered up by years of "progress" which, when cleared off, might yet lead us back to something new, which paths are of inventive thought; they have not been taken.

D) The museum makes paths clear, numerous ones of inventive thought no one has taken, which might be because they've been covered up by years of "progress" and need to be cleared off, after which they—the paths, that is—might still lead us back to something new.

CONTINUE

Questions 34 - 44 are based on the following passage.

This passage is adapted from A. A. Milne, "Goldfish," originally published in 1920.

Goldfish are a symbol of tranquility or futility according to their position in the home. Outside the home, they may have stood for 34 <u>courage, constancy, or devoting one's life to a cause;</u> I cannot tell. I may only speak of them as I find 35 <u>them now; in</u> the garden or in the drawing-room. In their lily-leaved pool, they remind me of sundials and lavender and 36 <u>old delightful things</u>. But in their cheap glass bowl, they remind me of doilies and sofas and all that is hopeless. It is hard that the goldfish himself should have so little choice in the matter.

34

A) NO CHANGE

B) acting with courage, constancy, or with devotion;

C) a life of courage or of constancy or devotion;

D) dare-devil courage, for constancy or for devotion;

35

A) NO CHANGE

B) them now: which is to say, in

C) them now: in

D) them now in

36

Which choice best supports a central argument of the paragraph and sets up the next sentence?

A) NO CHANGE

B) all that is old and delightful.

C) all that is peaceful.

D) all that is wonderful.

CONTINUE

In addition to their free will, you must have pondered why, of all diets, we should feed them ants' eggs. I 37 suppose—I am lamentably ignorant on these matters, that there was a time when goldfish roamed the sea or the river, fighting for existence, and Nature showed them the food which suited them. I have often come across ants' nests in my travels, but never when swimming. 38 In rivers, pools, and lakes I have wandered, but Nature has never put ants' eggs in my way.

Yet, since it would seem that he has acquired the taste, it can only be that the taste has come to the goldfish with captivity. The old wild goldfish (this is my theory: see figure 1) was a terrible beast. 39 He could not have been kept within the limits of the terrace pool. Kept in the

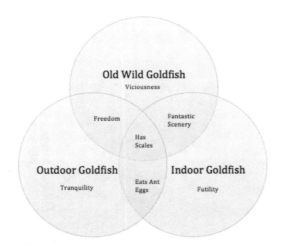

37

A) NO CHANGE

B) suppose I am lamentably ignorant on these matters,

C) suppose; I am lamentably ignorant on these matters;

D) suppose (but I am lamentably ignorant on these matters) that

38

A) NO CHANGE

B) In rivers, pools, and lakes, I have wandered

C) In, rivers, pools, and lakes I have wandered,

D) In rivers, pools, and, lakes I have wandered,

39

Which choice is best supported by information in the diagram?

A) NO CHANGE

B) Practically the only thing he would have in common with his docile brethren is a set of scales.

C) He did not take his lack of freedom lightly.

D) The freedom and fantastic scenery he enjoyed made him vicious.

CONTINUE

terrace pool, he 40 <u>dragged</u> in the shrieking child as she leant to feed him. Ants' eggs were given him to quell his spirit, and, just as a man, given the need, can get up a passion even for the vilest of medicines, 41 <u>similarly,</u> the goldfish has grown in captivity to welcome the once-hated omelette.

Let us consider now the goldfish in the house: 42 <u>his diet is the same, but how different his surroundings!</u> The drawing-room may not

---

40

A) NO CHANGE

B) would drag

C) has dragged

D) will drag

41

A) NO CHANGE

B) thus

C) so

D) thence

42

Which choice provides the best transition from the previous paragraph to this one?

A) NO CHANGE

B) his life is nothing like that of the outdoor goldfish!

C) he loves ants' eggs for entirely different reasons.

D) the goldfish outside may have a bigger space, but the indoor goldfish has the most incredible view!

CONTINUE ➡

seem much to you, but to him this impressionist picture through the curved glass must be amazing. Let not the outdoor goldfish boast of his freedom. What does the outside fish know of the vistas which open to his happier 43 brother? The indoor goldfish passes jauntily from china dog to ottoman and from ottoman to piano. Ah, here is life! It may be that in the course of years he will get bored by it (indeed, for that reason I always advocate giving him a glance at the dining-room on Wednesdays), but his first day in the bowl must be the opening of an undreamt of heaven to him.

      44 Alas, that I could be like that most glorious of symbols, the goldfish!

43

Which choice most effectively combines the sentences at the underlined portion?

A) brother as he passes jauntily from china dog to ottoman and from ottoman to piano?

B) brother, the very same brother who jauntily passes wonder after wonder as he swims from china dog to ottoman and then from ottoman to piano?

C) brother, whilst he passes jauntily from china dog to ottoman and from ottoman to piano?

D) brother, who gets to pass so much great

44

Which choice most effectively concludes the passage in a way that flows logically from the previous paragraph and relates to the beginning of the passage?

A) NO CHANGE

B) Given these brief facts on goldfish, I hope it is now clear that their position in the house determines what they represent: tranquility or futility.

C) Now that I have thought it out, I can see that I was wrong about the indoor goldfish. I recognize now that he is not a symbol of futility; he is a symbol of fortune.

D) The outdoor goldfish on his first day in the pool, however, would likely not appreciate the freedom he has over his indoor companion.

STOP

**If you finish before time is called, you may check your work on this section only.
Do not turn to any other section.**

No Test Material On This Page

Math Test – No Calculator
25 Minutes, 20 Questions

DIRECTIONS

For questions 1 – 15, solve each problem, choose the best answer from the choices provided, and fill in the corresponding circle on your answer sheet. **For questions 16 – 20,** solve the problem and enter your answer in the grid on the answer sheet. You may use any available space in your test booklet for scratch work.

NOTES

1. The use of a calculator **is not permitted**.

2. All variables and expressions used represent real numbers unless otherwise noted.

3. Figures provided in this test are drawn to scale unless otherwise indicated.

4. All figures lie in a plane unless otherwise indicated.

5. Unless otherwise indicated, the domain of a given function f is the set of all real numbers for x for which $f(x)$ is a real number.

REFERENCE

$A = \pi r^2$
$C = 2\pi r$

$A = lw$

$A = \frac{1}{2}bh$

$c^2 = a^2 + b^2$

Special Right Triangles

$V = lwh$

$V = \pi r^2 h$

$V = \frac{4}{3}\pi r^3$

$V = \frac{1}{3}\pi r^3 h$

$V = \frac{1}{3}lwh$

The number of degrees of arc in a circle is 360.
The number of radians of arc in a circle is 2π.
The sum of the measures in degrees of the angle of a triangle is 180.

CONTINUE

1

Tommy wants to purchase concert tickets from an online website. The website charges a one-time service fee for processing the purchase of the tickets. The equation $P = 7x + 22$ represents the total amount P, in dollars, Tommy will pay for x tickets. What does 22 represent?

A) The total amount, in dollars, Tommy will pay for one ticket

B) The price of one ticket, in dollars

C) The total amount, in dollars, Tommy will pay for any number of tickets

D) The amount of the service fee, in dollars

2

Which of the following is equivalent to $4(x + 9) - 6$?

A) $2(2x + 18) - 18$

B) $4(x + 5) - 8$

C) $2(2x + 16) - 2$

D) $4(x + 2) + 28$

3

A video game console company is selling a new console in a standard edition and a collector's edition. The box of the standard edition has a volume of 45 cubic inches, and the box of the collector's edition has a volume of 60 cubic inches. The company receives an order for 235 consoles and the total volume of the order to be shipped is 3,500 cubic inches. Which of the following systems of equations can be used to determine the number of standard edition games, a, and collector's edition games, c, that were ordered?

A) $235 - a = c$
$45c + 60a = 3500$

B) $235 - a = c$
$45a + 60c = 3500$

C) $a - c = 235$
$45a + 60c = 3500$

D) $a - c = 235$
$45c + 60a = 3500$

4

What is the sum of the complex numbers $3 + 4i$ and $6 + 11i$, where $i = \sqrt{-1}$?

A) 24

B) $24i$

C) $18 + 44i$

D) $9 + 15i$

CONTINUE

5

$$25x^2 - 4 = (ax + b)(ax - b)$$

In the equation above, a and b are constants. Which of the following could be the value of b^2?

A) 4

B) -4

C) 2

D) -2

6

Which of the following is the graph of the equation $y = \frac{1}{2}x - 3$ in the xy-plane?

A)

B)

C)

D)

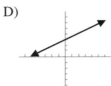

7

If $x = \frac{4}{5}y$ and $x = 16$, what is the value of $2y - 17$?

A) -2.2

B) 15

C) 23

D) 33

CONTINUE

8

x	$a(x)$	$b(x)$
5	-4	1
6	-3	-9
7	-2	-5
8	1	7
9	4	5

The table above shows some values of the functions a and b. For which value of x is $a(x) - b(x) = x$?

A) 6

B) 7

C) 8

D) 9

9

If $\sqrt{t} + \sqrt{25} + \sqrt{4} = \sqrt{121}$, what is the value of t?

A) $\sqrt{4}$

B) $\sqrt{92}$

C) 4

D) 16

10

Which of the following is equivalent to $\frac{5x^2 + 15x}{5x + 10}$?

A) $x + 5$

B) $x + 1 - \frac{10}{5x+10}$

C) $2x + \frac{10}{5x+10}$

D) $x - \frac{10}{5x+10}$

11

Maggie is training for the Olympics. Her goal is to swim an average of at least 75 kilometers per week for 5 weeks. She swam 48 kilometers the first week, 66 kilometers the second week, 79 kilometers the third week, and 81 kilometers the 4th week. Which inequality can be used to represent the number of kilometers, x, Maggie should swim on the 5th week to meet her goal?

A) $\frac{48}{5} + \frac{66}{5} + \frac{79}{5} + \frac{81}{5} + x \geq 75$

B) $48 + 66 + 79 + 81 + x \geq 5(75)$

C) $48 + 66 + 79 + 81 \geq 75x$

D) $\frac{48+66+79+81}{4} + x \geq 75$

CONTINUE

12

$$3x^2 - 6x = w$$

In the equation above, w is a constant. If the equation has no real solutions, which of the following could be the value of w?

A) 5

B) 2

C) -3

D) -5

13

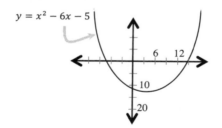

$y = x^2 - 6x - 5$

Which of the following is an equivalent form of the equation of the graph shown in the xy-plane above from which the coordinate of vertex A can be identified as constants in the equation?

A) $y = (x - 3)^2 - 14$

B) $y = (x - 5)(x - 1)$

C) $y = (x - 6)(x + 1)$

D) $y = x(x - 6) - 5$

14

A construction company is buying tile and grout from its supplier. The supplier will deliver no more than 550 pounds in a shipment. Each box of tile weighs 25.7 pounds, and each container of grout weights 13.25 pounds. The construction company wants to buy at least three times as many boxes of tile as containers of grout. Let t represent the number of boxes of tile, and let g represent the number of containers of grout, where t and g are nonnegative integers. Which of the following systems of inequalities best represent this situation?

A) $25.7t + 13.25g \leq 550$
$\quad t \geq 3g$

B) $25.7t + 13.25g \leq 550$
$\quad 3t \geq g$

C) $77.1t + 13.25g \leq 550$
$\quad t \geq 3g$

D) $77.1t + 13.25g \leq 550$
$\quad 3t \geq g$

15

Which of the following is equivalent to $(x + \frac{y}{5})^2$?

A) $x^2 + \frac{y^2}{5}$

B) $x^2 + \frac{y^2}{25}$

C) $x^2 + \frac{2xy}{5} + \frac{y^2}{25}$

D) $x^2 + \frac{xy}{5} + \frac{y^2}{25}$

CONTINUE ➡

16

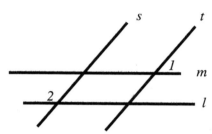

In the figure above, lines l and m are parallel and lines s and t are parallel. If the measure of $\angle 2$ is $\angle 125°$, what is the measure of $\angle 1$?

17

$$\frac{4}{7}p = \frac{12}{5}$$

What value of p is the solution of the equation above?

18

If $a = 5\sqrt{7}$ and $3a = \sqrt{7x}$, what is the value of x?

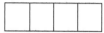

19

In triangle ABC, the measure of $\angle B$ is $90°$, $AB = 9$ and $AC = 15$. Triangle DEF is similar to triangle ABC, where vertices $D, E,$ and F correspond to vertices $A, B,$ and C, respectively, and each side of triangle is DEF is $\frac{1}{3}$ the length of the corresponding side of triangle ABC. What is the value of $\sin D$?

20

A rectangle was altered by increasing its length by 50 percent and decreasing its width by x percent. If these alterations decreased the area of the rectangle by 15 percent, what is the value of x? (Round to the nearest tenth)

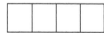

STOP
If you finish before time is called, you may check your work on this section only.
Do not turn to any other section.

Math Test – Calculator
55 Minutes, 38 Questions

DIRECTIONS

For questions 1 – 30, solve each problem, choose the best answer from the choices provided, and fill in the corresponding circle on your answer sheet. **For questions 31 – 38**, solve the problem and enter your answer in the grid on the answer sheet. You may use any available space in your test booklet for scratch work.

NOTES

1. The use of a calculator **is permitted**.

2. All variables and expressions used represent real numbers unless otherwise noted.

3. Figures provided in this test are drawn to scale unless otherwise indicated.

4. All figures lie in a plane unless otherwise indicated.

5. Unless otherwise indicated, the domain of a given function f is the set of all real numbers for x for which $f(x)$ is a real number.

REFERENCE

$A = \pi r^2$
$C = 2\pi r$

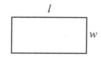

$A = lw$

$A = \frac{1}{2}bh$

$c^2 = a^2 + b^2$

Special Right Triangles

$V = lwh$

$V = \pi r^2 h$

$V = \frac{4}{3}\pi r^3$

$V = \frac{1}{3}\pi r^3 h$

$V = \frac{1}{3}lwh$

The number of degrees of arc in a circle is 360.
The number of radians of arc in a circle is 2π.
The sum of the measures in degrees of the angle of a triangle is 180.

CONTINUE

1

	Tea	Coffee	Total
Men	8	13	21
Women	5	12	17
Total	13	25	38

The table above shows the kinds of beverages that men and women prefer to drink in the morning. What fraction of men prefers to drink coffee in the morning?

A) $\frac{13}{21}$

B) $\frac{13}{38}$

C) $\frac{13}{25}$

D) $\frac{21}{38}$

2

$$(x^2 + 4) - (-2x^2 + 5)$$

Which of the following expressions is equivalent to the one above?

A) $-x^2 + 9$

B) $-x^2 - 1$

C) $3x^2 + 9$

D) $3x^2 - 1$

3

A certain package requires 5 centimeters of tape to be closed securely. What is the maximum number of packages of this type that can be secured with 6 meters of tape? (1 meter =100 cm)

A) 120

B) 150

C) 300

D) 600

4

A market researcher selected 300 people at random from a group of people who indicated that they liked a certain recording artist. The 300 people were shown a Broadway show based on the recording artist and then asked whether they liked or disliked the Broadway show. Of the surveyed, 75% said they disliked the show. Which of the following inferences can appropriately be drawn from this survey result?

A) Most people who dislike the artist will like this show.

B) Most people who like this artist will dislike the show.

C) At least 75% of people who go see the shows will dislike this show.

D) At least 75% of people who like recording artists will dislike this show.

CONTINUE

287

5

Which of the following ordered pairs (x, y) satisfies the inequality $4x - y > 4$?

   I. $(1, 1)$
   II. $(2, 4)$
   III. $(3, 2)$

A) I only

B) III only

C) I and II only

D) II and III only

6

In the equation $(ax - 5)^2 = 49$, a is a constant. If $x = -4$ is one solution to the equation, what is a possible value of a?

A) 3

B) 2

C) -3

D) $-\frac{1}{2}$

CONTINUE

Questions 7 and 8 refer to the following information.

Hours of Sunlight Intake vs. Height of Plant

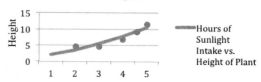

Hours of sunlight

The scatterplot above shows the height of plants in centimeters, with respect to their average hours of sunlight intake. The line of best fit is also shown.

7

According to the scatterplot, which of the following statements is true about the relationship between a planet's average hours of sunlight intake and its height?

A) Plants that intake more sunlight tend to have shorter heights.

B) Plants that intake less sunlight tend to have taller heights.

C) Plants that intake less sunlight tend to have shorter heights.

D) Plants that intake more sunlight tend to have fuller flowers.

8

A botanist has discovered a new plant that takes in an average of 4.5 hours of sunlight per day. According to the line of best fit, which of the following best approximates the height of the plant in centimeters?

A) 1.6

B) 5.5

C) 8.7

D) 10.2

CONTINUE

9

$$6ax + 6b - 9 = 15$$

Based on the equation above, what is the value of $ax + b$?

A) 1

B) 4

C) 36

D) 144

10

Juliet spent 35% of her 8-hour workday answering phone calls. How many minutes of her workday did she spend answering phone calls?

A) 2.8

B) 21

C) 148

D) 168

11

Dara is at a fruit stand and he is deciding what fruit to buy. He notices that the oranges and apples are on sale. He wants to only buy 25 fruit in total and he only has $12.25. The apples cost $0.75 each and oranges cost $1.25. Which of the following systems of equations can be used to determine the number of apples, a, and the number of oranges, x, Dara bought?

A) $25 - x = a$
   $0.75a + 1.25x = 12.25$

B) $25 - x = a$
   $0.75x + 1.25a = 12.25$

C) $a - x = 25$
   $0.75a + 1.25x = 12.25$

D) $a - x = 25$
   $0.75x + 1.25a = 12.25$

12

A customer paid $42.00 for a jacket after a 7.25 percent sales tax was added. What was the price of the jacket before the sales tax was added?

A) $24.35

B) $39.16

C) $38.95

D) $45.05

CONTINUE

13

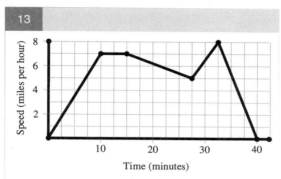

Valerie hiked on a trail for forty minutes, and her time and speed are shown on the graph above. According to the graph, which of the following statements is NOT true concerning Valerie's hike?

A) Valerie ran at a constant speed for 5 minutes.

B) Valerie's speed reached maximum during the last 20 minutes.

C) Valerie's speed was decreasing for a longer period of time than it was increasing.

D) Valerie's speed increased at a constant rate during the last 10 minutes.

14

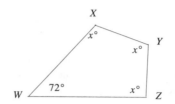

In the figure above, what is the value of $2x$?

A) 288

B) 96

C) 192

D) 72

CONTINUE

15

If 25 one-cent coins were stacked on top of each other in a column, the column would be approximately $4\frac{4}{5}$ inches tall. At this rate, which of the following is closest to the number of one-cent coins it would take to make an 11-inch-tall column?

A) 12

B) 60

C) 40

D) 120

16

If $a - b = 6$ and $\frac{b}{6} = 4$, what is the value of $a + b$?

A) 24

B) 30

C) 42

D) 54

17

$$y = 152 + 8.99x$$

The equation above models the total cost y, in dollars, that a company charges a customer to rent a jet ski for one day and drive the jet ski for x hours. The total cost consists of a flat fee plus a charge per hour ridden. When the equation is graphed in the xy-plane, what does the y-intercept of the graph represent in terms of the model?

A) A flat fee of $152

B) A charge per hour of $8.99

C) Total daily charges of $160.99

D) A charge per hour of $152

CONTINUE

18

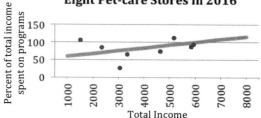

Income and Percent of Total Expenses Spent on Programs for Eight Pet-care Stores in 2016

The scatterplot above shows data for eight pet-care stores along with the line of best fit. For the store with the least percent of total expenses spent on programs, which of the following is closest to the difference of the actual percent and the percent predicted by the line of best fit?

A) 25%

B) 50%

C) 75%

D) 100%

Questions 19 and 20 refer to the following information.

$$\text{Ideal gas law: } T = \frac{PV}{nR}$$

$$\text{Density: } D = \frac{M}{V}$$

The equation above is the ideal gas law equation and the equation below is the equation for density. Both equations are used in both chemistry and physics.

19

Based on the ideal gas law formula, what is P in terms of T?

A) $P = \frac{TV}{nR}$

B) $P = \frac{nRT}{V}$

C) $P = \frac{nRV}{T}$

D) $P = \frac{nR}{TV}$

20

Based on both equations, which of the following is equivalent to V^2?

A) $\frac{PTM}{nRD}$

B) $\frac{PTD}{nRM}$

C) $\frac{nRTD}{PM}$

D) $\frac{nRTM}{PD}$

CONTINUE

21

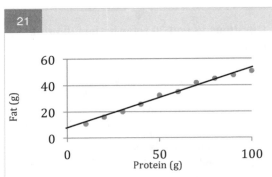

The scatterplot above shows the numbers of grams of both total protein and fat for ten protein bars. The line of best fit for the data is also shown. According to the line of best fit, which of the following is closest to the predicted increase in the total fat in grams for every increase of 1 gram in total protein?

A) 0.5

B) 1.0

C) 1.5

D) 2.5

22

Percent of Residents Who Earned a Bachelor's Degree or Higher

County	Percent of residents
County A	43.5%
County B	27.3%
County C	17.1%
County D	35.8%
County E	38.3%
County F	22.9%
County G	32.4%
County H	19.7%
County I	15.8%

A survey was given to residents of all counties in the state of California asking if they had earned a bachelor's degree or higher. The results from 9 of the counties are given the table above. The median percent of residents who earned a bachelor's degree or higher for all counties in California was 26.78%. What is the difference between the median percent of residents who earned a bachelor's degree or higher for these 9 counties and the median for all counties in California?

A) 0.52%

B) 3.88%

C) 5.62%

D) 11.52%

CONTINUE

23

A cylindrical can containing mushrooms is filled to the top with a cream sauce before it is sealed. The base of the can has an area of 68 cm^2, and the height of the can is 12 cm. If 210 cm^3 of cream sauce is needed to fill the can to the top, which of the following is closest to the total volume of the mushrooms in the can?

A) 3.8 cm^3

B) 606 cm^3

C) 816 cm^3

D) 1026 cm^3

24

$$h(t) = 7t^2 + 15t + 110$$

The function above models the height h, in feet of an object above ground t seconds after being launched straight up in the air. What does the number 110 represent in the function?

A) The initial height, in feet, of the object

B) The maximum height, in feet, of the object

C) The minimum height, in feet per second, of the object

D) The maximum speed, in feet per second, of the object

CONTINUE

Questions 25 and 26 refer to the following information.

Macronutrient	Food calories	Kilojoules
Protein	7.0	46.0
Fat	7.0	46.0
Carbohydrate	15.0	98.6

The table above gives the typical amount of energy per gram, expressed in both food calories and kilojoules, of the three macronutrients in food.

25

If c food calories is equivalent to k kilojoules, of the following, which best represents the relationship between c and k?

A) $c = 6.6k$

B) $k = 0.66c$

C) $k = 6.6c$

D) $ck = 6.6$

26

If the 450 food calories in a chocolate bar came directly from f grams of fat, p grams of protein, and c grams of carbohydrates, which of the following expresses c in terms of p and f?

A) $c = 30 + \frac{7}{15}(p + f)$

B) $c = 30 - \frac{7}{15}(p - f)$

C) $c = 30 - \frac{7}{15}(p + f)$

D) $c = 30 + \frac{7}{15}(p - f)$

27

The world's population has grown at an average rate of 2.3 percent per year since 1963. There were approximately 8 billion people in the world in 1983. Which of the following functions represents the world's population, P, in billions of people, t years since 1983?

A) $P(t) = 8\,(1.023)^t$

B) $P(t) = 8 + 1.023t$

C) $P(t) = 8\,(1.23)^t$

D) $P(t) = 8 + 1.23t$

CONTINUE ➡

28

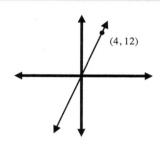

(4, 12)

In the xy-plane above, a point (not shown) with coordinates (a, b) lies on the graph of the linear function f. If a and b are positive integers, what is the ratio of b to a?

A) 1 to 4

B) 4 to 1

C) 1 to 3

D) 3 to 1

29

A circle in the in the xy-plane has equation $(x - 2)^2 + (y + 1)^2 = 16$. Which of the following points does NOT lie in the interior of the circle?

A) (2, -1)

B) (-1,-2)

C) (4,-3)

D) (-1,3)

30

Year	Subscriptions Sold
2010	7,530
2011	8,420

The manager of an online news service received the report above on the number of subscriptions sold by the service. The manager estimated that the percent increase from 2010-2011 would be quadruple the percent increase from 2011 to 2012. How many subscriptions did the manager expect would be sold in 2012?

A) 8,668.80

B) 8,642.20

C) 7,752.50

D) 9,415.19

CONTINUE

31

At a teashop in San Francisco, a 2-ounce package of black dragon pearl tea costs $15.00. If a customer paid $150.00, how many pounds of tea did the customer purchase? (16 ounces=1 pound)

32

Line a is shown in the xy-plane below. What is the slope of line a?

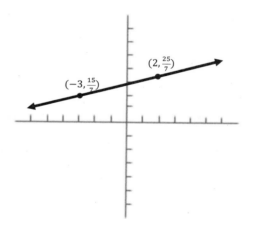

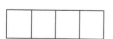

33

The score on a test is obtained by subtracting the number of incorrect answers from twice the number of correct answers. If a student answered 75 questions and obtained a score of 60, how many questions did the student answer correctly?

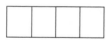

34

Point C is the center of the circle above. What fraction of the area of the circle is the area of the region of the smaller arc?

CONTINUE

35

$$y = x^2 + 6x - 27$$
$$y = 6x - 2$$

If the ordered pair (x, y) satisfies the system of equations above, what is one possible value of x?

36

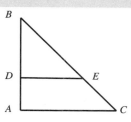

In the figure above, $\cos B = \frac{4}{5}$.

If BC = 20 and DA = 8, what is the length of $\overline{DE}$?

Questions 37 and 38 refer to the following information.

	5 out of 5	4 out of 5	3 out of 5	2 out of 5	1 out of 5	0 out of 5	Total
Day 1	2	3	4	3	2	1	15
Day 2	4	1	6	2	1	1	15
Day 3	1	4	3	4	2	1	15
Total	7	8	13	9	5	3	45

The same 15 contestants, on each of 3 days, answered 5 questions in order to win a prize. Each contestant received 1 point for each correct answer. The number of contestants receiving a given score on each day is shown in the table above.

37

What was the mean score of the contestants on Day 1?

38

No contestant received the same score on two different days. If a contestant is selected at random what is the probability that the selected contestant received a score of 3 on Day 2 or Day 3, given that the contestant received a score of 3 on one of the three days?

STOP

If you finish before time is called, you may check your work on this section only.
Do not turn to any other section.

No Test Material On This Page

Essay

ESSAY BOOK

DIRECTIONS

The essay gives you an opportunity to show how effectively you can read and comprehend a passage and write an essay analyzing the passage. In your essay, you should demonstrate that you have read the passage carefully, present a clear and logical analysis, and use language precisely.

Your essay must be written on the lines provided in your answer booklet; except for the Planning Page of the answer booklet, you will receive no other paper on which to write.

You have <u>50 minutes</u> to read the passage and write an essay in response to the prompt provided inside this booklet.

As you read the passage below, consider how Fredrick Douglas uses

- evidence, such as facts or examples, to support claims.

- reasoning to develop ideas and to connect claims and evidence.

- stylistic or persuasive elements, such as word choice or appeals to emotion, to add power to the ideas expressed.

Adapted from John F. Kennedy, *We Choose To Go To The Moon*, delivered to the American public at Rice Stadium in Houston, Texas on September 12, 1962.

1 Despite the striking fact that most of the scientists that the world has ever known are alive and working today, despite the fact that this Nation's own scientific manpower is doubling every 12 years in a rate of growth more than three times that of our population as a whole, despite that, the vast stretches of the unknown and the unanswered and the unfinished still far outstrip our collective comprehension.

2 No man can fully grasp how far and how fast we have come, but condense, if you will, the 50,000 years of man's recorded history in a time span of but a half-century. Stated in these terms, we know very little about the first 40 years, except at the end of them advanced man had learned to use the skins of animals to cover them. Then about 10 years ago, under this standard, man emerged from his caves to construct other kinds of shelter. Only five years ago man learned to write and use a cart with wheels. Christianity began less than two years ago. The printing press came this year, and then less than two months ago, during this whole 50-year span of human history, the steam engine provided a new source of power.

3 Newton explored the meaning of gravity. Last month electric lights and telephones and automobiles and airplanes became available. Only last week did we develop penicillin and television and nuclear power, and now if America's new spacecraft succeeds in reaching Venus, we will have literally reached the stars before midnight tonight.

4 This is a breathtaking pace, and such a pace cannot help but create new ills as it dispels old, new ignorance, new problems, new dangers. Surely the opening vistas of space promise high costs and hardships, as well as high reward.

5 So it is not surprising that some would have us stay where we are a little longer to rest, to wait. But this city of Houston, this State of Texas, this country of the United States was not built by those who waited and rested and wished to look behind them. This country was conquered by those who moved forward--and so will space.

6 William Bradford, speaking in 1630 of the founding of the Plymouth Bay Colony, said that all great and honorable actions are accompanied with great difficulties, and both must be enterprised and overcome with answerable courage.

7 If this capsule history of our progress teaches us anything, it is that man, in his quest for knowledge and progress, is determined and cannot be deterred. The exploration of space will go ahead, whether we join in it or not, and it is one of the great adventures of all time, and no nation which expects to be the leader of other nations can expect to stay behind in the race for space.

8 Those who came before us made certain that this country rode the first waves of the industrial revolutions, the first waves of modern invention, and the first wave of nuclear power, and this generation does not intend to founder in the backwash of the coming age of space. We mean to be a part of it--we mean to lead it. For the eyes of the world now look into space, to the moon and to the planets beyond, and we have vowed that we shall not see it governed by a hostile flag of conquest, but by a banner of freedom and peace. We have vowed that we shall not see space filled with weapons of mass destruction, but with instruments of knowledge and understanding.

9 Yet the vows of this Nation can only be fulfilled if we in this Nation are first, and, therefore, we intend to be first. In short, our leadership in science and in industry, our hopes for peace and security, our obligations to ourselves as well as others, all require us to make this effort, to solve these mysteries, to solve them for the good of all men, and to become the world's leading space-faring nation.

10 There is no strife, no prejudice, no national conflict in outer space as yet. Its hazards are hostile to us all. Its conquest deserves the best of all mankind, and its opportunity for peaceful cooperation many never come again. But why, some say, the moon? Why choose this as our goal? And they may well ask why climb the highest mountain? Why, 35 years ago, fly the Atlantic?

11 We choose to go to the moon. We choose to go to the moon in this decade and do the other things, not because they are easy, but because they are hard, because that goal will serve to organize and measure the best of our energies and skills, because that challenge is one that we are willing to accept, one we are unwilling to postpone, and one which we intend to win, and the others, too.

12 It is for these reasons that I regard the decision last year to shift our efforts in space from low to high gear as among the most important decisions that will be made during my incumbency in the office of the Presidency.

Write an essay in which you explain how John F. Kennedy builds an argument to persuade his audience to support the national effort to send humans to the Moon. In your essay, analyze how Kennedy uses one or more of the features listed in the box above (or features of your own choice) to strengthen the logic and persuasiveness of his argument. Be sure that the analysis focuses on the most relevant features of the passage.

Your essay should not explain whether you agree with Kennedy's claims, but rather explain how Kennedy builds an argument to persuade his audience.

FOR
PLANNING
ONLY

Sample

Exam

B

Tried & True Tutoring

Reading Test
65 Minutes, 52 Questions

DIRECTIONS

Each passage or pair of passages below is followed by a number of questions. After reading each passage or pair, choose the best answer to each question based on what is stated or implied in the passage or passages and in any accompanying graphics (such as a table or graph).

Questions 1-10 are based on the following passage.

This passage is adapted from Bram Stoker, *Dracula*. Originally published in 1897.

Soon we were hemmed in with trees, and again great frowning rocks guarded us boldly on either side. Though we were in shelter, we could
Line
5 hear the rising wind, for it moaned and whistled through the rocks, and the branches of the trees crashed together as we swept along. It grew colder and colder still, and fine, powdery snow began to fall, so that soon we and all around us were covered with a white blanket. The keen
10 wind still carried the howling of the dogs, though this grew fainter as we went on our way. The baying of the wolves sounded nearer and nearer, as though they were closing round on us from every side. I grew dreadfully afraid, and the
15 horses shared my fear. The driver, however, was not in the least disturbed; he kept turning his head to left and right, but I could not see anything through the darkness.

Suddenly, away on our left, I saw a faint
20 flickering blue flame. The driver saw it at the same moment; he at once checked the horses, and, jumping to the ground, disappeared into the darkness. I did not know what to do, the less as the howling of the wolves grew closer; but while
25 I wondered the driver suddenly appeared again, and without a word took his seat, and we resumed our journey. I think I must have fallen asleep and kept dreaming of the incident, for it seemed to be repeated endlessly, and now looking back, it is
30 like a sort of awful nightmare. Once the flame

appeared so near the road, that even in the darkness around us I could watch the driver's motions. He went rapidly to where the blue flame arose—it must have been very faint, for it did not
35 seem to illumine the place around it at all—and gathering a few stones, formed them into some device. Once there appeared a strange optical effect: when he stood between me and the flame he did not obstruct it, for I could see its ghostly
40 flicker all the same. This startled me, but as the effect was only momentary, I took it that my eyes deceived me straining through the darkness.

At last there came a time when the driver went further afield than he had yet gone, and
45 during his absence, the horses began to tremble worse than ever and to snort and scream with fright. I could not see any cause for it, for the howling of the wolves had ceased altogether; but just then the moon, sailing through the black
50 clouds, appeared, and by its light I saw around us a ring of wolves, with white teeth and lolling red tongues, with long, sinewy limbs and shaggy hair. They were a hundred times more terrible in the grim silence which held them than even when
55 they howled. For myself, I felt a sort of paralysis of fear. It is only when a man feels himself face to face with such horrors that he can understand their true import.

The horses jumped about and reared, and
60 looked helplessly round with eyes that rolled in a way painful to see; but the living ring of terror encompassed them on every side; and they had perforce to remain within it. I called to the coachman to come. I shouted and beat the side of
65 the calèche, hoping by the noise to scare the

CONTINUE ➡

wolves from that side, so as to give him a chance of reaching the trap. How he came there, I know not, but I heard his voice raised in a tone of imperious command, and looking towards the
70 sound, saw him stand in the roadway. As he swept his long arms, as though brushing aside some impalpable obstacle, the wolves fell back and back further still. Just then a heavy cloud passed across the face of the moon, so that we
75 were again in darkness.

When I could see again the driver was climbing into the calèche, and the wolves had disappeared. This was all so strange and uncanny that a dreadful fear came upon me, and I was
80 afraid to speak or move. The time seemed interminable as we swept on our way, now in almost complete darkness, for the rolling clouds obscured the moon.

1

The "white blanket" (line 9) most likely refers to

A) a man-made item.

B) a weather phenomenon.

C) the mood of the horses.

D) something in the narrator's memory.

2

Which statement best describes a technique the narrator uses in the first paragraph to heighten the sense of danger?

A) The narrator underscores the horses' fear through their actions and manner.

B) The narrator indicates the nervousness of the usually calm driver in his looking in all directions.

C) The narrator implies through the noises of animals that he is moving away from the safety of civilization and into more dangerous territory.

D) The narrator demonstrates that the rocks, trees, and wind are working against the men and the horses.

3

Which of the following can be most reasonably inferred from the passage about the driver?

A) He has excellent night vision.

B) His hearing is impaired.

C) He wants the narrator's blood.

D) He does not like the narrator.

4

Which choice provides the best evidence for the answer to the previous question?

A) Lines 15-18 ("The driver, however… darkness")

B) Lines 20-27 ("The driver saw… journey")

C) Lines 33-37 ("He went… device")

D) Lines 67-75 ("How he… darkness")

5

The purpose of the narrator's statement about falling asleep ("I think… awful nightmare," lines 27-30) is to

A) show how terrible the ride was by equating it to a nightmare and indicating the narrator's exhaustion brought on by fear.

B) characterize the driver as repetitive and boring and the narrator as antisocial.

C) cast doubt as the whether the driver is human or not.

D) emphasize how strange, surreal, and terrible the carriage ride was.

6

The "strange optical effect" mentioned in lines 37-38 refers to

A) a blue flame that did not illuminate the area around it.

B) a flame seen through something solid.

C) the straining of the narrator's eyes in the darkness.

D) a device made out of stones.

7

As used in line 52, "sinewy" most nearly means

A) delicate.

B) stringy.

C) lean.

D) hairy.

8

The horses as portrayed in the passage can best be described as

A) terrified but determined to remain loyal.

B) paralyzed by fear.

C) demonstrating steadfast discipline and bravery through a difficult situation.

D) staying with the carriage only to avoid being hurt.

9

Which choice provides the best evidence to the answer to the previous question?

A) Lines 43-48 ("At last… ceased altogether")

B) Lines 53-58 ("They were a hundred… import")

C) Lines 59-61 ("The horses… painful to see")

D) Lines 61-63 ("but the living… within it")

10

The main purpose of the narrator's description of the driver's actions in the fifth and sixth paragraphs (lines 59-83) is to

A) demonstrate how much the driver cares for his horses.

B) hint at the driver's strange powers.

C) indicate the narrator's confusion about the event described in the passage.

D) cast doubt on the reliability of the narrator's senses.

CONTINUE

Questions 11-20 are based on the following passages.

Passage 1 is adapted from Adam Smith, *An Inquiry into the Nature and Causes of the Wealth of Nations.* Originally published in 1776. Passage 2 is adapted from a speech on communism delivered by Moses Hess in Elberfeld, Germany in 1845.

Passage 1

Line
5

It is the necessary, though very slow and gradual consequence of a certain propensity in human nature which has in view no such extensive utility; the propensity to truck, barter, and exchange one thing for another.

It is common to all men, and to be found in no other race of animals, which seem to know neither this nor any other species of contracts. Two greyhounds, in running down the same hare, have sometimes the appearance of acting in some sort of concert. Each turns her towards his companion, or endeavors to intercept her when his companion turns her towards himself. This, however, is not the effect of any contract, but of the accidental concurrence of their passions in the same object at that particular time. Nobody ever saw a dog make a fair and deliberate exchange of one bone for another with another dog. When an animal wants to obtain something either of a man or of another animal, it has no other means of persuasion but to gain the favor of those whose service it requires. A puppy fawns upon its dam, and a spaniel endeavors by a thousand attractions to engage the attention of its master who is at dinner, when it wants to be fed by him. Man sometimes uses the same arts with his brethren, and when he has no other means of engaging them to act according to his inclinations, endeavors by every servile and fawning attention to obtain their good will. He has not time, however, to do this upon every occasion. In civilized society he stands at all times in need of the cooperation and assistance of great multitudes. In almost every other race of animals each individual, when it is grown up to maturity, is entirely independent, and in its natural state has occasion for the assistance of no other living creature. But man has almost constant occasion for the help of his brethren, and it is in vain for him to expect it from their benevolence only. He will be more likely to prevail if he can interest their self-love in his favor, and show them that it

is for their own advantage to do for him what he requires of them. Whoever offers to another a bargain of any kind proposes to do this. It is not from the benevolence of the butcher, the brewer, or the baker that we expect our dinner, but from their regard to their own interest. We address ourselves not to their humanity, but to their self-love and never talk to them of our own necessities but of their advantages.

Passage 2

There is no point in talking to you about the intellectual, moral and physical misery of today's society. Any man with a heart, however favorable his position, will agree with me, when he looks at this world of misery, that our life is not happy. I just want to draw to your attention that the basic cause of all the ills of present-day society, which is normally attributed to the imperfection of human nature, is in fact the lack of organization of human society. I have already also often heard it said that the idea of communism, fine and true in itself, is unfortunately unrealizable.

The idea of communism, gentlemen, with which everyone says he agrees, is the life-law of love applied to social life. The law of love is innate in man, as in all life, but attempts to apply this law to social life will only be made when men's consciousness of their life has begun to mature in them, when they come to see more and more clearly their own existence, when they understand more and more clearly that it is precisely and solely in love that energy, the energy of life, creative energy, lies. When men compare their own inner understanding of life with, on the one hand, the life of nature they find that here their life-consciousness is everywhere confirmed, that love, which they recognize as their life, is equally the real life of nature; but when, on the other hand, they compare their conception of life, now confirmed and enriched by the natural sciences, with social life, they find with horror that here, in their own world, nothing conforms to this law of life and that everything contradicts it—in a word, they discover that they are living in a perverted world!

No living being comes into existence fully developed. Rather, everything first develops in the course of time. This development is called the history, the genesis of a being. Gentlemen, if you now find the idea of communism fine and true in itself this is because your life-consciousness has already come to maturity, because you recognize that the true life consists only of love.

11

As it is used in line 15, "concurrence" most nearly means

A) harmony.

B) occurrence.

C) influence.

D) disagreement.

12

According to Passage 1, why do people sometimes not "gain the favor of those whose services [they require]" (lines 21-22) in the same way animals do?

A) They don't need to gain favor with the same frequency as animals.

B) They are too self-interested.

C) They don't have enough time.

D) They don't have as great an ability as animals to do so.

13

According to Passage 1, one major difference between animals and people is that

A) people do not always live according to their true natures.

B) animals are more self-sufficient than people when they grow up.

C) people use money whereas animals do not.

D) animals must rely more on their physical abilities than people must.

14

Which choice provides the best evidence for the answer to the previous question?

A) Lines 18-25 ("When an animal… fed by him")

B) Lines 25-30 ("Man sometimes… good will")

C) Lines 30-31 ("He has not… every occasion")

D) Lines 38-44 ("But man has… requires of them")

15

As it is used in line 64, "unrealizable" most nearly means

A) unlikely.

B) unimaginable.

C) impossible.

D) harmful.

16

According to Passage 2, communism will be implemented only when

A) capitalism falls.

B) greed no longer has a place in man's heart.

C) society is better organized.

D) people gain maturity and understanding.

17

Which choice provides the best evidence for the answer to the previous question?

A) Lines 54-61 ("Any man… of human society")

B) Lines 67-75 ("The law… lies")

C) Lines80-86 ("But when… perverted world")

D) Lines 90-94 ("Gentlemen, if… only of love")

18

Which of the following structures do Passages 1 and 2 share?

A) Each passage relates a personal story to promote an economic system the author favors.

B) Each passage discusses man's commonality with nature to explain society as it is or should be.

C) Each passage tells a fictional tale about animals as an allegory to explain the nature of human beings.

D) Each passage makes a moral argument to support its author's position on how society should function.

19

Based on Passage 1, which choice gives Adam Smith's most likely response to what Moses Hess says about love in lines 67-68 and 75-80?

A) Love in nature is an appearance that occurs when more than one creature would benefit by acting together toward the same goal or when one creature wants something from another.

B) What appears to be love between human beings is often no more than one offering servile and fawning attention to others in order to gain their good will; love amongst a whole species in natural only animals.

C) The law of man is unrelated to "all life" just as the "real life of nature" has no bearing on the life of man.

D) As man must rely on the cooperation and assistance of great multitudes, he must endeavor to emulate the love that exists in nature.

20

Based on Passage 2, which issue stated in Passage 1 would Moses Hess most likely say is true but fixable?

A) "Nobody ever saw a dog make a fair and deliberate exchange of one bone for another with another dog" (lines 16-18)

B) "In civilized society he stands at all times in need of the cooperation and assistance of great multitudes" (lines 31-34)

C) "But man has almost constant occasion for the help of his brethren" (lines 38-39)

D) "It is in vain for him to expect it from their benevolence only" (lines 39-40)

Questions 21 - 30 are based on the following passage.

This passage is adapted from E. W. Scripture, "Cross-Education." Originally published in *Appleton's Popular Science Monthly*, March 1900. The figures are from the same source.

Some years ago I arranged a rubber bulb to connect with a bottle, from which rose a long, vertical glass tube. The bottle contained mercury, and the long tube reached nearly to the bottom.

Line 5 When anybody squeezed the bulb the mercury was forced up the vertical tube. It was what is known as a mercury-dynamometer.

During experiments with this dynamometer, what was more natural than to think of trying

10 what would happen if one hand were practiced daily in squeezing the bulb? So one of our graduate students was set to work in the following manner: on the first day she squeezed the bulb as hard as possible with the left hand,

15 while an assistant noted the height of the mercury. Immediately thereafter she took a record with the right hand. Then, on the following days, she practiced the right hand by squeezing ten times on each occasion. On the last day she

20 again tested the left hand, which had not been practiced in the meantime.

The left hand had gained about fifty percent in strength through practice of the right hand (see Figure 1). This peculiar phenomenon of

25 transference of the effects of practice from one side to the other I have ventured to call "cross-education."

Let us ask in what this education consists. On this point some curious observations have been

30 made by Prof. W. W. Davis. The subject of his experiment began by raising a five-pound dumb-bell by flexing the arm at the elbow; this called into play chiefly the biceps and forearm muscles. This was done as many times as possible with the

35 right arm, and then, after a rest, with the left arm. The subject then entered upon a practice extending from two to four weeks; this consisted in lifting the weight with the right arm only. At the end both arms were tested as at the start.

40 The results were strange enough (see Figure 2). The unpracticed left arm gained in power as

we expected, but it also gained in size. All subjects had gained power in the unpracticed left arm, three of them largely and three slightly. All

45 but one had gained in the size of the unpracticed left biceps. Strangely enough, those who had gained most in power had gained least in size. The gains in power were unquestionably mostly central—that is, in the nerve centers—and not in

50 the muscles. Yet there was also a strange but unquestionable gain in the size of the muscles at the same time.

We have arrived at the second step of the ladder: the gain by practice which shows itself in

55 cross-education consists in a development of higher nerve centers connected with the two sides of the body. We must next ask: is this effect of practice confined to symmetrical organs, or does it extend to other organs? This question was

60 answered by another of Professor Davis's experiments.

The experiment consisted in testing the effect of educating one of the feet to tap as rapidly as possible on a telegraph key. There were three

65 keys of this kind, any one of which would register. One key each was arranged for tapping with the big toes; the third key could be tapped by either right or left index finger.

On the first day all four digits—right and left

70 index fingers and right and left large toes—were carefully tested in tapping as rapidly as possible. Thereafter the right large toe was practiced daily in tapping for several weeks, the other digits being left unpracticed. At the end all four digits

75 were again tested. Four of the six persons experimented upon showed a gain for the right large toe; the other two showed a slight loss, due unquestionably to "over-practice." All of those who gained for the right large toe gained for the

80 other digits also. Thus we have reached the third step—the effects of practice are extended to various parts of the body.

Beyond the third step the experimental investigations have not yet advanced, but I

85 believe the ladder of cross-education will be slowly climbed by psychological investigators; if they find at the top a principle of value and wide application, surely the climb will have been worth the time and trouble.

CONTINUE ➡

Figure 1

	DAY								
	First	Second	Third	Fourth	Fifth	Sixth	Seventh	Eight	Ninth
	Inches	Inches	Inches	Inches	Inches	Inches	Inches	Inches	Inches
Right hand	28.8	33.7	35.6	36.6	40.9	44.7	47.0	48.8	48.6
Left hand	29.9	....	....	....	....	....	....	....	42.3

Figure 2

SUBJECT.	GAINS IN GIRTH.		GAINS IN POWER.	
	Right biceps.	Left biceps.	Right arm.	Left arm.
G	5 mm.	-5 mm.	820 flexions.	200 flexions.
J	2 "	0 "	400 "	225 "
K	4 "	2 "	724 "	514 "
H	13 "	6 "	950 "	30 "
B	6 "	11 "	900 "	75 "
I	8 "	3 "	750 "	75 "

21

Over the course of the passage, the main focus shifts from

A) instructions for making a scientific apparatus to experiments involving that apparatus.

B) a phenomenon discovered by the author to experiments on the phenomenon conducted by his assistants.

C) an overview of cross-education to the context in which it was discovered.

D) an event that drew the author to a phenomenon to experiments about that phenomenon.

22

As used in line 29, "curious" most nearly means

A) unexpected.

B) dubious.

C) unconventional.

D) inquisitive.

CONTINUE

23

Based on information in the passage, before the experiment described in the fourth and fifth paragraphs (lines 28-52), the author most likely would have expected

A) gains in left-hand power to be more even across participants.

B) participants' gains in muscle size to correspond to gains in power.

C) gains in power to be more from muscle growth than from nerve centers.

D) gains in left-arm power of about fifty percent.

24

Which choice provides the best evidence for the answer to the previous question?

A) Lines 22-23 ("The left hand… the right hand")

B) Lines 40-44 ("The results… three slightly")

C) Lines 44-47 ("All but one… least in size")

D) Lines 48-52 ("The gains… same time")

25

The main purpose of the analogy of the ladder (lines 53-54 and 80-86) is to

A) emphasize the hard work that has gone into making discoveries about cross-education as well as the importance of continuing this hard work.

B) clarify the results of the experiments explained in the passage.

C) illustrate the progress made so far in studying cross-education and indicate that there's further to go.

D) deliver a counterargument to the opponents of cross-education theory.

26

Based on information in the passage, it is most likely that sometimes a person can improve their ability to perform a simple action with their left index finger by

A) refraining from performing that action too many times with their right big toe.

B) performing that action with their right index finger as many times as possible over the course of several months.

C) performing a series of related actions with both of their index fingers for a few weeks.

D) resting their right index finger before starting.

27

Which choice provides the best evidence for the answer to the previous question?

A) Lines 34-39 ("This was done… at the start")

B) Lines 72-77 ("Thereafter the right… large toe")

C) Lines 77-80 ("the other two… digits also")

D) Lines 80-82 ("Thus we have… of the body")

28

According to figure 1, the left hand

A) gained no strength until the ninth day.

B) grew about 12 inches by the ninth day.

C) gained slightly less strength than the right hand every day.

D) was stronger than the right hand at the beginning of the experiment.

CONTINUE

29

Which of the following subjects from figure 2 contradict(s) the statement in lines 44-46 ("All but one… left biceps.")?

A) subject G

B) subject B

C) subjects G and J

D) subjects B and H

30

Which of the following is a strange result of the weight-lifting experiment demonstrated in figure 2 but not in the fifth paragraph (lines 40-52)?

A) The subjects whose right arms gained the most power gained the least power in their left arms.

B) Greater gains in biceps girth corresponded to lesser gains in power.

C) Each subject's right arm gained more power than that subject's left arm.

D) Some of the subjects gained more girth in their left biceps than in their right.

Questions 31-41 are based on the following passage.

This passage is adapted from Crystal Eastman, "Now We Can Begin." Originally published in 1920. The supplemental figures are from the Bureau of Labor Statistics, "Women's median earnings 82 percent of men's in 2016." Originally published 2017.

Most women will agree that August 23, the day when the Tennessee legislature finally enacted the Federal suffrage amendment, is a day
Line
5   to begin with, not a day to end with. Men are saying perhaps "Thank God, this everlasting woman's fight is over!" But women, if I know them, are saying, "Now at last we can begin." In fighting for the right to vote most women have tried to be either non-committal or thoroughly
10 respectable on every other subject. Now they can say what they are really after; and what they are after, in common with all the rest of the struggling world, is freedom.

Freedom is a large word.
15   What, then, is "the matter with women"? What is the problem of women's freedom? It seems to me to be this: how to arrange the world so that women can be human beings, with a chance to exercise their infinitely varied gifts in
20 infinitely varied ways, instead of being destined by the accident of their sex to one field of activity—housework and child-raising. And second, if and when they choose housework and child-raising, to have that occupation recognized
25 by the world as work, requiring a definite economic reward and not merely entitling the performer to be dependent on some man.

This is not the whole of feminism, of course, but it is enough to begin with. "Oh, don't
30 begin with economics," my friends often protest, "Woman does not live by bread alone. What she needs first of all is a free soul." And I can agree that women will never be great until they achieve a certain emotional freedom, a strong healthy
35 egotism, and some un-personal sources of joy — that in this inner sense we cannot make woman free by changing her economic status. What we can do, however, is to create conditions of outward freedom in which a free woman's soul
40 can be born and grow. It is these outward conditions with which an organized feminist movement must concern itself.

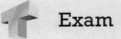

Freedom of choice in occupation and individual economic independence for women:
45 How shall we approach this next feminist objective? First, by breaking down all remaining barriers, actual as well as legal, which make it difficult for women to enter or succeed in the various professions, to go into and get on in
50 business, to learn trades and practice them, to join trades unions. Chief among these remaining barriers is inequality in pay. Here the ground is already broken. This is the easiest part of our program.
55   Second, we must institute a revolution in the early training and education of both boys and girls. It must be womanly as well as manly to earn your own living, to stand on your own feet. And it must be manly as well as womanly to
60 know how to cook and sew and clean and take care of yourself in the ordinary exigencies of life. I need not add that the second part of this revolution will be more passionately resisted than the first. Men will not give up their privilege of
65 helplessness without a struggle. The average man has a carefully cultivated ignorance about household matters — from what to do with the crumbs to the grocer's telephone number — a sort of cheerful inefficiency which protects him
70 better than the reputation for having a violent temper. It was his mother's fault in the beginning, but even as a boy he was quick to see how a general reputation for being "no good around the house" would serve him throughout life, and half-
75 consciously he began to cultivate that helplessness until today it is the despair of feminist wives.

Figure 1

Occupations in which women's median earnings as a percentage of men's median earnings are the lowest, 2016

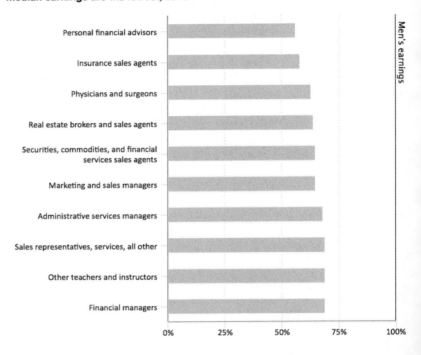

Figure 2

Occupations in which women's median earnings as a percentage of men's median earnings are the highest, 2016

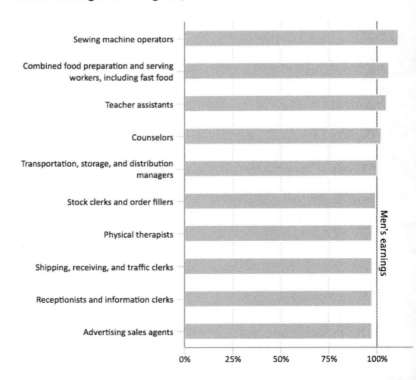

CONTINUE

31

This passage primarily serves to

A) announce a major victory for the feminist movement.

B) introduce feminism as a national movement.

C) explain why women have not received equal treatment to men.

D) propose new goals for the feminist movement.

32

Which of the following does the author state in the passage as a problem?

A) the inequality in election to political offices between men and women

B) women's lack of access to higher education

C) the disparity between women's abilities and options

D) women being expected to work harder than men for less money

33

Which choice provides the best evidence for the answer to the previous question?

A) Lines 16-22 ("It seems to me… child-raising")

B) Lines 22-27 ("And second…on some man")

C) Lines 43-46 ("Freedom of choice… feminist objective")

D) Lines 46-52 ("First, by… inequality in pay")

34

The author includes the quotations in the fourth paragraph (lines 28-42) most likely to

make the topic of the passage more relatable by sharing a personal story.

explain why the feminist movement should not focus on economics.

put the arguments of the previous paragraph into context.

offer a counterargument to a previous

35

As used in line 35, "egotism" most nearly means

A) arrogance.

B) sense of self-interest.

C) desire for independence.

D) selfishness.

36

As used in line 61, "exigencies" most nearly means

A) desires.

B) actions.

C) trials.

D) needs.

37

The author most clearly implies that men's inability to care for themselves is

A) taught to them as the manly way of life.

B) inherited from their fathers.

C) somewhat purposely developed.

D) a strange way of showing their love for women.

38

Which choice provides the best evidence for the answer to the previous question?

A) Lines 22-27 ("And second… on some man")

B) Lines 57-58 ("It must be… your own feet")

C) Lines 59-65 ("And it must…without a struggle")

D) Lines 71-77 ("It was his… feminist wives")

39

Based on Figure 2, in 2016 women employed as counselors

A) earned on average about the same amount of money as men employed as counselors.

B) earned slightly more than women employed as physical therapists.

C) earned a median salary slightly higher than that of men employed as counselors.

D) earned a median salary slightly higher than the median salary of working US males in 2016.

40

Based on information in the passage and the two figures, if she were still alive, the author might most reasonably conclude that between 1920 and 2016 the feminist movement

A) succeeded in making more jobs available to women but failed in making what had been women's tasks "manly."

B) succeeded in earning equal pay for women in some occupations but failed to make men less helpless around the house.

C) failed to free women's souls but succeeded in opening women's job opportunities to more than one field of activity.

D) took great strides toward but had not yet achieved political equality with men.

41

Based on information in the passage, which of the following would the author most like to see on one the figures?

A) data for college enrollment by gender

B) housework and child-raising as occupations

C) the median salaries for each occupation in dollars

D) some occupations for which women's median salaries doubled men's

CONTINUE →

Questions 42 - 52 are based on the following passage.

This passage is adapted from "Ancient Art of Weaving Ready to Head to Mars and Beyond." Originally published 2017 on NASA's website.

Weaving processes created millennia ago are part of the most cutting-edge technology on NASA's Orion spaceship that may one day
Line shield humans from heat as they ride all the way
5 to Mars and back.

That same technology is finding a home on Earth as well, enabling thicker, denser composite materials for race cars, among other applications.
10 It started with a connection problem: there are points across Orion's heat shield surface that must link the crew capsule to its service module and, ultimately, the rocket. "At these points, you have to use a very strong, robust
15 material," explains materials engineer Jay Feldman, technical lead for the 3-D Multifunctional Ablative Thermal Protection System (3D-MAT) at NASA's Ames Research Center.
20 But great insulators are often not particularly strong. Luckily, Feldman and other engineers at Ames were already working with partners at weaving company Bally Ribbon Mills on next-generation heat-shielding material.
25 Together, they were developing a three-dimensional quartz-fiber composite, woven using classic shuttle looms upgraded for the modern era.

Three-dimensional woven composites
30 offered big advantages over layered 2-D woven composites used in previous spacecraft. "When you have fibers going in all three directions, it's very, very strong," explains Feldman. "And we can also tailor the composition so it has relatively
35 low thermal conductivity."

Bally Ribbon Mills, in Bally, Pennsylvania was a natural partner for the project. A leading U.S. manufacturer of two and three-dimensional textiles, the company's client
40 list includes the U.S. Air Force, Formula One racing teams and biomedical companies.

The firm's expertise extends back to 1923, when the family-owned company started out weaving silk hat bands. Three generations
45 later the company had evolved into a high-tech

custom engineering firm, explains Mark Harries, part of the fourth generation of his family to run the textile company. "That's when we really found our niche," Harries says.
50 The NASA partnership, and the resulting material, have generated a lot of excitement at the space agency, prompting a January 2015 visit to the mill by then-NASA Administrator Charles Bolden, who declared: "From this day on, the
55 path to Mars goes through Bally, Pennsylvania."

For Orion, the threads are made of quartz, which is an excellent insulator and also capable of transmitting electrical signals.

Bally Ribbon Mills had to design new
60 equipment to meet NASA's needs: a thicker textile and, to improve compression strength, the same number of fibers going in all three directions. The final product "is like a brick," says senior textile engineer Curt Wilkinson.
65 But the design is truly elegant, says Ethiraj Venkatapathy, project manager and chief technologist for the Entry Systems and Technologies Division at Ames. "The material can be a structure, it can be a thermal protection
70 system, it can be a shock absorber, and it can carry loads," he says, a contrast to designs that tend to focus on just one discipline.

Already the designers of Orion are looking at other spots where the 3D-MAT
75 material may be incorporated. And outside NASA, government agencies and aerospace companies have expressed interest. The work for NASA has also increased the product line the company offers in more frequently used
80 materials, like carbon fiber, to its long-standing clients, including Formula One car manufacturers.

Yet underneath the high-tech add-ons, the core of the process is the same type of shuttle
85 looms the company used for silk in the 1920s. It's an evolution that has kept nearly 300 jobs in central Pennsylvania, where most of the other textile mills have long gone out of business.

"We incorporate modern electronic
90 components, and we also build and incorporate our own take-up systems, but the loom itself is extremely old," Wilkinson says. "Using the same age-old steps of weaving, we're now weaving material that's going to go to Mars."

42

The main purpose of the passage is to

A) demonstrate the varied needs of NASA that are met by a cutting-edge woven material.

B) explain the process by which weaving makes space-age materials.

C) announce a new heat shield for NASA's future shuttles.

D) discuss an old technique being used to create new technologies.

43

The main purpose of the third paragraph (lines 10-19) is to

A) suggest a specific solution to a long-term problem.

B) indicate the problem that caused NASA to seek technology like that described in the passage.

C) demonstrate how amazing new technology described later in the passage is by stating a few of the many considerations that make space travel so complicated.

D) show that weaving makes a very strong, robust material.

44

The passage implies that new woven composites are superior to other insulators because the new woven composites

A) have relatively low thermal conductivity.

B) are three-dimensional.

C) are stronger.

D) do not allow any heat into the shuttle.

45

Which of the following statements from the passage does Feldman's assertion in lines 33-35 ("And we can... thermal conductivity) most strongly support?

A) Lines 1-5 ("Weaving processes... and back")

B) Lines 6-9 ("That same technology... other applications")

C) Lines 56-58 ("For Orion... electrical signals")

D) Lines 63-64 ("The final product... Curt Wilkinson")

46

By his statement in lines 54-55 ("From this day... Bally, Pennsylvania), Charles Bolden most likely means that

A) he expects NASA to begin and continue launching shuttles from Bally, Pennsylvania.

B) material developed in Bally, Pennsylvania will make Mars missions feasible.

C) astronauts will continue to be trained in Bally, Pennsylvania for the foreseeable future.

D) the most important parts of future shuttles will be manufactured in Bally, Pennsylvania.

47

Based on the passage, which of the following statements about the three-dimensional quartz material used on the Orion spaceship is most likely true?

A) The thick material would block electrical transmissions.

B) The efficiency of the material would allow NASA to use thinner portions of it.

C) The material is very good at conducting heat.

D) Doubling the fibers going in one direction would weaken the compound.

CONTINUE ▶

48

Which choice provides the best evidence for the answer to the previous question?

A) Lines 31-33 ("When you have… very strong")

B) Lines 56-59 ("For Orion… electrical signals")

C) Lines 59-63 ("Bally Ribbon Mills… three directions")

D) Lines 68-71 ("The material… carry loads")

49

The writer describes the design of the three-dimensional quartz-fiber composite as "truly elegant" (line 65) to indicate that the material

A) has a pleasing appearance.

B) offers a single solution that fills several needs.

C) is graceful and stylish.

D) protects against extreme temperatures.

50

As used in line 72, "discipline" most nearly means

A) subject.

B) system of rules.

C) control.

D) problem.

51

It can be most reasonably inferred from the passage that

A) many workers from other textile mills quit their jobs to work at Bally Ribbon Mills.

B) NASA and Formula One car manufacturers use all the same Bally Ribbon materials for their products.

C) Bally Ribbon Mills uses techniques or machinery developed for NASA projects to make products for other companies.

D) Formula One car manufacturers hope to start making spaceships.

52

Which choice provides the best evidence for the answer to the previous question?

A) Lines 68-71 ("The material… carry loads")

B) Lines 73-75 ("Already the designers… may be incorporated")

C) Lines 77-82 ("The work for… car manufacturers")

D) Lines 85-88 ("It's an evolution… out of business")

STOP

**If you finish before time is called, you may check your work on this section only.
Do not turn to any other section.**

Writing and Language Test
35 Minutes, 44 Questions

DIRECTIONS

Each passage or pair of passages below is followed by a number of questions. For some questions, you will consider how the passage might be revised to improve the expression of ideas. For other questions, you will consider how the passage might be edited to correct errors in sentence structure, usage, or punctuation. A passage or a question may be accompanied by one or more graphics (such as a table or graph) that you will consider as you make revising and editing decisions.

Some questions will direct you to an underlined portion of the passage. Other questions will direct you to a location in a passage or ask you to think about the passage as a whole.

After reading each passage, choose the answer to each question that most effectively improves the quality of writing in the passage or that makes the passage conform to the conventions of standard written English. Many questions include a "NO CHANGE" option. Choose that option if you think the best choice is to leave the relevant portion of the passage as it is.

Questions 1-11 are based on the following passage.

This passage is adapted from A. A. Milne, "The Charm of Golf," originally published in 1920.

When he reads of the 1 prominent doings of famous golfers, the bad golfer has no envy in his heart. For by this time he has discovered the great secret of golf. 2 Before he began to play he wondered wherein lay the fascination of it, now he knows. Golf is so popular simply because it is the best game in the world at which to be bad.

1

A) NO CHANGE
B) high-profile
C) preeminent
D) notable

2

A) NO CHANGE
B) Whereas before
C) Since before
D) However before

CONTINUE

Consider what it is to be bad at cricket. You have bought 3 all manner of protective gear, a new pair of pads, and gloves of the very latest design. Do they let you use them? No. After one ball they send you back into the pavilion.

Consider what it is to be bad at lawn tennis. 4 True you have spent less money on equipment, but how often do you get to use it? How often does your partner cry "Mine!" and shove you out of the way? Is there pleasure in playing football badly? You may spend the full eighty minutes in your new shoes, but your relations with the ball will be distant. They do not give you a ball to yourself in football.

But how different a game is golf. At golf it is the bad player who gets the most strokes. However good his opponent, the bad player has the right to play out each hole to the end; he will get 5 bigger than his share of the game.

3

A) NO CHANGE

B) a helmet, a bat, and some protective headward.

C) a large stick with which to hit the ball, new pads of the latest design, and a hardwood bat that will surely be the envy of the pitch.

D) a large stick with which to hit the ball, a hard hat to protect your head, and shoes with nasty spikes to help you run faster.

4

A) NO CHANGE

B) True, the ball does not hurt as much if it hits you, but consider the threat such close proximity to a vicious competitor poses.

C) True, you are allowed to hold on to your new racket all through the game, but how often are you allowed to employ it usefully?

D) While you only look bad in front of three others (if there are no spectators), one of them poses a threat to your health that should not be overlooked.

5

A) NO CHANGE

B) more then his share

C) a greater share then his

D) more than his share

6 Since he will have the chance to drive off every tee, so he need have no fears that his new driver will not be employed. He will have as many swings with it as the excellent golfer—more, if he misses the ball altogether upon one or two tees.

Above all, there is this to be said for golfing mediocrity—the bad player can make the strokes of the good player. 7 The poor golfer, at some time or other, has played to perfection the course's every hole, provided he has golfed on said course frequently enough. He has driven a ball 250 yards; he has made superb approaches; he has run down the long putt. 8 It is possible that perhaps any of these things might suddenly happen to him again. 9 This being the case, it is not his fate to have to sit in the club after his

---

6

A) NO CHANGE

B) Because he will have the chance to drive off every tee:

C) Since he will have the chance to drive off every tee;

D) He will have the chance to drive off every tee, so

7

A) NO CHANGE

B) If he has golfed frequently enough, the poor golfer has, some time or other, played every hole on the course to perfection.

C) The poor golfer to perfection has, some time or other, if he has golfed frequently enough, played every hole on the course.

D) At one time or another, the poor golfer, which is to say the player who struggles to golf well, has played every hole to perfection as long as he has golfed frequently enough.

8

A) NO CHANGE

B) All of these will

C) Any of these things might

D) Perhaps any of these things might

9

A) NO CHANGE

B) However,

C) By the same token,

D) All things considered,

CONTINUE ➡

second round and listen to the 10 <u>wonderful deeds</u> of others. He can join in too. He can say with perfect truth, "I once carried the ditch at the fourth with my second," or "I remember when I drove into the bunker guarding the eighth green."

11 <u>A bad player at cricket is not so lucky.</u>

10

A) NO CHANGE

B) daring do

C) impressive feats

D) wowing facts

11

The writer would like to conclude with a specific example that flows naturally from the rest of the paragraph, supports the central argument of the passage, and acknowledges an example from earlier in the passage. Which choice most effectively accomplishes these goals?

A) NO CHANGE

B) But if the bad tennis player says, "I remember when I took five games and a set from Federer before he came back to edge me out in the end," he is nothing but a liar.

C) A bad footballer has likely never accomplished anything so great as a good footballer.

D) Even so, it would be wonderful to be a good golfer one day.

CONTINUE

Questions 12-22 are based on the following passage.

This passage is adapted from Garth Brown, "How Do You Eat Raw Meat?"

The short answer is 12 *don't*: the longer answer is *very carefully*.

Cooking meat has become a cultural norm for a variety of reasons. 13 Cooked meat tastes good, and it has more available calories than raw meat. Cooking makes tough cuts tender. 14 Even so, these days the single biggest reason most people cook food is safety. Heat can kill all the pathogenic bacteria commonly found on foods. While cold isn't an adequate kill step for most pathogens, it can stop or retard bacterial growth. So far as I know, freezing will stop the reproduction of all pathogens.

15 As you can tell, foods can be dangerous. Experts recommend that potentially dangerous food, including any meat, be kept cold

12

A) NO CHANGE

B) *don't*, the longer answer is *very carefully*.

C) *don't*; the longer answer is *very carefully*.

D) *don't*—the longer answer—*very carefully*.

13

A) Cooked meat tastes good, has more available calories than raw meat, and makes tough cuts tender.

B) Having more available calories, tasting better, and making tough cuts tender, cooking meat is the way to go.

C) Cooking meat flavorizes, calorizes, and tenderizes.

D) Cooking meat makes it taste better, makes calories more available, and makes tough cuts tender.

14

A) NO CHANGE

B) On the other hand,

C) Considering this,

D) This being the case,

15

A) NO CHANGE

B) One should always strive to stop the reproduction of pathogens.

C) Temperature guidelines are based on this information.

D) Freezing may, however, render meat less delicious.

CONTINUE

until it is prepared, at which point it should be cooked; 16 it should left to rest between 40 and 140 degrees Fahrenheit to maximize safety.

And yet, there is a way to not only render raw meat safe at room temperature, but to make it absolutely delicious, and that is curing. Curing meat involves 17 a combination of salt, time, and sometimes fermentation which work together to render the food free of pathogens, or so I've read. As I set out to make dry cured sausages for the first time, 18 my biggest mental hurdle was the idea of leaving it right in the middle of the food danger zone for weeks on end. The most terrifying prospect, however, was botulism.

16

A) NO CHANGE

B) it should be cooked to a temperature of 140 degrees Fahrenheit.

C) the surface temperature of the meat should be allowed to rise above 140 degrees Fahrenheit.

D) it should be between 40 and 140 degrees Fahrenheit for as short a time as possible to limit pathogens.

17

A) NO CHANGE

B) a combination of, salt, time, and sometimes fermentation, which

C) a combination of salt, time, and sometimes fermentation, which

D) a combination of salt, time, and sometimes fermentation, that

18

Which choice most effectively expresses the mindset of the writer in a way that is supported by the assertions of the previous paragraphs?

A) NO CHANGE

B) I was pretty nervous about using too much salt.

C) the idea fermentation terrified me.

D) I wondered why I had always subjected my meats to such high temperatures.

CONTINUE

Here's a fun fact—the word *botulism* derives from the Latin word *botulus*, which means sausage. These days botulism is overwhelmingly associated with poorly canned goods. It's a pathogen that is basically everywhere, but it requires particular conditions to thrive. Before the widespread advent of canned goods, however, aged sausage 19 <u>fits</u> the bill.

Luckily, there are curing 20 <u>salts—</u> <u>nitrites and nitrates,</u> that can prevent botulinum growth when used appropriately. So the processes that work together to render an aged sausage safe to eat are manifold, or at least threefold. Curing salts inhibit botulinum while allowing the growth of beneficial bacteria. Beneficial bacteria such as lactobacillus lower the acidity, which inhibits the growth of pathogens. As the sausage dries, its available water decreases, which also kills off pathogens. The end result is a reliably safe, delicious product. It's also meat that is, in a sense, still raw. 21 <u>No one has ever heated it,</u> <u>frozen it, and it has even been encouraged to</u> <u>foster a huge colony of bacteria.</u> It feels illicit, almost like black magic, to violate basically every conventional precept of food safety and yet to end

19

A) NO CHANGE

B) fit

C) should have fit

D) fitted

20

A) NO CHANGE

B) salts; nitrites and nitrates,

C) salts—nitrites and nitrates—

D) salts: nitrites, and nitrates,

21

A) NO CHANGE

B) It has never been heated, never been cooked, and has even been encouraged by the temperature to foster a huge colony of bacteria.

C) No one has ever cooked it, it hasn't been frozen, and the temperature encourages a huge colony of bacteria.

D) It has never been heated, it has not been frozen, and it even has been encouraged to foster a huge colony of bacteria.

CONTINUE ➡

up with something so uniquely wonderful as a result.

22 Unless you will be curing your own meats, all you need know is of their deliciousness and safety (if the curing has been done properly). So if all this talk about potentially lethal bacteria hasn't scared you into overcooking your food, go ahead and enjoy a botulus today.

22

A) NO CHANGE

B) If you will not be making your own cured meat, all you need to know is that it's delicious and, if properly done, safe.

C) If you will not be curing your own meats, safe and delicious is all you need to know about what they are if done properly.

D) It is delicious and, done properly, safe is all that you need to know about cured meat unless you will be doing the curing yourself.

CONTINUE

Questions 23-33 are based on the following passage.

This passage is adapted from Kate M. Foley, "The Attitude of the Public Toward the Blind," originally published in 1919.

23 No one can deny the idea that all blind people are so much happier than sighted people. This belief comes, I suppose, as a result of the feeling of the average human being that, if deprived of eyesight, he could never be induced to laugh again. One of my foreign pupils said to me when I spoke of his cheerful attitude, "Madam, I laugh that I may not weep." This is the key to much of the cheerfulness of the blind. People feel so sorry for the blind that they are often unable to address them at 24 all, or, when they do speak, convey a whole world of well-meant, but misdirected sympathy in a few ill-chosen words. This misdirected sympathy is one of the hardest things the blind adult has to bear.

25 A prevalent idea among so-called well-informed men and women is that a loss of eyesight carries with it a total inability to engage in any of the world's work. Anything done by the blind, 26 he or she thinks, from recognizing a voice to remembering a street number, is a

---

23

A) NO CHANGE

B) If there is one thing that makes me angrier than anything else, it is

C) I am very thankful for

D) To begin, I wish to mention a popular fallacy concerning the blind:

24

A) NO CHANGE

B) all or, when they do speak, convey a whole world of well-meant

C) all or, when they do speak, convey a whole world of well-meant,

D) all, or when they do speak convey a whole world of well-meant

25

A) NO CHANGE

B) A prevalent idea among so-called well-informed men and women are

C) An idea among so-called well-informed men and women prevail

D) Prevalent among so-called well-informed men and women, an idea prevails

26

A) NO CHANGE

B) they think,

C) one thinks,

D) these think,

CONTINUE ➡

wonder, and this attitude is very trying to the blind adult who is striving to adjust to new conditions. The commiseration and incredulous words of his friends 27 is one of the 28 principle trials that the blind adult is called upon to bear. They are sorry, honestly sorry, and want so much to help, but, to the 29 mind's of sighted people's, blindness is the greatest of all afflictions, and loss of eyesight is accompanied by a corresponding loss of physical ability and mental vigor.

　　　As a class I honestly believe that blind people are more courageous than seeing people, and I am sure that a greater demand is made upon their stock of courage. 30 This demand will be

---

27

A) NO CHANGE

B) are one

C) are some

D) comprise much

28

A) NO CHANGE

B) principal

C) cheif

D) mane

29

A) NO CHANGE

B) minds of sighted people's,

C) sighted peoples' minds,

D) minds of sighted people,

30

At this point, the writer is considering adding the following sentence.

> It is possible they have this demand to thank for their courage.

Should the writer make this addition here?

A) Yes, because it might make sighted people feel better for putting demands on the blind.

B) Yes, because it responds to a question the reader is likely to have formulated.

C) No, because it is pure speculation on the part of the writer.

D) No, because it undermines the writer's main goal in this paragraph.

CONTINUE ➡

lessened when the public learns to look upon blindness as a physical, not a mental handicap, and when, instead of compelling people so handicapped to sit on the sidelines holding their broken 31 swords, it leads them forward, places a new sword in their hands, and brings them the glad tidings, that they are needed on the firing line. Loss of eyesight is always 32 reprehensible, but it is not so terrible as the isolation which generally follows it, an isolation due, in large measure, to misplaced sympathy on the part of the public, generous to a fault in bestowing alms, but slow to believe in the ability of the blind. 33 When the public is brought to look upon the blind as men and women just as eager to work and interested in things as when they saw them through the natural medium, their handicap would be lessened and their lives much happier.

31

A) NO CHANGE

B) swords, it leads them forward, places a new sword in their hands, and brings them the glad tidings that they are needed on the firing line.

C) swords it leads them forward, places a new sword in their hands, and brings them the glad tidings that they are needed on the firing line.

D) swords, it leads them forward; places a new sword in their hands, and brings them the glad tidings, that they are needed on the firing line.

32

A) NO CHANGE

B) diabolical,

C) unfortunate,

D) crestfallen,

33

A) NO CHANGE

B) The public should be

C) As the public might be

D) If the public could be

CONTINUE

Questions 34 - 44 are based on the following passage.

This passage is adapted from G. K. Chesterton, "On Lying in Bed," originally published in 1909.

Lying in bed would be an altogether perfect and supreme experience if only one had a brush long enough to paint on the ceiling. I think that this might be managed with several buckets of paint and a 34 broom, to that purpose the white ceiling would be of the greatest possible use. In fact, it is the only use I can think of for a white ceiling.

If not for the beautiful experiment of lying in bed, I might never have discovered it. 35 For years I've searched them for blank spaces to draw on— paper is much too small for any really grand design—but to no avail; it seemed there was no suitable space for me in the modern house. When I tried to find these fine clear spaces in the modern rooms such as we all live in, I was continually disappointed. I examined the walls. 36 Beyond recognition with wallpaper, I lamented the uninteresting, monotonous images I

34

A) NO CHANGE

B) broom, to which

C) broom, to whose

D) broom with a

35

A) NO CHANGE

B) I, for years, have, as paper is much too small for any really grand design, been looking for some blank spaces to draw on that are larger, and where better to look in these modern times than in a house?

C) Many a modern house has been searched for blank spaces over the years by me since paper is much too small for any really grand design

D) As paper is too small for any really grand design, I have been looking for blank spaces in a modern house to draw on for years.

36

A) NO CHANGE

B) Already covered with wallpaper,

C) Finding them covered with wallpaper,

D) Utterly wallpapered,

CONTINUE ▶

saw. Everywhere that I went forlornly with my pencil or my paint brush, I found that others had unaccountably been there before 37 me, spoiling the walls, the curtains, and the furniture with their childish, and barbaric designs.

38 Nowhere did I find a really clear space for sketching until this occasion when I prolonged the process of lying on my back in bed beyond the proper limit. Then the light of that white ceiling broke upon my vision. To my distress, 39 I found the canvas, but no dice.

37

A) NO CHANGE

B) me, spoiling the walls, the curtains, and ruining the furniture with their childish, barbaric

C) me, spoiling the walls, the curtains, and the furniture with their childish, barbaric

D) me spoiling the walls, the curtains, and the furniture with their childish barbaric

38

A) NO CHANGE

B) Lying in bed was the only remedy from these terrible images.

C) I decided, and I congratulate myself on the decision, that the wise man goes to bed early; I would be wise for perhaps the first time in my life.

D) Those designs infuriate me to this day!

39

A) NO CHANGE

B) the canvas long sought by this pitiable wretch seemed within my grasp, yet cruel fortune hath a woeful plan wrought and unfurled.

C) now that it is seen, it is found to be unattainable.

D) my plan was ixnayed.

CONTINUE ➡

40 [1] The tone now commonly taken toward the practice of lying in bed is negative and unhealthy. [2] Getting up early follows practical wisdom, but there is nothing good about it or bad about its opposite. [3] **41** <u>Some bad people get up early, and some good people do not.</u> [4] Instead of being regarded, as it ought to be, as a matter of

---

40

At this point, the writer is considering adding the following sentence.

> My proposal to lie down and paint on the ceiling with the bristly end of a broom has been discouraged— never mind by whom.

Should the writer make this addition here?

A) Yes, because it sets up a transition from the previous sentence to the next paragraph.

B) Yes, because it provides another example that supports the central argument of the paragraph.

C) No, because it does not adequately respond to an obvious counterargument.

D) No, because it is irrelevant to the paragraph.

41

The writer would like to support the claim of the previous sentence with some specific examples. Which choice most effectively accomplished these goals?

A) NO CHANGE

B) When I must, I wake up early, but I prefer to prolong the experience of lazy repose as I am quite certain would nearly everyone who gives it a proper go around.

C) Nuns get up early in the morning, and priests, I have it on the best authority, rise even earlier.

D) Misers get up early in the morning, and burglars, I am informed, get up the night before.

CONTINUE

personal convenience and adjustment, lying in bed 42 came to be regarding by many as if it were a part of essential morals to get up early in the morning. 43

For those who study the great art of lying in bed there is one emphatic caution to be added: if you do lie in bed, be sure you do it without any reason or justification at all. If a healthy man lies in bed, let him do it without a rag of excuse; then he will get up a healthy man. 44 Notwithstanding this, if he does it for some secondary reason, if he has some scientific explanation, he may get up a hypochondriac.

42

A) NO CHANGE

B) has come to be regarded

C) is to be regarded

D) will have been regarded

43

A) where it is now.

B) before sentence 1.

C) after sentence 1.

D) before sentence 3.

44

A) NO CHANGE

B) Wherefore

C) By the same token,

D) On the other hand,

STOP
**If you finish before time is called, you may check your work on this section only.
Do not turn to any other section.**

No Test Material On This Page

Math Test – No Calculator
25 Minutes, 20 Questions

DIRECTIONS

For questions 1 – 15, solve each problem, choose the best answer from the choices provided, and fill in the corresponding circle on your answer sheet. **For questions 16 – 20**, solve the problem and enter your answer in the grid on the answer sheet. You may use any available space in your test booklet for scratch work.

NOTES

1. The use of a calculator **is not permitted**.

2. All variables and expressions used represent real numbers unless otherwise noted.

3. Figures provided in this test are drawn to scale unless otherwise indicated.

4. All figures lie in a plane unless otherwise indicated.

5. Unless otherwise indicated, the domain of a given function f is the set of all real numbers for x for which $f(x)$ is a real number.

REFERENCE

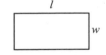

$A = \pi r^2$
$C = 2\pi r$

$A = lw$

$A = \frac{1}{2}bh$

$c^2 = a^2 + b^2$

Special Right Triangles

$V = lwh$

$V = \pi r^2 h$

$V = \frac{4}{3}\pi r^3$

$V = \frac{1}{3}\pi r^3 h$

$V = \frac{1}{3}lwh$

The number of degrees of arc in a circle is 360.
The number of radians of arc in a circle is 2π.
The sum of the measures in degrees of the angle of a triangle is 180.

CONTINUE

1

$$5x - 11 + 2x - 3x + x + 14 = 8 + 2x + 2 - 4$$

In the equation above, what is the value of x?

A) $-\frac{2}{3}$

B) $\frac{10}{3}$

C) 1

D) 3

2

The width of a rectangular wall is w feet. The width of the wall is 4 feet shorter than its length. Which of the following expresses the area in feet, of the wall in terms of w?

A) $w^2 + 4w$

B) $4w + 8$

C) $w^4 + 8$

D) $2w + 4$

3

$$2x + 3y = 13$$
$$x = 2 + 3y$$

Which ordered pair (x, y) satisfies the system of equations shown above?

A) $(2, 3)$

B) $(5, 1)$

C) $(-4, -2)$

D) $(8, 2)$

4

Which of the following complex numbers is equal to $(6 + 10i) - (4i^2 - 6i)$ for $i = \sqrt{-1}$?

A) $-10 + 4i$

B) $10 + 16i$

C) $-2 - 4i$

D) $2 + 16i$

CONTINUE

5

If $f(x) = \frac{x^2-x-6}{x+2}$, what is $f(-3)$?

A) 12

B) 6

C) 0

D) -6

6

A company that photographs food purchases camera equipment for $62,400. The equipment depreciates in value at a constant rate for 12 years, after which it is considered to have no monetary value. How much is the camera equipment worth 5 years after it is purchased?

A) $26,000

B) $36,400

C) $41,600

D) $57,200

7

$$x^2 - 4x + 10$$

Which of the following is equivalent to the expression above?

A) $(x + 2)^2 + 6$

B) $(x + 2)^2 - 6$

C) $(x - 2)^2 - 6$

D) $(x - 2)^2 + 6$

CONTINUE

8

Steve is working this summer as a part of a crew on a yacht. He earned \$12 per hour for the first 10 hours he worked this week. Because of his performance, his captain raised his salary to \$14 per hour for the rest of the week. Steve saves 80% of his earnings from each week. What is the least number of hours he must work the rest of the week to save at least \$320 for the week?

A) 20

B) 37

C) 45

D) 14

9

$$\left(\frac{x^2 y^{-\frac{1}{3}}}{x^{-2} y^{-3}}\right)^{-\frac{1}{3}}$$

Which of the expressions below is equivalent to the expression above?

A) $\dfrac{\sqrt[3]{x^4}}{y \sqrt[9]{y}}$

B) $\dfrac{\sqrt[9]{y}}{\sqrt[6]{y}\,\sqrt[3]{x^4}}$

C) $\dfrac{\sqrt[9]{y}}{y \sqrt[3]{x^4}}$

D) $\dfrac{\sqrt[6]{y}}{\sqrt{y^3}\,\sqrt[3]{x^4}}$

10

A catering company is going to hire at least 13 staff members for its upcoming event. The staff will be made up of members, who will be paid \$370 per week, and managers, who will be paid \$840 per week. The company's budget for paying the employees is no more than \$8,550 per week. They must hire at least 4 staff members and at least 2 managers. Which of the following systems of inequalities represents the conditions described if x is the number of staff members and y is the number of managers?

D) $370x + 840y \geq 8,350$
    $x + y \leq 13$
    $x \geq 4$
    $y \geq 2$

C) $370x + 840y \leq 8,550$
    $x + y \leq 13$
    $x \leq 4$
    $y \leq 2$

B) $370x + 840y \leq 8,850$
    $x + y \geq 13$
    $x \geq 4$
    $y \geq 2$

A) $370x + 840y \geq 8,350$
    $x + y \leq 13$
    $x \geq 4$
    $y \geq 2$

11

$$ax^3 + bx^2 + cx + d = 0$$

In the equation above, $a, b, c,$ and d are constants. If the equation has roots -2, 4, and -7, which of the following is a factor of $ax^3 + bx^2 + cx + d$?

A) $x - 2$

B) $x + 4$

C) $x - 7$

D) $x - 4$

CONTINUE

12

The function f is defined by $f(x) = (x - 2)(x + 8)$. The graph of the xy-plane is a parabola. Which of the following intervals contains the x-coordinate of the vertex of the graph of f?

A) $-2 < x < 8$

B) $-8 < x < 2$

C) $2 < x < 4$

D) $2 < x < 8$

13

Which of the following expressions is equivalent to $\frac{x^2+5x-12}{x-4}$?

A) $x + 1 - \frac{8}{x-4}$

B) $x + 9 + \frac{24}{x-4}$

C) $x + 1 - \frac{16}{x-4}$

D) $x + 9 - \frac{48}{x-4}$

14

A shipping service restricts the dimensions of the boxes it will ship for a certain type of service. The restriction states that for boxes shaped like a rectangular prisms, the sum of the perimeter of the base of the box and the height of the box cannot exceed 170 inches. The perimeter of the base is determined using the width and length of the box. If a box has a height of 50 inches and its length is 3 times the width, which inequality shows the available width x, in inches, of the box?

A) $0 < x \leq 27\frac{1}{2}$

B) $0 < x \leq 30$

C) $0 < x \leq 12$

D) $0 < x \leq 15$

15

The expression $\frac{1}{4}x^2 - 2$ can be written as $\frac{1}{4}(x - a)(x + a)$, where a is a positive constant. What is the value of a?

A) $2\sqrt{2}$

B) $\sqrt{2}$

C) 4

D) 8

CONTINUE

16

If $5x + 12 = 27$, what is the value of $x + 6$?

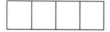

17

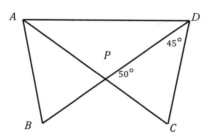

In the figure above (not drawn to scale), $\overline{AC}$ and $\overline{BD}$ intersect at point P, $BP = CP$, and $AP = PD$. What is the measure, in degrees, of $\angle BDA$? (Disregard the degree symbol when gridding your answer)

18

The number of radians in a 1080-degree angle can be written as $x\pi$, where x is a constant. What is the value of x?

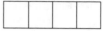

19

The graph of a line in the xy-plane passes through the point $(2, 6)$ and crosses the x-axis at the point $(3,0)$. The line crosses the y-axis at the point $(0, b)$. What is the value of b?

20

$$(6786 + 100y^2) - 12(8y^2 - 110)$$

The expression above can be written in the form $ay^2 + b$, where a and b are constants. What is the value $a + b$?

STOP

If you finish before time is called, you may check your work on this section only.
Do not turn to any other section.

Math Test – Calculator
55 Minutes, 38 Questions

DIRECTIONS

For questions 1 – 30, solve each problem, choose the best answer from the choices provided, and fill in the corresponding circle on your answer sheet. **For questions 31 – 38**, solve the problem and enter your answer in the grid on the answer sheet. You may use any available space in your test booklet for scratch work.

NOTES

1. The use of a calculator **is permitted**.

2. All variables and expressions used represent real numbers unless otherwise noted.

3. Figures provided in this test are drawn to scale unless otherwise indicated.

4. All figures lie in a plane unless otherwise indicated.

5. Unless otherwise indicated, the domain of a given function *f* is the set of all real numbers for *x* for which *f(x)* is a real number.

REFERENCE

$A = \pi r^2$
$C = 2\pi r$

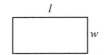

$A = lw$

$A = \frac{1}{2}bh$

$c^2 = a^2 + b^2$

Special Right Triangles

$V = lwh$

$V = \pi r^2 h$

$V = \frac{4}{3}\pi r^3$

$V = \frac{1}{3}\pi r^3 h$

$V = \frac{1}{3}lwh$

The number of degrees of arc in a circle is 360.
The number of radians of arc in a circle is 2π.
The sum of the measures in degrees of the angle of a triangle is 180.

CONTINUE ➡

1

$$(4x^2 - 6) - (-2x^2 + 4x - 8)?$$

Which expression is equivalent to the equation above?

A) $2x^2 - 4x - 14$

B) $2x^2 + 4x - 2$

C) $6x^2 - 4x + 2$

D) $6x^2 + 4x - 14$

2

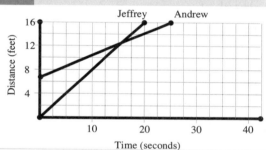

The graph above shows the positions of Andrew and Jeffery during a swim race. Andrew and Jeffery each swim at a constant rate, and Andrew was given a head start to shorten the distance he needed to swim across the pool. Jeffery finished the race in 20 seconds, and Andrew finished the race in 25 seconds. According to the graph, Andrew was given a head start of how many feet?

A) 5

B) 7

C) 10

D) 12

3

To make a bakery's signature oatmeal and raisin cookies, a baker needs 14.8 pounds of oatmeal for 64 cookies. How many ounces of oatmeal are needed to make one cookie? (1 pound= 16 ounces)

A) 0.23

B) 0.27

C) 3.70

D) 4.32

4

A cellular service company charges its a customers a onetime setup fee of $40 plus x dollars for each month. If a customer paid $1,024 for the first 12 months, including the set up fee, what is the value of x?

A) 26

B) 45

C) 75

D) 82

CONTINUE

5

$$8x < 6y + 12$$

Which of the following inequalities is equivalent to the inequality above?

A) $4x - 2y < 6$

B) $3x - 4y < 6$

C) $2x - 3y < 3$

D) $4x - 3y < 6$

6

Source	Percent of Surveyed
Department Store	27%
Specialty Store	18%
Internet	25%
Grocery Store	15%
Television	9%
Other	6%

The table above shows a summary of 800 responses to a survey question. Based on the table, how many of those surveyed get most of their household items from either a specialty store or the Internet?

A) 320

B) 344

C) 360

D) 456

CONTINUE

7

The members of a city council wanted to assess the opinions of all city residents about converting an open field into a community recreation center. The council surveyed a sample of 200 city residents who are athletic. The survey showed that the majority of those sampled were in favor of the recreation center. Which of the following is true about the survey?

A) The survey sample is not a good representation of the all of the residents in the city.

B) The survey sample should have consisted of more residents who are athletic.

C) The survey sample should have consisted entirely of residents who are not athletic.

D) It shows that the majority of the city residents are in favor of the community recreation center.

8

	Dressing	
	Ranch	Italian
Croutons	8	5
Bacon Bits	4	9

The table above shows salad dressings and toppings chosen by people at a family party. Each person chose one dressing and one topping. Of the people who chose ranch dressing, what fraction chose croutons as a topping?

A) $\frac{2}{3}$

B) $\frac{4}{13}$

C) $\frac{1}{3}$

D) $\frac{6}{13}$

CONTINUE

9

The total area of a coastal city is 117.8 square miles, of which 22.3 square miles is water. If the city had a population of 732,000 people in the year 2015, which of the following is closest to the population density, in people per square mile of land area, of the city at that time?

A) 5,225

B) 6,256

C) 7,665

D) 32,825

10

Camilla is planning to travel for the summer. Her first trip is going to last 25 days longer than her second trip, and the two trips combined will last 93 days in total. How many days did the first trip last?

A) 31

B) 34

C) 59

D) 68

11

$$3x - 4y = -5$$
$$-10x + 4y = 12$$

For the solution (x, y) to the system of equations above, what is the value of $x + y$?

A) $\frac{1}{2}$

B) $-\frac{1}{2}$

C) $-1\frac{1}{2}$

D) $1\frac{1}{2}$

CONTINUE

Questions 12-14 correspond to the following information.

The table below shows the height of an orchid over time.

Day	Height
0	0.00
7	12.93
14	25.25
21	47.76
28	78.10
35	111.00
42	159.5
49	205.5
56	238.30
63	242.10
70	249.50
77	250.80
84	251.50

12

Over which of the following time periods is the average growth rate of the orchid greatest?

A) Day 0 to 21

B) Day 21 to 42

C) Day 42 to 63

D) Day 63 to 84

13

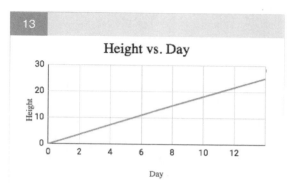

Height vs. Day

The function above, f, defined by $h(t) = xt + y$, where x and y are constants, models the height, in centimeters, of the orchid after t days of growth during a time period in which the growth is approximately linear. What does y represent?

A) The predicted number of centimeters the orchid grows each day during the period.

B) The predicted height, in centimeters, of the orchid at the beginning of the period.

C) The predicted height, in centimeters, of the orchid at the end of the period.

D) The predicted total increase in height, in centimeters, of the orchid at during the period.

14

The growth rate of the orchid from day 21 to 35 is nearly constant. On this interval, which of the following equations best models the height h, in centimeters, of the orchid t days after it begins to grow?

A) $h = 2.1t - 15$

B) $h = 0.22t - 43$

C) $h = 7.8t - 22$

D) $h = 4.5t - 47$

CONTINUE

15

x	1	3	4	5	7
y	$\dfrac{13}{6}$	$\dfrac{45}{6}$	$\dfrac{61}{6}$	$\dfrac{77}{6}$	$\dfrac{109}{6}$

Which of the following equations relates y and x for the values in the table above?

A) $y = \frac{1}{2} \cdot \left(\frac{16}{3}\right)^x$

B) $y = \frac{8}{3} \cdot \left(\frac{1}{2}\right)^x$

C) $y = \frac{8}{3}x - \frac{1}{2}$

D) $y = \frac{16}{3}x - \frac{19}{3}$

16

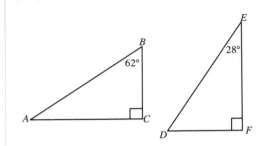

Triangles ABC and DEF are shown above. Which of the following is equal to the ratio $\frac{DF}{DE}$?

A) $\frac{BC}{AB}$

B) $\frac{AB}{BC}$

C) $\frac{BC}{AC}$

D) $\frac{AC}{BC}$

CONTINUE

Questions 17-19 refer to the following information.

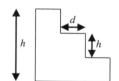

Note: This figure is not drawn to scale.

When designing a stairway, an architect uses the following formula: $4h + 2d = 48$. In the formula height is h, in inches, and d is the depth, in inches. For any given stairway, the heights are the same and the depths are the same for all steps in that stairway.

The number of steps in a stairway is the number of its risers. For example, there are 5 steps in the stairway in the figure above. The total rise of a stairway is the sum of the riser heights as shown in the figure.

17

Which of the following expresses the depth in terms of the height?

A) $d = 4(12 - h)$

B) $d = \frac{1}{4}(12 - h)$

C) $d = \frac{1}{2}(12 - h)$

D) $d = 2(12 - h)$

18

Some building codes require that, for indoor stairways, the depth must be at least 10 inches and the height must be at least 3 inches. According to the formula given, which of the following inequalities represents the set of all possible values for the height that meets this code requirement?

A) $h \geq 7$

B) $7 \leq h \leq 10$

C) $3 \leq h \leq 7$

D) $3 \leq h \leq 10$

19

An architect wants to use the formula given above to design a stairway with a total rise of 7 feet, a height between 5 and 6 inches, and an odd number of steps. With the architect's constraints, which of the following must be the depth, in inches, of the stairway?

A) 12.8

B) 13.5

C) 12.0

D) 14.0

CONTINUE

20

What is the sum of the solutions to
$(x - 0.32)(x + 4) = 0$?

A) 4.32

B) 3.68

C) -4.32

D) -3.68

21

A study was done on the length of different types of land snakes. A random sample of snakes was caught and marked in order to ensure none were recorded more than once. The sample contained 120 Milk Snakes, of which 20% were longer than 60 inches. Which of the conclusions is best supported by the sample data?

A) The majority of all the snakes on land are less than 60 inches long.

B) Approximately 20% of all land snakes is more than 60 inches long.

C) Approximately 20% of all milk snakes is more than 60 inches long.

D) The average length of all the land snakes is approximately 60 inches.

22

Electoral Votes	Frequency
15	3
18	1
20	2
22	1
29	2
38	1
55	1

In 2012, there were 18 states with 15 or more electoral votes, as shown in the table above. Based on the table, what was the median number of electoral votes for the 21 states?

A) 22

B) 20

C) 15

D) 29

CONTINUE

23

A customer's monthly electrical bill was $23.56. Due to a rate increase, his monthly bill is now $27.47. To the nearest tenth, by what percent did the amount of the customer's electrical bill increase?

A)   14.2%

B)   14.4%

C)   16.6%

D)   16.9%

24

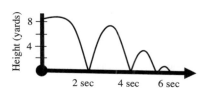

Height of a ball in feet t seconds after being dropped

As part of an experiment, a ball was thrown from a window and allowed to bounce repeatedly off the ground until it came to rest. The graph above represents the relationship between the time elapsed after the ball was dropped and the height of the ball above the ground. After it was dropped, how many times was the ball at a height of 6 yards?

A) Three

B) Four

C) Five

D) Six

CONTINUE

25

x	$f(x)$
0	8
2	9
8	12

Some values of the linear equation f are shown in the table above. What is the value of $f(6)$?

A) 8

B) 9.5

C) 10

D) 11

26

In the xy-plane, the point (a, z) lies on the line with equation $y = x + b$, where b is a constant. The point with coordinates $(4a, 3z)$ lies on the line with equation $y = 5x + b$. If $z \neq 0$, what is the value of $\frac{a}{z}$?

A) $\frac{19}{2}$

B) $\frac{2}{19}$

C) $\frac{21}{4}$

D) $\frac{4}{21}$

27

In the xy-plane, graph of $2x^2 - 6x + 2y^2 + 2y = 45$ is a circle. What is the center of the circle?

A) $(1.5, -0.5)$

B) $(-1.5, -0.5)$

C) $(2.25, 0.25)$

D) $(2.25, -0.25)$

CONTINUE

28

Two different points on a number line are both 8 units from the point with coordinate -3. The solution to which of the following equations gives the coordinates of both points?

A) $|x - 3| = 8$

B) $|x + 3| = 8$

C) $|x - 8| = 3$

D) $|x + 8| = 3$

29

A motor powers a model car so that after starting from rest, the car travels t inches in s seconds, where $t = 25s\sqrt{s}$. Which of the following gives the average speed of the car, in inches per second, over the first s seconds after it starts?

A) $5s$

B) $5\sqrt{s}$

C) $25\sqrt{s}$

D) $\dfrac{5s}{\sqrt{s}}$

30

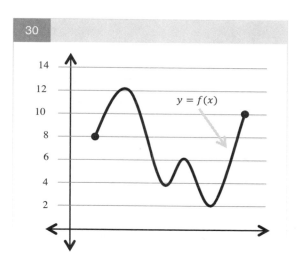

$y = f(x)$

x	-3	-2	-1	0	2	5	6	8
$g(x)$	0	1	2	3	5	8	9	11

The complete graph of the function f and a table of values for the function g are shown above. The minimum value of f is k. What is the value of $g(k)$?

A) 11

B) 8

C) 5

D) 0

CONTINUE

31

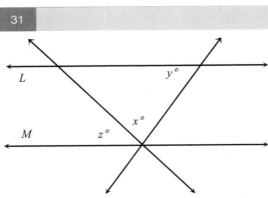

In the figure above, lines L and M are parallel, $y = 40$, and $z = 30$. What is the value of x?

32

A group of friends decided to divide the $1400 cost of a trip equally among themselves. When two more people join their trip, the friends decided to divide the total price of $1400 equally among the new total number of people interested in the trip, but each friend's share of cost decreased of $35. How many friends were in the group originally?

33

$$3(5x - 14) - (39 + 3x) = 15$$

What value of x satisfies the equation above?

34

Students in chemistry lab use graduated cylinders with an internal radius of 3 inches and an internal height between 5.75 inches and 6 inches. What is one possible volume, rounded to the nearest cubic inch, of a graduated cylinder the students use for their experiments?

CONTINUE

35

In the xy-plane, the graph of $y = 6x^2 - 35x$ intersects the graph of $x = y$ at the points $(0, 0)$ and (a, a). What is the value of a?

37

Morgan deposited x dollars in her investment account on March 21, 2003. The amount of money in the account doubled each year until she had \$1200 dollars in her investment account on March 21, 2008. What is the value of x?

36

The line with the equation $\frac{4}{3}x + \frac{5}{7}y = 1$ is graphed in the xy-plane. What is the x-coordinate of the x-intercept of the line?

38

An animation company is forming a committee to discuss plans for a future project. Of those invited to join the committee, 15% are interns, 45% are computer and IT specialists, 25% are talent program specialists, and the remaining 18 people are senior engineers. How many more computer and IT specialists were invited to join the committee than talent program specialists?

STOP

**If you finish before time is called, you may check your work on this section only.
Do not turn to any other section.**

No Test Material On This Page

Essay

ESSAY BOOK

DIRECTIONS

The essay gives you an opportunity to show how effectively you can read and comprehend a passage and write an essay analyzing the passage. In your essay, you should demonstrate that you have read the passage carefully, present a clear and logical analysis, and use language precisely.

Your essay must be written on the lines provided in your answer booklet; except for the Planning Page of the answer booklet, you will receive no other paper on which to write.

You have <u>50 minutes</u> to read the passage and write an essay in response to the prompt provided inside this booklet.

As you read the passage below, consider how Fredrick Douglas uses

- evidence, such as facts or examples, to support claims.

- reasoning to develop ideas and to connect claims and evidence.

- stylistic or persuasive elements, such as word choice or appeals to emotion, to add power to the ideas expressed.

Adapted from Fredrick Douglass, *Speech on Women's Suffrage*, delivered to the International Council of Women in Washington, D.C., April 1888.

1 All good causes are mutually helpful. The benefits accruing from this movement for the equal rights of woman are not confined or limited to woman only. They will be shared by every effort to promote the progress and welfare of mankind every where and in all ages. It was an example and a prophecy of what can be accomplished against strongly opposing forces, against time-hallowed abuses, against deeply entrenched error, against worldwide usage, and against the settled judgment of mankind, by a few earnest women, clad only in the panoply of truth, and determined to live and die in what they considered a righteous cause.

2 I do not forget the thoughtful remark of our president in the opening address to this International Council, reminding us of the incompleteness of our work. The remark was wise and timely. Nevertheless, no man can compare the present with the past, the obstacles that then opposed us, and the influences that now favor us, the meeting in the little Methodist chapel forty years ago, and the Council in this vast theater today, without admitting that woman's cause is already a brilliant success. But, however this may be and whatever the future may have in store for us, one thing is certain—this new revolution in human thought will never go backward. When a great truth once gets abroad in the world, no power on earth can imprison it, or prescribe its limits, or suppress it. It is bound to go on till it becomes the thought of the world. Such a truth is woman's right to equal liberty with man. She was born with it. It was hers before she comprehended it. It is inscribed upon all the powers and faculties of her soul, and no custom, law or usage can ever destroy it. Now that it has got fairly fixed in the minds of the few, it is bound to become fixed in the minds of the many, and be supported at last by a great cloud of witnesses, which no man can number and no power can withstand.

3 The women who have thus far carried on this agitation have already embodied and illustrated Theodore Parker's three grades of human greatness. The first is greatness in executive and administrative ability; second, greatness in the ability to organize; and, thirdly, in the ability to discover truth. Wherever these three elements of power are combined in any movement, there is a reasonable ground to believe in its final success; and these elements of power have been manifest in the women who have had the movement in hand from the beginning. They are seen in the order which has characterized the proceedings of this Council. They are seen in the depth and are seen in the fervid eloquence and downright earnestness with which women advocate their cause. They are seen in the profound attention with which woman is heard in her own behalf. They are seen in the steady growth and onward march of the movement, and they will be seen in the final triumph of woman's cause, not only in this country, but throughout the world.

Write an essay in which you explain how Fredrick Douglass builds an argument to persuade his audience that women should have the right to vote. In your essay, analyze how Douglass uses one or more of the features listed in the box above (or features of your own choice) to strengthen the logic and persuasiveness of his argument. Be sure that the analysis focuses on the most relevant features of the passage.

Your essay should not explain whether you agree with Douglass's claims, but rather explain how Douglass builds an argument to persuade his audience.

FOR
PLANNING
ONLY

Page 5
- December
- One month
- Every

Page 7
- 540
- 1080
- 5 passages, 52 multiple choice questions
- 44 multiple choice questions

Page 8
- Correct = 1
- Incorrect = 0
- Blank = 0
- Never
1. False
2. Never

Page 10
- 5 passages
- Prose
- Social Studies
- Science

Page 12
1. Whole Passage
2. Prose, Social Studies, Science
3. Command of Evidence
4. 12 lines, not including the lines given
5. Count 6 lines up and 6 lines down from the line numbers given
6. Score Zone Reading

Reading Practice 1: Pages 16-17
1. B
2. C
3. D
4. A
5. C
6. C
7. B
8. C
9. D
10. B
11. C

Reading Traps: Pages 20-23
1. C (Trap: B)
2. A (Trap: C)
3. B(Trap: A
4. B (Traps: A, C)
5. C (Trap: A)
6. D (Traps: A, B, C)
7. C (Trap: B)

Reading Practice 2: Pages 24-26
1. D
2. C
3. B
4. A
5. C
6. B
7. C
8. D
9. C
10. B

Reading Practice 3: Pages 32-33
1. B
2. C
3. D
4. A
5. D
6. B
7. C
8. A
9. D
10. B

Reading Practice 4: Pages 36-37
1. C
2. A
3. D
4. B
5. B
6. A
7. A
8. C
9. C
10. A

Reading Practice 5: Pagse 38-40
1. D
2. B
3. B
4. D
5. C
6. A
7. A
8. B
9. C
10. C
11. D

Reading Practice 6: Pages 42-43
1. C
2. B
3. A
4. D
5. B
6. B
7. A
8. D
9. D
10. C

Reading Practice 7: Pages 45-46
1. B
2. C
3. D
4. A
5. C
6. C
7. B
8. D
9. B
10. A
11. D

Reading Practice 8: Pages 48-49
1. D
2. D
3. B
4. A
5. C
6. B
7. C
8. A
9. B
10. D

Reading Practice 9: Pages 51-52
1. D
2. A
3. B
4. C
5. D
6. A
7. B
8. B
9. C
10. D
11. C

Reading Practice 10: Pages 54-55
1. D
2. D
3. B
4. C
5. B
6. A
7. C
8. A
9. D
10. B

Page 58
1. If it has a question, it is a Question Question
2. Grammar
3. Recognizing types of questions quickly

Page 59
1. Punctuation
2. Verb tense
3. Verb tense, apostrophes
4. Pronouns, verb tense

Page 60
1. Complete
2. Fragment
3. Fragment
4. Complete

Page 61 – Answers may vary
1. Period, semicolon, dash, or comma+FANBOYS
2. Dash, colon, or comma
3. Comma ONLY
4. Dash, colon, or semicolon

Page 62 – Answers may vary
1. Some days, when it is very sunny, my mom, brother, and I like to go to the small private beach near our house, but we stay home if it's raining.
2. Neil DeGrasse Tyson, an author, astrophysicist, and researcher, is a very interesting, funny man.

Punctuation Practice 1: Pages 64-67
1. B; commas
2. A; commas, apostrophes
3. A; sentence punctuation, commas, incomplete sentences
4. B; commas
5. D; sentence punctuation
6. C; sentence punctuation, commas
7. C; sentence punctuation, commas
8. D; commas
9. C; sentence punctuation, apostrophes
10. D; apostrophes
11. A; commas
12. D; incomplete sentences
13. B; sentence punctuation
14. B; commas
15. D; sentence punctuation
16. D; commas
17. C; sentence punctuation
18. B; apostrophes
19. C; incomplete sentences, sentence punctuation
20. C; sentence punctuation
21. D; sentence punctuation commas

Punctuation Practice 2: Pages 68-71
1. D; incomplete sentences, sentence punctuation
2. C; sentence punctuation
3. B; sentence punctuation, apostrophes
4. D; sentence punctuation, apostrophes
5. B; apostrophes, sentence punctuation
6. D; incomplete sentences
7. B; apostrophes
8. B; sentence punctuation, commas
9. B; incomplete sentences
10. C; sentence punctuation
11. D; sentence punctuation, apostrophes
12. B; sentence punctuation
13. D; sentence punctuation, commas
14. C; apostrophes, capitalization (surprise!)
15. D; sentence punctuation
16. C; sentence punctuation

Punctuation Practice 3: Pages 72-76
1. C; incomplete sentences, sentence punctuation
2. B; sentence punctuation
3. A; sentence punctuation, apostrophes
4. A; commas
5. A; sentence punctuation
6. C; apostrophes
7. D; sentence punctuation, commas
8. D; commas, apostrophes
9. D; commas
10. B; sentence punctuation
11. C; incomplete sentences, sentence punctuation
12. B; commas
13. D; apostrophes
14. D; commas, apostrophes
15. C; sentence punctuation
16. A; incomplete sentences, apostrophes
17. D; sentence punctuation, commas, apostrophes
18. B; sentence punctuation, apostrophes

Page 78
- replaces
- I, me, you, him, he, her, she, it
- We, us, you, they, them
1. their soccer gear
2. it met
3. his injuries
4. it produces

Page 79
- Subject
- Object
- David, the store
- I, we, you, it, he, she, they, who
- Me, us, you, it, him, her, them, whom

Page 80
- Talk, think, be
1. The three of us are running…
2. …the number of voters is…
- when it happened
3. …she had started college…
4. …has been improving greatly.

Pronouns & Verbs Practice 1: Pages 81-85
1. D; subject vs. object pronouns, verb tense
2. D; verb tense
3. C; subject-verb agreement, verb tense
4. A; pronoun number, verb tense
5. C; subject vs. object pronouns, verb tense
6. D; subject-verb agreement, verb tense
7. D; subject vs. object pronouns, pronoun number
8. C; pronoun number, clear pronouns
9. D; clear pronouns, incomplete sentences (surprise!)
10. C; verb tense
11. B; clear pronouns, pronoun number
12. C; verb tense
13. A; verb tense
14. B; subject-verb agreement
15. C; verb tense
16. D; subject vs. object pronouns
17. D; verb tense
18. D; subject-verb agreement, verb tense
19. B; subject vs. object pronouns
20. B; verb tense
21. C; pronoun clarity
22. D; pronoun number
23. D; verb tense
24. D; pronoun number, pronoun clarity

Pronouns & Verbs Practice 2: Pages 86-89
1. A; verb tense
2. C; subject vs. object pronouns
3. B; verb tense, subject-verb agreement
4. D; verb tense
5. A; pronoun number, verb tense
6. B; verb tense
7. D; pronoun clarity
8. D; subject-verb agreement, verb tense

9. C; pronoun clarity
10. D; subject vs. object pronouns, pronoun number
11. C; subject vs. object pronouns, pronoun number
12. B; verb tense
13. D; verb tense
14. C; verb tense
15. A; pronoun clarity, verb tense
16. B; verb tense

Pronouns & Verbs Practice 3
Pages 90-95
1. C; pronoun number
2. A; verb tense
3. C; verb tense
4. B; verb tense
5. D; subject vs. object pronouns
6. D; pronoun number
7. B; verb tense
8. C; verb tense
9. C; verb tense
10. C; pronoun number
11. C; verb tense
12. C; verb tense
13. B; subject vs. object pronouns
14. D; verb tense
15. D; verb tense
16. C; subject vs. object pronouns, verb tense
17. C; verb tense
18. B; verb tense
19. B; subject-verb agreement
20. C; verb tense
21. C; pronoun number
22. D; verb tense
23. A; verb tense
24. C; subject vs. object pronouns, subject-verb agreement
25. C; verb tense
26. D; verb tense
27. C; verb tense
28. B; pronoun number
29. D; verb tense

Page 97 (Answers may vary)
1. … has a world tour.
2. … too aware of myself.
3. …Kanye West, Kendrick Lamar, and even Justin Bieber.
4. … a rapper as she is a singer.

Page 98 (Answers may vary)
1. Like Justin Bieber's…
2. …that of Star Wars…
3. …than his sister's…
4. …those of Jane Austen.
5. Despite the fact that Skylar finished his homework, his dad would not allow him…
6. This morning while riding my bike, I saw a dog.
7. After Jonathan went camping for the weekend, his clothes…
8. As I hiked towards the summit, blisters…

Writing Logically Practice 1:
Pages 99-103
1. D; misplaced modifiers
2. D; redundancy
3. D; redundancy
4. B; misplaced modifier
5. C; misplaced modifiers
6. D; redundancy
7. B; redundancy, faulty comparisons, parallelism

8. C; redundancy, faulty comparisons
9. C; parallelism
10. D; parallelism
11. D; redundancy
12. A; misplaced modifier
13. D; misplaced modifier
14. B; parallelism, redundancy
15. C; redundancy
16. D; misplaced modifier
17. D; parallelism
18. C; redundancy
19. C; parallelism
20. D; parallelism

Writing Logically Practice 2
Page 104-107
1. D; redundancy
2. D; parallelism
3. C; misplaced modifier
4. D; redundancy
5. D; faulty comparison
6. D; redundancy
7. C; faulty comparison
8. B; redundancy
9. D; redundancy
10. C; paralellism
11. C; paralellism
12. D; faulty comparisons
13. D; redundancy
14. C; misplaced modifier
15. D; redundancy
16. D; redundancy
17. D; parallelism
18. B; parallelism

Page 109 (Answers may vary)
1. Since she wanted to score a 1550 on the SAT, Jackie studied for an hour per day leading up to the test.
2. Despite being too nervous to sleep the night before the test, Jackie still scored well.
3. …his parents insisted on him applying to several safety schools in order to make sure…

In order for Jesse to not miss the bus, he arrived at the station a half-hour early, because last time he missed the bus by accident.

Page 112 (Sentences may vary)
- Also: greement
- Alternatively: disagreement
- As such: result
- Consequently: result
- Finally: result
- For example: example
- Furthermore: agreement
- Hence: result
- However: disagreement
- In other words: example
- In contrast: disagreement
- Likewise: agreement
- Moreover: agreement
- Nevertheless: disagreement
- Previously: result
- Similarly: agreement
- Therefore: result
- Thus: result
- Whereby: result
1. However, I listen…
2. Similarly, Taylor Swift…

Word Choice Practice 1
Pages 113-117
1. D; usage
2. B; tone
3. B; tone
4. C; tone
5. B; concise wording
6. B; transition words, idioms
7. C; commonly confused words
8. A; transition words
9. D; tone
10. D; commonly confused words
11. C; commonly confused words
12. D; tone, concise wording
13. C; usage
14. C; commonly confused words
15. C; usage
16. B; usage
17. D; usage
18. A; transition words
19. D; tone, usage
20. A; usage
21. C; usage, concise wording

Word Choice Practice 2:
Page 118-122
1. D; tone
2. B; tone, usage
3. D; usage
4. D; transition words
5. C; tone, usage
6. D; usage
7. D; usage
8. C; transition words
9. B; usage
10. C; usage, tone
11. C; commonly confused words
12. D; transition words, concise wording
13. A; usage
14. B; usage, idioms
15. B; usage, concise wording
16. D; transition words
17. A; awkward wording (surprise!)
18. B; tone

Page 124 (Answers may vary)
1. Goal: end passage with restatement of writer's claim
   Look for: one that matches writer's claim
2. Goal: give second supporting example similar to the one already given
   Look for: one that matches the one already given
3. Goal: fit with tone
   Look for: same tone
4. Goal: effective transition from previous paragraph
   Look for: something linking the two topics

Question Questions Practice 1
Pages 126-130
1. C; goal: establish the paragraph's main point
2. D; goal: set up the following examples
3. D; deleting sentences
4. D; adding sentences
5. A; combine sentences
6. A; transition sentence
7. B; combine sentences
8. B; goal: tie example to the paragraph's argument
9. B; goal: tie example to the paragraph's argument

10. D; goal: relate example to the previous paragraph
11. B; goal: add specificity to example and endear kittens to reader
12. D; sentence placement
13. C; goal: use argument to make a call for action

Question Questions Practice 2
Pages 131-135
1. C; goal: succinctly establish central point
2. D; goal: transition
3. B; goal: indicate contradiction
4. A; goal: set up examples
5. B; combine sentences
6. C; adding sentences
7. D; sentence placement
8. A; goal: transition from last paragraph and establish main point
9. D; deleting sentences
10. B; goal: final example
11. C; goal: show confusion, etc.

Page 141
1. prime
2. 9, 8
3. integer, positive. negative
4. 18
5. 6
6. irrational
7. -1/7

Page 142
5. C
6. D

Page 143
1. 3
2. D
3. D

Page 144
1. 3, 6, or 9
2. 41

Math Tricks Practice 1:
Pages 145-146
1. A
2. B
3. B
4. D
5. C
6. D
7. B
8. A
9. C
10. A

Math Tricks Practice 2:
Pages 147-148
1. B
2. A
3. A
4. D
5. C
6. D
7. B
8. A
9. C
10. A

Page 150
1. (n/2) - 3 = n + 4
2. 6(12) - 22

Page 151
1. 3
2. D
3. D

Page 152
1. 12
2. 29
3. $88,200

Page 153
1. $P = \dfrac{RT}{\frac{v}{n} - b} - a\left(\dfrac{n}{v}\right)^2$
2. B

Page 154
1. 8 or -2
2. x < 7 or x > -2
3. 6 or -6
4. x ≤ 1 or x ≥ -1

Algebra Fun-Damentals Practice 1:
Page 155-156
1. D 6. C
2. A 7. D
3. B 8. C
4. C 9. B
5. A 10. C

Algebra Fun-Damentals Practice 2:
Pages 157-158
1. A 6. B
2. C 7. A
3. B 8. A
4. A 9. D
5. D 10. A

Algebra Fun-Damentals Practice 3:
Pages 159-160
1. B 6. D
2. B 7. B
3. D 8. D
4. C 9. A
5. D

Page 162
1. linear
2. nonlinear
3. nonlinear
4. linear

Page 163
1. b = 7, x = 7/3
2. 12.2 kg
3. x = -12
4. y = 3, x = 2

Page 164
1. $\sqrt{74}$
2. 13
3. 6.5
4. 500 ft

Page 165
1. (- ½, 4 ½)
2. (-4, -6)

Linear Equations Practice 1:
Pages 166-167
1. D 6. D
2. C 7. B
3. C 8. A
4. C 9. C
5. A 10. A

Linear Equations Practice 2:
Page 167-168
1. A 6. B
2. C 7. C
3. D 8. C
4. D 9. C
5. D 10. A

Page 171
1. x = 2, (2, 3)
2. x = ½

Page 172
1. 44
2. 2.30
3. 12

Systems of Equations Practice 1:
Pages 173-174
1. B 6. B
2. A 7. D
3. D 8. D
4. A 9. B
5. C 10. A

Systems of Equations Practice 2:
Page 175-176
1. B 6. C
2. C 7. A
3. D 8. B
4. C 9. A
5. C 10. D

Page 178
- Parabola

Page 179
1. a) $x^2 - x - 12$
   b) $x^2 - 4$
   c) $x^3 - x^2 - 7x + 15$
2. a) (x − 2)(x − 3)
   b) (x − 3)(x − 3)
   c) 2(x + 2)(x + 4)
3. 4/3, -2
4. ½ ± $\sqrt{21}$

Page 180
1. (2, 1)
2. (3, -1)

Quadratic Equations Practice 1:
Pages 181-182
1. B 6. D
2. C 7. C
3. A 8. D
4. D 9. B
5. B 10. A

Quadratic Equations Practice 2:
Pages 183-184
1. D 6. C
2. D 7. C
3. D 8. C
4. B 9. A
5. B 10. B

Page 186
1. $l = 120$, $m = 120$, $n = 60$, $o = 60$, $p = 120$, $q = 120$, $r = 60$
2. C

Page 187
Equilateral: 2nd box
Isosceles: 3rd box
Right: 1st box ($a^2 + b^2 = c^2$)
45-45-90: 4th box
30-60-90: 5th box

Page 188
1. 6
2. 4.5
3. x = 10, y = 4
4. 4, 18

Page 189
1. 360
   #SAT_hack: 3$\sqrt{2}$
2. 54, 27
3. 62, 30

Page 190
Circumference: (2π r) or (π d)
Area: (π r²)
1. 144π, 24π
2. 24π, 4π

Geometry Practice 1:
Pages 191-193
1. B 6. A
2. A 7. A
3. B 8. D
4. C 9. C
5. C 10. B

Geometry Practice 2:
Pages 194-196
1. D 6. B
2. B 7. C
3. C 8. D
4. C 9. A
5. D 10. A

Page 198
- Whole, part
- Part, part
1. 8/33, 2 to 3 or 2:3
2. ¾, ¼
3. 3.6×10^4
4. 6

Page 199
1. inversely 3. directly
2. inversely 4. directly

Page 200
1. B
2. 15%

Ratios, Fractions, and Proportions Practice 1:
Pages 201-202
1. D 6. D
2. B 7. A
3. C 8. B
4. B 9. C
5. C 10. A

Ratios, Fractions, and Proportions Practice 2:
Pages 203-204
1. A 6. B
2. D 7. A
3. C 8. C
4. B 9. C
5. B 10. C

Page 206
- 10.5
1. 93%
2. 2

Page 208
1. 20
2. 2017 & 2018

Page 210
1. People at the playground are more likely to have children – sample size is biased.
2. During the day, people with jobs are unlikely to answer the phone – biased method
3. D

Statistics & Data Practice 1:
Pages 211-213
1. D 6. D
2. A 7. C
3. B 8. D
4. B 9. B
5. A 10. A

Statistics & Data Practice 2:
Pages 214-216
1. D 6. C
2. D 7. D
3. C 8. B
4. A 9. D
5. B 10. B

Statistics & Data Practice 3:
Pages 217-219
1. B 6. A
2. C 7. D
3. C 8. C
4. A 9. A
5. D

Page 221
1. add; x^5
2. subtract; x^4
3. multiply; x^6
Table:
   $x^{½} = \sqrt{x}$
   $x^{¾} = \sqrt[3]{(x^4)}$ (cube root of x^4)
   $x^{-¾} = 1/\sqrt[3]{(x^4)}$
   $x^0 = 1$

Page 222
1. 11
2. 3
3. 0
4. $85.84
5. 3.17 g

Page 223
Table:
   $i^1 = \sqrt{-1}$
   $i^2 = -1$
   $i^3 = -\sqrt{-1}$
   $i^2 = 1$
   $i^5 = \sqrt{-1}$ (cycle restarts)
1. C
2. 16/5

Exponents, Roots & i Practice 1:
Pages 224-225
1. C 6. B
2. A 7. A
3. A 8. A
4. B 9. C
5. D 10. B

Exponents, Roots & i Practice 2:
Pages 226-227
1. A 6. B
2. B 7. C
3. D 8. D
4. D 9. A
5. B 10. A

Page 232
1. FALSE
2. analytical
3. 1-4 by two graders in 3 areas: reading, analysis, writing

Sample Exam A

Reading Test: P. 246	Writing & Language Test: Page 262	Math without Calculator Test: Page 280	Math with Calculator Test: Page 286
1. B	1. D	1. D	1. A
2. C	2. B	2. C	2. D
3. A	3. D	3. B	3. A
4. A	4. D	4. D	4. B
5. D	5. C	5. A	5. B
6. B	6. B	6. B	6. C
7. C	7. B	7. C	7. C
8. D	8. C	8. A	8. C
9. D	9. D	9. D	9. B
10. B	10. A	10. B	10. D
11. A	11. A	11. B	11. A
12. C	12. D	12. D	12. B
13. C	13. C	13. A	13. D
14. C	14. B	14. A	14. C
15. A	15. B	15. C	15. B
16. D	16. B	16. 55	16. D
17. D	17. A	17. 21/5 or 4.2	17. A
18. B	18. A	18. 225	18. B
19. B	19. C	19. 4/5, 0.8	19. D
20. A	20. D	20. 43.3	20. D
21. C	21. D		21. A
22. D	22. B		22. A
23. C	23. D		23. B
24. B	24. A		24. A
25. D	25. B		25. C
26. A	26. D		26. C
27. C	27. B		27. A
28. A	28. C		28. D
29. B	29. D		29. D
30. B	30. D		30. A
31. B	31. C		31. 1.25
32. B	32. D		32. 2/7
33. B	33. A		33. 45
34. C	34. D		34. 0.208, 0.21, 5/24
35. D	35. C		35. 5
36. C	36. C		36. 6
37. D	37. D		37. 2.8
38. B	38. A		38. 9/15 or 0.6 or 0.60
39. D	39. B		
40. A	40. B		
41. D	41. C		
42. B	42. A		
43. C	43. A		
44. B	44. C		
45. A			
46. B			
47. D			
48. D			
49. A			
50. B			
51. C			
52. D			

Sample Exam B

Reading Test:
P. 306

1. B
2. C
3. A
4. A
5. D
6. B
7. C
8. D
9. D
10. B
11. A
12. C
13. B
14. C
15. C
16. D
17. B
18. B
19. A
20. D
21. D
22. A
23. B
24. C
25. C
26. A
27. C
28. D
29. C
30. A
31. D
32. C
33. A
34. D
35. B
36. D
37. C
38. D
39. C
40. A
41. B
42. D
43. B
44. C
45. A
46. B
47. D
48. C
49. B
50. D
51. C
52. C

Writing & Language Test:
Page 322

1. D
2. B
3. D
4. C
5. D
6. D
7. B
8. C
9. A
10. C
11. B
12. C
13. D
14. A
15. C
16. D
17. C
18. A
19. B
20. C
21. D
22. B
23. D
24. A
25. A
26. B
27. C
28. B
29. D
30. D
31. B
32. C
33. D
34. B
35. D
36. C
37. C
38. A
39. C
40. A
41. D
42. B
43. C
44. D

Math without Calculator Test:
Page 338

1. C
2. A
3. B
4. B
5. D
6. B
7. D
8. A
9. C
10. C
11. D
12. B
13. B
14. D
15. A
16. 9
17. 25
18. 6
19. 18
20. 8,110

Math with Calculator Test:
Page 344

1. C
2. B
3. C
4. D
5. D
6. B
7. A
8. A
9. C
10. C
11. B
12. B
13. B
14. D
15. C
16. A
17. D
18. C
19. A
20. D
21. C
22. B
23. C
24. A
25. D
26. B
27. A
28. B
29. C
30. C
31. 110
32. 8
33. 8
34. 162, 163, 164, 165, 166, 167, 168, 169, 170
35. 6
36. ¾ or 0.75
37. 37.5
38. 24

NOTES

Here's to a Successful SAT!

400 to 1600 is the new scoring statistics.
Teaching Tried & True Methods and we're keeping it simplistic.
Math strategies are explicit. It's nothing subliminal,
We're stealing points here and there like an SAT criminal!

Reading Strategies we're teaching. It's what you are needing,
Tutors are seasoned, and your score boost we're guaranteeing.
We're working with students, and we understand kids,
Our curriculum is flawless, made by test prep geniuses.

We're the best at this test. It's our secret sauce.
Turn you from a novice into an SAT Boss!
Put our test prep games into the Hall of Fame.
We set a goal, and we aim to maximize your score change.

Our credentialed methods of teaching are Tried & True.
Since 2007, we know exactly what to do!
Being a junior in high school is stressful as can be.
But together Tried & True and You - here's to a successful SAT!